Planemakers:2

WESTLAND

David Mondey

JANE'S

Copyright © David Mondey 1982

First published in the United Kingdom in 1982 by
Jane's Publishing Company Limited
238 City Road, London EC1V 2PU

ISBN 0 7106 0134 4

Designed by Geoffrey Wadsley

Computer typesetting by
Method Limited, Woodford Green, Essex

Printed in Great Britain by
Biddles Limited, Guildford, Surrey

CONTENTS

ACKNOWLEDGEMENTS

No company history can be created without very considerable assistance from the company concerned, and I am most grateful for the generous help received from Westland's (alphabetically) Jim Baird, Fred Ballam, Peter Batten, David Gibbings . . . and Uncle Mike Farlam and all. My sincere friend John W.R. Taylor must be remembered for, as always, his advice, encouragement, and kindly help. There is also a host of other people, but I would mention in particular Wing Commander Frank Merchant, RAF (Retd), who had some good ideas when I had none; members of the staff of the Yeovil Library, and Taunton County Library, and County Records Office, who went to endless trouble to dig out dusty reference material; and last, but not least, the Committee of the Friends of Yeovil Museum who delayed the start of a monthly meeting to offer help and advice to a complete stranger. All of the illustrations, with the exception of a small number which are separately identified in their captions, are reproduced from photographs in Westland's photographic library and I am most grateful for permission to use them in this history.

To all those mentioned above, and others whose names I have not recorded, I trust you will find this book a suitable reward for your endeavours.

D.M. Surbiton, 1981

1. FOUNDATION

Yeovil, in Somerset, cradled by gentle hills, and with golden-coloured houses fashioned from the famous Ham Hill limestone, was to remain a small market town typical of Britain's 'West Country' until the middle of the 19th century. For its people busily engaged in agriculture, and in the glove making industry which, according to county records, had first been established in the area in 1361, it must have been a relatively untroubled place in which to live. The impact of the early stages of the Industrial Revolution passed by with little effect on the life of Yeovil and its surrounding villages and, like many similar small towns in Britain, it was not until the tentacles of the railway octopus began to stretch out across the country, from 1840 onwards, that the first real signs of change were to be seen.

During this latter period a citizen of Yeovil, James Bazeley Petter, was married, and received as a wedding gift from his father an established ironmongery business in the town. Both the business and his marriage prospered, the latter to the extent of 15 children. The third and fourth of these were twin boys, Percival Waddams and Ernest Willoughby, and they are very much a part of this history. While they were growing up, and busily occupied with school life and schoolboy activities, 'JB' was even more actively engaged in the expansion of his business to feed his growing family. By the 1870s this was known as Petter and Edgar, with a partner needed to help as changing times began to bring mechanisation to the agricultural scene. No longer just simply an ironmonger, 'JB' was now involved as an agricultural implement maker, engineer, and iron founder with a foundry, to become known as the Yeovil Foundry, established on the north side of Huish, more or less where Douglas Seaton's showrooms and garage are now situated. One of the products of the foundry was castings for the Nautilus grate, which was to become famous after being selected by Queen Victoria for installation in the fireplaces of Balmoral Castle and Osborne House. It was to this foundry that son Percy came after leaving Yeovil Grammar School, there to learn the art of casting and the repair of agricultural machinery and by 1893 he had become its manager.

Although no one could then have appreciated the significance of that appointment, it represented the real beginning of the company which is the subject of this book. Percy was interested in the 'horseless carriage' that had been developed on the continent, and could see no reason why something equally as good should not be built in Britain. With the help of one Mr Jacobs, foreman of the foundry, he designed and built a single-cylinder oil engine to serve as the power unit for such a vehicle. He was to comment later that the success of this engine owed more to Mr Jacobs' skill than his own. When running satisfactorily, it was installed in a chassis built by the local carriage builders, Hill & Boll, and thus the people of Yeovil were to see one of the first functional motor cars to be built in this country when it was demonstrated in 1895. There seemed every chance that further interest would be shown in this vehicle, and 'JB' established the Yeovil Motor Car and Cycle Co Ltd, with a new factory being built in Reckleford. This was to become the Nautilus Works, still standing today and used as a bus garage, with traces of its former glory still to be seen.

In its issue of 3 April 1896, the publication *Engineer* gave a technical description of the Petter horseless carriage and during the following year, probably as a result of interest aroused by this article, the new company built 12 of these vehicles. Later examples were powered by an improved twin-cylinder engine, and one of these was entered in a competition held at the Crystal Palace. Percy, now joined by his brother Ernest, felt certain they would win, but when they failed to gain any special recognition for their design, both returned to Yeovil very much deflated. Clearly, they needed to look in a new direction if the business was to grow in prosperity but, before leaving this road vehicle episode, it is interesting to record that during November 1897 the company supplied two electrically-powered carriages of similar type. Built to the order of a battery manufacturer, one of these took part in the Lord Mayor's Show in London.

Back in Yeovil, their disappointment behind them, the Petters looked more closely at their creation. It did not take very long for them to appreciate that, without much doubt, the most significant feature of the horseless carriage was its oil engine. It was decided to develop this power unit for agricultural use, with the result that a new engine of 1.1 kw (1.25 hp) output, to become known as the Petter Patent Oil Engine, was exhibited and demonstrated at the Royal Show of 1899. Within two years the private limited company of James B. Petter & Sons had been established, and by which time a range of oil engines with power outputs ranging from 1.1 to 16.4 kW (1.25 to 22 hp) were available. In the following year, the company produced an agricultural tractor, powered by a 22.4 kW (30 hp) horizontal oil engine. B.J. Jacobs, whose skill had helped to develop the first successful engine, was not forgotten; he was to become Chief Engineer of the company, and remained with Petters until his death in 1936. Among the fascinating features of historical research are the intermeshed threads that one comes across, often related but not directly linked: here is one of them. B.J.

Jacobs had members of the Stringfellow family at Chard, Somerset, as his friends. This was the family of John Stringfellow, renowned in Britain's early aviation history.

By 1910, when Petters Limited was established as a public company, the scope and activities of the business had become centred on the production of engines of all sizes. An Almanack of 1913 records that by 1912 the Nautilus Works employed about 500 people, and that some 1,500 engines were being produced annually. To maintain such production rates a large volume of castings were needed, and the capacity of the company's foundry was being strained to the utmost. The site at Reckleford had been built over by the beginning of 1913, and it was not possible to find the space needed there. To resolve this situation it was decided to seek a site for a new, larger foundry, and leading to the acquisition of an area of meadowland in West Hendford on the west side of the town. At the same time, additional adjacent land was purchased on which to build a garden village that would house the company's workforce. The new foundry was built and ready for use in early 1914, at which time it was one of the largest in Britain. Further expansion of the Nautilus Works was also impossible, and to cater for the requirements of the growing business, work had also begun on the construction of new buildings at the West Hendford site to provide increased production facilities.

It is impossible to conjecture whether this move would have occurred if there has been a better appreciation of the fact that, within some 18 months of acquiring this site,

Britain would be at war with Germany. Apart from the aviation activities in which the company was to be become involved within a year of the beginning of the First World War, the demands for Petter engines were to reach unprecedented figures, so it was fortunate that these plans materialised.

To preserve continuity, it is as well to relate now some later activities of Petters Limited which, by the end of the war, was associated with Vickers and producing engines of up to 298 kW (400 hp). One between-wars activity is worth recording, namely the co-partnership of Douglas Seaton and Petters in the design and production of the 7.5 kW to 13.4 kW (10 to 18 hp) Seaton/Petter motor cars, produced in small numbers from 1926 to 1933. This represents another of the interesting threads entangled within any history for, as mentioned earlier, Douglas Seaton's business now occupies the site of the former Yeovil Foundry. But despite such parochial activities, the name of Petters Limited was to become known internationally, the company's diesel and petrol engines delivered worldwide. They were used for agriculture; civil engineering applications that involved hoists and pumps; drainage and irrigation; electricity generation; in mines and oilfields; to power motor vehicles and works locomotives; and for refrigeration and water supply. They were also used quite extensively for marine applications that ranged from the smallest private motor boats, to barges, drifters and trawlers. In early 1939 the Yeovil Foundry and Nautilus Factory were finally closed when the company became part of the Brush Group, and production

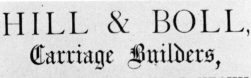

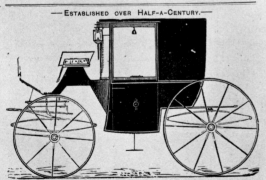

James B. Petter advertisement text:

Experienced
Smiths,
Hot Water Fitters,
Plumbers,
Gas Fitters,
Tin-Plate Workers,
Bell Hangers.

Heating Apparatus,
Kitchen Ranges,
Stoves,
Chimney Pieces,
Grates,
Fenders,
Tile Hearths.

Wrought and Cast
Ironwork,
Fencing,
Gates,
Wirework.

ENGINEERING.
Sanitary,
Gas,
Horticultural,
Agricultural,
Dairy,
Domestic,
Electric,
Waterworks.

Electric Lighting,
Electric Bells,
Telephones.

Cutlery,
Electro-Plate,
Table Lamps,
Floor Lamps.

Bedsteads,
Baths,
Perambulators.

Travelling Boxes,
Portmanteaus,
Hand Bags.

Oils, Colours, Bar Iron,
Tools, &c.

JAMES B. PETTER
YEOVIL.

PATENT LIFTING FIRE,
50 PER CENT. OF FUEL SAVED.

Ironmonger, Ironfounder,
AND
Implement Manufacturer.

TELEGRAMS PETTER, YEOVIL.

Above left: **Petters shop in Yeovil High Street about the turn of the century** (*Yeovil Museum*)

Above: **A Petter advertisement of the 1890s** (*Yeovil Almanack*)

Left: **Hill and Boll advertisement** (*Yeovil Almanack*)

Hill & Boll advertisement text:

HILL & BOLL,
Carriage Builders,
KINGSTON & PARK ROAD, YEOVIL
AND
SOUTH STREET, SHERBORNE.

— ESTABLISHED OVER HALF-A-CENTURY. —

Patent Cee Spring Carts a Specialite,

NOT TO BE SURPASSED FOR SMARTNESS OR COMFORT.

CARRIAGES of every description built on the Newest and most
Improved principles. Inspection at their Works solicited.

LARGE STOCK OF NEW AND SECOND-HAND CARRIAGES ALWAYS ON HAND.

ESTIMATES GIVEN FOR REPAIRS.

Carriages Taken in Exchange and Arrangements made for Easy Purchase

BEST SEASONED MATERIAL,
SUPERIOR WORKMANSHIP AND FINISH GUARANTEED.

was transferred to Loughborough, Leicestershire. The final move came in 1947 when Petters became established in Staines, Middlesex. Still active in 1981, and now a member of the Hawker Siddeley Group, the company concentrates on the production of air pumps and Thermo King refrigeration units, high-powered engines being built by another member of the group.

There is some satisfaction in recording this virtually unbroken history, with Petter industry extending over a period of more than 100 years. It is a success story that is to be repeated by the subsidiary Westland Aircraft Works that, because of wartime demands, became established on the West Hendford site in 1915.

2. THE FIRST WORLD WAR

Westland Aircraft Works was established on the West Hendford site in 1915, and how and why this occurred is perhaps best explained in the words of Ernest Petter, writing in the company's *Monthly News* in 1936, by which time he had become Sir Ernest. After referring, perhaps inaccurately, to the naming of the company, he continued: '. . . The circumstances that led up to this incident were as follows. Mr Lloyd George a few days previously, it being the second year of the war, had made in Parliament a very serious speech, in which he frankly exposed the inadequacy and unsuitability of the munitions available for carrying on the war.

'The writer hastily convened a Board meeting of Petters Limited, then a comparatively small company manufacturing oil engines, and the Board passed a resolution by which they placed at the disposal of the Government the whole of their manufacturing resources, to make anything or everything the Government might call for from them. A copy of this resolution was the same day sent to the War Office and the Admiralty. From the former, nothing was heard, but almost the next day a telegram came from the Admiralty asking that two representatives might go up for a conference. The writer, accompanied by his brother Mr P.W. Petter, accordingly went to London and were received by five gentlemen, at least three of whom were Lords of the Admiralty, who stated that the great need of the Navy was seaplanes, and were we willing to make them?

'We explained that our experience and factory were not exactly in line with their requirements, but we were willing to attempt anything which would help the Country. "Good," said they, "You are the fellows we want; we will send you the drawings and give you all the help we can. Get on with it." So we got on with it . . . when the Armistice was declared in 1918, 1,100 aeroplanes had been turned out.'

The statements of Sir Ernest and his brother, Percy, do not agree entirely in fact, but then this is so often true when memory is used to recall long forgotten events. Of course, Percy confirms his brother's words in principle, and he relates the continuation of this story when the company was

Single-seat Sopwith 1½-Strutter

instructed to send representatives to Short Brothers at Rochester, Kent, to find out the kind of task that was expected of them.

'. . . I must confess that my heart nearly failed me when I saw its nature, (the particular manufacturing processes expected of them) but my brother John, and Mr Warren were sure of their ability to supervise construction of such machines, and in the first instance were put in charge of the works. However, I was not satisfied that their experience was adequate for this difficult undertaking. A year or so earlier, when the position of Works Manager of the engine business was open, among other applicants, I had interviewed a Mr Robert Arthur Bruce who was the Manager of the British & Colonial Aeroplane Company at Bristol, but though I had not thought that management of the engine business was suitable for him, I now kept thinking that if only we could get hold of him he was the man for this aircraft business. Unfortunately I could not get in touch until one day it occurred to me to see if he was a member of the Institution of Mechanical Engineers, and finding his name in the Directory I wrote to him.'

The reason for Percy Petter's initial failure to contact Bruce was that he was no longer employed by the British & Colonial (later Bristol) Aeroplane Company. Instead, he was then serving as a Lieutenant RNVR, and had been posted as resident Admiralty inspector to the Sopwith Aviation Company at its Kingston upon Thames factory. Approaches were made to the Admiralty to emphasise the need that Petters had for this experienced engineer to knock the new factory into shape and, appreciating the situation and also requiring the potential output of this Yeovil manufacturer, it was agreed to release him to take up the post offered. Thus, in July 1915, Robert the Bruce, as he was inevitably known,

arrived to take up his appointment as the manager of the new Westland Aircraft Works.

Already this narrative is slightly out of context, for how and why did Petters Limited become Westland Aircraft Works? Thy 'why' is comparatively easy, for the Board considered that the new project needed a separate title from that of the established oil-engine manufacturing company. Although wholly owned by Petters Limited, it was thought that it should be operated as a separate self-supporting company. How it became named Westland Aircraft Works appears to be an insoluble problem, for so many conflicting stories of its 'christening' have been related that it seems impossible to accept any one as being strictly true. Sir Ernest in the opening paragraph to his article in the company's *Monthly News* of 1936 recorded that: 'Twenty-one years ago last April, three men walked down to the corner of a field just outside Yeovil, where there was a small farm hut. One of the three, the only survivor, and the author of this little story, opened the door of the hut and solemnly said: "This is the Westland Aircraft Works."' If this is accurate, he presumably acquired the name Westland from his brother Percy's wife. This is suggested in the 22nd Henson and Stringfellow Memorial Lecture given to the Yeovil Branch of the Royal Aeronautical Society by Harald Penrose who, in course of time, became the company's test pilot, and finally one of its senior executives. In that lecture he commented . . . 'At a little ceremony one Saturday afternoon in 1913 Percy Petter, his wife, and two of his small daughters, Norah and Kathleen, were present when the first turfs were cut for the foundation(s) of the new foundry, and

D.H.4 with Eagle III engine

D.H.9A with Liberty engine

as this was the West side of Yeovil Mrs Petter chose the name 'Westland' for the proposed garden village and works'.

There are several other explanations, including that which refers to a map of 1332, showing a road called Westelane, running through the area called Northover Fields where the factory now stands. Another interesting lead is suggested by records in the County library, which in establishing that Yeovil was a pioneer housing authority recorded: 'In January 1912 work began on Yeovil's first fifty municipal houses at the Eastland No.1 site'. Was there also a Westland site? Perhaps one day the answer will be known, but Westland Aircraft Works it was, and the embryo concern was soon deeply involved in the problem of producing its first batch of sub-contracted aircraft. As Percy Petter's comment had implied, this was no easy project for a company with experience limited to the design and manufacture of robust, and often heavy engines.

One of the very first steps involved the transfer from Petters Ltd of a young man named Arthur Davenport. An engine designer, he was given the new appointment of Chief Draughtsman, and his first task involved a stay at Short Brothers, where he made the necessary production drawings for the Short 184 seaplane, of which the company had received an order for twelve. The newly-recruited staff of the factory, comprising a nucleus of engineers from the Nautilus Works, plus a variety of local tradesmen, were soon to acquire new skills. By January 1916 the first example was completed, and with the confidence gained from this initial

success, production of aircraft was to continue at a reasonable speed, and to a commendable quality.

The fourth aircraft to be completed at Yeovil, which duly acquired the Naval serial number 8359, was the only one of the Navy's seaplanes to be airborne during the Battle of Jutland, operating from HM Seaplane Carrier *Engadine*. In this action the Short seaplane, piloted by Flt-Lt F.J. Rutland, with Asst Paymaster G.S. Trewen as his observer spotted, and reported by radio, movements of the German fleet. When this news was received subsequently at the Yeovil works it gave new confidence to the workforce, proving to their satisfaction that they were capable of building aircraft as good as those from any other source.

The problems experienced in dealing with this first production contract, small though it was, demonstrated that the choice of Robert Bruce to guide the activities of the new project had been a good one. He soon proved to be a giant in capability, creating a large and significant aircraft works from the small workshop that he found when he took up his appointment. Technical problems, however complex, were taken in his stride, and innumerable people have commented on his warm personality which welded together a loyal workforce. It was fortunate that this was so, for there were plenty of problems to be faced before Britain would once again be at peace.

As production of the Short 184s was nearing its end, the company received a new contract to build 20 Short 166 seaplanes. Although of earlier vintage than the 184, only six examples had been built by Shorts, but whereas they had been intended as torpedo-bombers, those to be built by Westland were to be without torpedo carrying and launching gear. This posed some problems for the small drawing office, but these were compounded considerably when it

was discovered that there was nothing like a complete set of production drawings to work from. Although it created a crisis at the time, in the long run it was to prove fortunate, compelling the company to expand the capability of its own drawing office. The first of the 166s was delivered in July 1916, these being crated to travel by rail to Hamble, Hampshire, where they were flight tested by Sydney Pickles, a well-known pre-war sporting pilot, and freelance test pilot.

This might be considered a clumsy way of carrying out flight testing, but there was of course no suitable stretch of water within easy reach of the works that could be used for this purpose. In fact, there was not even an airfield from which they would be able to flight test landplanes. If the company intended to take seriously the possibility of becoming an established aircraft manufacturer, something equally ambitious had to be done. Accordingly, moves were made to acquire some of the adjoining area of Northover Fields which was then owned by the Yeovil and District Hospital Board. This was then typical farmland, incorporating hedges and ditches, but after it became the company's property, work was initiated to convert it into a reasonably level grass airfield. This entire operation was completed quite quickly, considering the size of the project and that it was wartime but, in fact, it was not quick enough. By the time that the airfield was ready for use, Westland had already completed its third sub-contract, covering the manufacture of Sopwith 1½-Strutter landplanes.

An initial contract for 50 of these aircraft was followed by one for an additional 25, and all of these were built during the Winter of 1916-17. This proved to be a much easier contract for Westland: not only were they beginning to gain a backlog of experience, but the Sopwith company provided first class production drawings, enabling manufacture to go ahead with virtually no delay. The fourth sub-contract, received from Airco (the Aircraft Manufacturing Company Ltd) was to represent a significant factor in Westland's future as an aircraft manufacturer.

Airco had been founded in early 1912 by George Holt Thomas, whose association with aviation had started as a promoter of flying events. In 1914 he secured as his Chief Designer a young man named Geoffrey de Havilland, who had gained previous experience with the Royal Aircraft Factory at Farnborough, and he began by designing for Airco a two-seat reconnaissance biplane which became designated D.H.1. An appreciation of de Havilland's early capability and of Holt Thomas' recognition of this fact, is that all of the aircraft designed for the company were recognised as de Havilland rather than Airco. The fourth of his designs for Airco, the D.H.4 day bomber, was to become regarded as one of the outstanding aircraft of the First World War and, for its day, was built in large numbers. British production totalled 1,449, built by Airco and six British sub-contractors, with more than three times this number being built in the USA.

As with the Sopwith contract, Westland received excellent production drawings, enabling construction to go ahead without unnecessary delay. To the extent that in early 1917, both D.H.4s and 1½-Strutters were on the factory floor at the same time, presenting a heart-warming sight to those who had worked so hard to get the company established as an aircraft manufacturer. Westland's contract covered the construction of 150 D.H.4s, but it is uncertain whether all of these were completed, and records suggest that the number delivered was nearer 140. Like all preceding aircraft, early production examples were crated for delivery by rail, but in the late afternoon of a showery April day in 1917, another well-known early pilot, B.C. Hucks, taxied a D.H.4 out across the newly-finished airfield and, to the cheers of the assembled workers, lifted it cleanly into the air. The following day it took to the air again, its destination France, and action on the Western Front.

Westland's work on the D.H.4 had been entirely satisfactory to Airco, and when the D.H.9 two-seat bomber was ordered into production, the company was again named as a sub-contractor. The D.H.9 needs more than passing mention, for its design was originated as a result of the daylight attacks on London that were being carried out by German bombers. The aim was to create a retaliatory bomber with longer range than the excellent D.H.4 and, because the need was urgent, it was decided to develop this from the D.H.4 design, retaining as much of the original structure as possible. The resulting aircraft however was unable to use its intended power plant, with the result that its performance was inferior to that of the D.H.4 which it was intended to replace. This was to result in serious losses when the type entered service on the Western Front, but despite this production continued, the type supplementing the D.H.4, but proving quite unsuitable for its originally intended long-range role. About 3,200 were built by Airco and 12 sub-contractors, and their construction in such numbers suggests that the intention was to overcome the enemy by quantity, rather than quality.

Westland-built Vickers Vimy (*F. Ballam*)

Of course, this shortcoming of the D.H.9 was not Westland's problem, which continued to do what had been requested and get on with production of these aircraft. Earlier, the D.H.4 had failed to demonstrate its potential until powered by a Rolls-Royce engine. Could a similar miracle be worked in the case of the D.H.9? Unfortunately, no. The demand for Rolls-Royce Eagle VIII engines considerably exceeded the supply, and Airco needed to think again to find a solution to the problems of the D.H.9. In America, the so-called Liberty engine had been developed by a consortium of motor car engine manufacturers, and it was decided to redesign the D.H.9 to accept this engine. But Airco was then deeply involved in design of the D.H.10 and had no drawing office capacity available. The task of redesigning the D.H.9 to accept the Liberty engine was handed over to Westland, marking a significant moment in the company's history, and ensuring that it was to survive throughout the lean post-war years.

At last there was a real job for Westland's drawing office to get its teeth into, and with experience of both the D.H.4 and D.H.9 behind them, the company decided to combine the best features of these two aircraft in the new design. The fuselage was modified to accept the new power plant, and other improvements made. When air-tested there was little

doubt that the resulting D.H.9A was fast, and indeed proved fast enough in service to fly over enemy territory without fighter escort. It was to become regarded as the outstanding strategic bomber aircraft of the First World War and brought Westland recognition as a capable design and construction organisation. It was to be the company's penultimate wartime contract.

The growing volume of production, especially during 1917, had shown that the works were not big enough, and the nucleus of buildings that had served at the beginning of the war began to expand. The final wartime sub-contract, received in August 1918, and covering the construction of 75 Vickers Vimy three-seat heavy bombers, was not to be completed. This, of course, was not known at the time that the contract was being negotiated, and to provide room for erection of these then giant aircraft, a new erecting shop, with an unsupported span of 42.67 m (140 ft), was built. At the time of its construction it was the largest building of its kind in Britain, and was to prove a valuable asset to the company during the post-war years. Westland was to build only 25 of the sub-contracted Vimys, for the Armistice brought cancellation of the wartime contracts. No doubt all members of the company, from the Managing Director to the humblest office boy, joined with the people of Yeovil and the nation in celebrating the end of the war. And, no doubt, there were far-seeing members of the company who wondered what course they were now to follow.

3. THE LEAN YEARS

Prior to the beginning of the First World War, Britain's aviation industry had been very small, with only limited demand for sporting aircraft, and the Army and Naval wings of the Royal Flying Corps in a very early stage of development. Indeed many military men had an unshakeable belief that a horse could do virtually as much as an aeroplane, at least on land, and in all weathers too. The demands of war however had converted the small industry into a giant, but the peace spelt disaster for many of these hugely expanded concerns. Westland, like many other companies, had only become an aircraft constructor because of Britain's wartime needs, but at least had a viable engine-building business to fall back on if necessary. This was not true of all the companies that had entered the industry for precisely the same reasons. Few had such an insurance policy for survival behind them, and tried unsuccessfully to pick up again the threads of the manufacturing trades that had provided their pre-war income. Almost certainly it was because of the assurance of the continuity of Petters Limited, that the company decided to take a risk on the development of the aircraft subsidiary. There was also one other factor that must have played an important part in the decision, namely a demand, however small, for continued production of the D.H.9A, and for the support of those aircraft which remained in RAF service.

During the war, Westland had developed three of their own designs in attempts to meet official specifications. The first of these was concerned with an Admiralty requirement for a single-seat scout seaplane, and for which the company built two N.1B prototypes under the company designations N 16 and N 17. By the time they had flown the requirement no longer existed, marking the first of a series of disappointments in endeavouring to satisfy service needs. The two seaplane prototypes were followed by a small single-seat fighter, designed to meet an RFC specification. Identified originally by the name of its chosen power plant, an A.B.C. Wasp, the insect had become a bird – the Wagtail – by the time that it was flown in April 1918. Power plant problems, essential modifications, and the resulting delay in completing competitive evaluation of the type against contenders from B.A.T. (the British Aerial Transport Company), and Sopwith, meant the war had come to an end by the time that Westland's design was declared the winner. The RAF had no funds available for new fighters, and once again the company failed to win a production contract despite the development of a successful contender. The third, and last of these wartime designs, intended to meet an RAF requirement for a replacement to the Bristol F.2B, was to gain another alliterative name, the Westland Weasel. It, and its contenders, were all based on a new A.B.C. radial engine named the 'Dragonfly', and which might aptly have been called the Mayfly, because it didn't very successfully. Having a pathetically short operational life that could be measured in less hours than could be indicated by the fingers of one hand, the engine, and the aircraft that were to have been powered by it, came to an ignominious end.

Westland, as well as the other manufacturers that decided to continue in the post-war aviation industry, needed no crystal ball to tell them there would be little future in developing new military designs. All of them, however, felt reasonably certain that, with wartime activities having demonstrated that aircraft were no longer the toys of wealthy sportsmen, there would be a growing demand for aircraft to provide civil services of various kinds. It was a mistake that was not confined to the manufacturers: users were of the same opinion and there was an early post-war rash of civil operations that were to prove that not only was there little demand for commercial air services, but that the general public had not yet become in the least air-minded. Almost a decade was to pass before there was any significant change in this attitude. And so, confident that a purpose-designed light transport would win orders, Westland launched itself into an era of post-war disappointments.

Early post-war air services, such as those between London and Paris, relied almost exclusively upon the use of ex-service aircraft, not all of which had received very sophisticated conversions for their new role. This was appreciated not only by the companies that were operating them, but also by the Department of Civil Aviation which, in August 1919, announced a competition with prizes totalling some £64,000 for the development of three categories of civil aircraft, comprising small, large, and seaplanes. Small was, indeed, small, meaning an aircraft for two persons, one of which was the pilot. Large also meant large for its day, required to carry 15 passengers and crew. Westland had, unfortunately, already built what we would now call a business aircraft, intended to accommodate three passengers in considerable comfort, plus a pilot, it therefore could not compete in any of the three categories. Despite the temptation of a not inconsiderable prize, with a government undertaking to buy the winning machine, Westland felt that it was too late to build a contender and decided to paddle its own canoe, naming its new design the Limousine. This, it was hoped, would give an impression of luxury.

In June 1919, Capt A.S.Keep, who had served with

Trenchard's Independent Air Force in France, joined Westland as the company's first test pilot. Of Australian origin, Stuart Keep was to take the prototype Limousine on its maiden flight in early July. When demonstrated to the Press, on 31 July, it was generally agreed that the company had created a most attractive aeroplane. The Westland directors were so enthusiastic at this reception that it was decided to proceed immediately with a production line of six aircraft to cope with the expected rush of orders.

In the meantime, the Society of British Aircraft Constructors had tackled the government's Department of Civil Aviation over the unrealistic seating capacities designated for the Small and Large classes of the proposed Civil Aircraft Competition. Their approach was successful, with the result that these categories were changed to embrace aircraft carrying between two and six passengers, and those which carried more than six passengers. The announcement of the changes encouraged Westland to enter a scaled up version of the Limousine, to accommodate a pilot and five passengers, with the resulting aircraft becoming designated as the Limousine III. Flown in the competition, held during 1920, the Limousine III proved good enough to take first place in the Small aircraft class, winning the government prize of £7,500. If the company needed confirmation of the excellence of their design, this was it, and there seemed nothing to prevent the Limousine from being built in considerable numbers. However, they had not then appreciated that the anticipated demand for civil transports was not going to materialise, and despite this competition success, and an enthusiastic Press reception for the earlier Limousine I/II, were once again faced with having to hide their disappointment. Perhaps they gained a small crumb of comfort from the fact that the Limousine III found its way to Newfoundland where, used successfully for fish and seal spotting duties, it was to be joined by three of the Limousine IIs in 1922.

No doubt taking a deep breath, Westland looked forward to the next stage of progress. In fact it proved to be one of the kind favoured by comedy script writers, representing one pace forward and about three backwards. However, it should be stressed that this was thrust upon them by a penniless RAF which, one way or another, had to provide the Navy with a land- or carrier-based three-seat spotter-reconnaissance aircraft. This requirement resulted in the creation of what was almost certainly the ugliest aircraft to come from the company's erecting sheds, the Westland Walrus. The lack of funds meant that an adaptation of the D.H.9A was called for and eventually 36 were built. These had barely entered service before a replacement was being sought as, being much underpowered as a result of the weight of the additional equipment that had been incorporated to make them suitable for the Navy's requirements, a number of them had been lost as a result of crashes, even on delivery flights from the Yeovil airfield. The next project was

at least original, with the company building to Air Ministry contract an early 'flying-wing' design which was designated the Dreadnought Postal Monoplane. Incorporating a wing that followed the proposals of the Russian inventor Woyevodsky, it represented a forward step into a region of unknown aerodynamic problems. On 8 May 1924, taxying tests of the new machine were carried out to everyone's satisfaction, and it was agreed that, weather permitting, the first flight would be made on the following day. It proved to be ideal, calm and sunny, with the lightest of breezes blowing. After a couple of fast taxi runs, the second terminated after a brief hop, Stuart Keep lined up for take-off and pushed the throttle wide open. The Lion engine responded with an appropriate roar, and slowly the strange machine gathered speed. A crowd had assembled to watch the take-off, and was rewarded by the sight of the wheels leaving the ground as the Dreadnought neared the Vimy shed. The aircraft began to climb steeply and suddenly, with horror, it was realised that it was an uncontrolled climb that could only result in the wing stalling. The starboard wing began to sink, and almost before there was time to shout in apprehension, the aircraft hit the ground with a tremendous crash, sending up clouds of dust as it slid and banged across the grass, the nose section (containing the cockpit) torn from the fuselage. Fortunately, the wreckage finally came to halt without catching fire. Yet another failure, but this one tragic, for Stuart Keep was to lose both legs as a result of the accident, and his flying days were over. Subsequently, he learned to cope with the difficulties of walking on two artificial legs, and was later to become the company's General Manager, finally retiring in 1935.

A replacement test pilot was needed, and thus Major Laurence Openshaw came to Westland. During the war he had served at Eastchurch, and the Admiralty's Isle of Grain experimental establishment, and was thus more than just a pilot. With the company having only limited requirements for flight testing at that stage of its growth, he was made responsible also for structural testing, and was asked to contribute the benefit of his experience in all design conferences. Openshaw had arrived at a difficult period in Westland's history when they, like many of their contemporaries, had reached a low ebb in production, the workshops desperate for work to keep the wheels turning. It was a period when many endeavoured to use their productive capacity to manufacture anything that the country would be prepared to buy. Some of those who found a successful product and outlet turned their backs on the aircraft industry for good, but Westland was fortunate in still having to meet RAF requirements in respect of the D.H.9A and, of course, had the strength of Petters behind it. It was at this time that the Seaton/Petter car project came on the scene, and with work needed for idle hands the prototype was developed by combining a chassis provided by Douglas Seaton, with a Petter two-stroke engine, and Westland designing and building a body that, reportedly, was probably one of the most unattractive ever to disgrace any motor car. Knowing these facts, it is not too difficult to understand why the Seaton/Petter car failed to become a best seller.

It was also a period of ebbtide in government spending, but some efforts were being made to help civil aviation to

survive. In 1922 the Air Council had announced a Light Aeroplane Competition, to be held at Lympne, Kent, during 1924, with the aim of fostering the development of a lightweight, economical aircraft. Like so many early projects of this nature, it was all a part of the endeavour to make people more air-minded, but in the case of the Light Aeroplane Competition served only to produce a batch of impractical aircraft, some positively dangerous. It was decided that Westland would participate, with the resulting design conference split by Robert Bruce who favoured a biplane configuration, and Arthur Davenport who championed the monoplane. A Solomon type judgement was reached, with an agreement to build prototypes of each. Thus were developed the biplane Woodpigeon and monoplane Widgeon, both flown during the late Summer of 1924. Perhaps Bruce was convinced of the superiority of the biplane configuration when, only five days after its first

flight, the Widgeon prototype was badly damaged as it sideslipped and hit the ground, fortunately without seriously injuring its pilot. In the long term, comparative evaluation of both Woodpigeon and Widgeon was to show that the performance of the monoplane configuration was superior, and leading eventually to the development of an improved Widgeon III. It was while participating in the 1927 Whitsun Flying Meeting at Bournemouth that the prototype Widgeon III brought a new tragedy for Westland. Competing in the first Handicap race on the Whit Monday, and flown by Laurence Openshaw, the Widgeon was one of eleven contenders bunched dangerously close together at a turning point. As they rounded the turn and gained the straight, the Widgeon was seen to collide with another aircraft, and both plunged to the ground. As a pall of black smoke rose into the air, it was clear there could be no survivors, and once again the company was without a test pilot. However, it should not be assumed that the Widgeon was an unstable monoplane: only a couple of Woodpigeons were built, but something like 30 Widgeons were constructed before production ended in 1929. One, (G-AAGH), remained in use as the company's communications aircraft for 19 years before being destroyed in 1948. Commenting upon its loss, Harald Penrose was to record in his beautiful book, *No Echo in the Sky*: '. . . there would still be other days and other flights, using

Left: Correspondence section 1919

Below left: Packing department 1919

Below: Westland N.1B wings folded

this aeroplane and that, but none so loved as the little Widgeon'.

Following the accident at Bournemouth, there was the problem of finding a replacement for Laurence Openshaw. Later in the year a long, lean and monocled Captain Louis Paget joined the company as its chief test pilot. A colourful character, with RAF service that included participation on the historic Cairo-Baghdad air mail route, he was to bring humour and flying experience to the company. Unlike his predecessors, however, he had received no scientific training. The first major project in which he became involved was the Westland Yeovil. This was a two-seat day bomber that the company regarded as being particularly important, representing the first opportunity that had been presented in the post-war years to tender for the design and construction of a military aircraft.

In August 1923, the Air Ministry had issued its Specification 26/23 calling for a two-seat long-range day bomber, and was to order three prototypes of each of the proposals, all to be powered by the Rolls-Royce Condor engine. As they began to take shape in the Vimy shop during the early Summer of 1925, a visitor joined the company on a temporary basis. This was Harald Penrose, who came to gain unpaid, practical experience, and who was later to become a significant part of Westland history. During that Summer the first two of Westland's prototypes were completed, the third in 1926. First to be ready for flight in June 1925 was J7508, but because the Air Ministry considered that Laurence Openshaw had insufficient recent experience of test flying, the maiden flight of the Yeovil was in the hands of one-time Parisian bank clerk, Captain Frank Courtney. He was to find no problems with the bomber during thirty minutes in the air, following take-off from the company's airfield, and it was agreed that the machine could be flown to Andover, where Openshaw would continue the development flights. The Yeovil was of majestic

Above: **Westland Weasel, rear view**

Above right: **Westland Limousine interior**

Right: **Westland Witch mock-up** (*F. Ballam*)

appearance for its day, standing tall on massive landing gear, and spanning some 18.29 m (60 ft), but despite meeting the Ministry's specification, the Hawker Horsley proved to be better. The three prototypes were to end their days as research aircraft, with no more examples being ordered. A small string of military prototypes followed in unsuccessful attempts to capture an Air Ministry production contract, but with the world getting close to the economic depression of the late 1920s and early 1930s, production contracts were as scarce as dinosaur's eggs. These aircraft included the Westbury twin-engine biplane fighter, Wizard single-seat monoplane fighter, and two-seat Witch day bomber. Of these, the Wizard was probably the most impressive, and when the prototype took part in the 1928 RAF Display at Hendon it was regarded as one of the stars of the show. A contract for an 'improved' Mk II prototype was to follow, but when its performance proved to be inferior to that of the original Wizard, all hopes of a contract had gone. For Westland this was a sore blow; there had been hopes that the Wizard would lead to great things, and to add to the difficulties of the times, work on the D.H.9A was beginning to run down. Unrecognised at the time, however, was the future demand for the offspring of a prototype that had flown in March 1927. Derived from the D.H.9A, which had for so long provided a degree of security to the aircraft activities, it was to represent a new page in the company's history.

4. GROWING ACTIVITIES

By the end of 1926 the Air Ministry had come to the conclusion that, however short of funds for new equipment, it could no longer delay at least a token attempt to replace some of its outmoded aircraft. This was inevitable if the RAF was to be able to deal efficiently and effectively with its growing responsibilities. One can imagine a senior civil servant expressing the opinion that whatever was done must be achieved in the most prudent manner possible, so that while new aircraft were needed, it was essential that they should be multi-purpose, reliable, and cheap. They were required, primarily, to replace the noble D.H.9A that had given so much valuable service, and the Specification 26/27 that was drawn up called for improved performance and greater load-carrying capability, and the desirable – but not imperative – use of an all-metal airframe. In order to keep costs to the absolute minimum, it was considered essential to use as many D.H.9A components as possible, for there were large quantities of parts and assemblies for these aircraft in RAF stores around the world. For the same reason, contenders were encouraged to use as power plant the Napier Lion engine, for the service also had large stocks of these.

With Britain's aviation manufacturers all anxious to secure any possible military contracts, it was not surprising that there was a big response to the 26/27 requirement, with Armstrong Whitworth, Bristol, de Havilland, Fairey, Gloster, Vickers, and Westland all doing their utmost to ensure that their design should be the one to gain success. Westland, of course, which had such a long association with the D.H.9A, was in a strong position, and produced a workmanlike biplane of good solid proportions which, basically, was a D.H.9A with a new fuselage. With regard to power plant they decided to take a gamble, turning their back on the favoured Lion, and installing instead a Bristol Jupiter radial engine. It was a gamble that paid off, for the Jupiter proved good enough for the Westland Wapiti prototype to demonstrate performance equal to the similarly-powered Vickers Valiant, but won hands down by incorporating far more D.H.9A components. The reward was an initial contract for twenty-five Wapiti Is.

Westland was jubilant at the result, and it is not unreasonable to suppose that there would have been something of a party if they had known then that the company was to build eventually 563 of these aircraft. Like the D.H.9A which they replaced, they were to give long and faithful service, used by the RAF on the North-West Frontier of India and over the deserts of Iraq, with eight squadrons serving in India, and three in the latter country. In addition, ten home-based squadrons were equipped with Wapitis, and although the majority had been retired by the beginning of the Second World War, about 80 were then still in service with the RAF in India.

While the Wapiti had been materialising, Westland had become involved in a strange family of aircraft, the tailless Pterodactyls. These derived from the work of Captain G.T.R. Hill, who had spent a long period of time studying the potential of this configuration which had been pioneered by J.W. Dunne. Following the construction and successful demonstration of a prototype aircraft of this configuration, the Air Ministry decided to give further encouragement, with the result that Westland was instructed to produce an improved prototype, under the guidance of Geoffrey Hill, who joined the staff of the company. Hill was academically and technically a brilliant man, and he steered the Pterodactyl project from a very tentative Mk I to the two-seat Pterodactyl V fighter prototype of 1934. Unfortunately, when the project had reached an interesting point, an internal shuffle of executives resulted in Geoffrey Hill tendering his resignation to the Board. With his going, and the growing pressures of the RAF's expansion programme, the Pterodactyl programme just faded away.

A growing appreciation of the fact that civil transport had something to offer was being promoted by the activities of pioneer pilots. The successful transatlantic solo flight from New York to Paris, accomplished by Charles Lindbergh in mid-1927, did more than anything else to make people understand that air transport was no longer a purely military, and often risky, activity. With civil air services beginning to grow, Westland decided to try and become involved in this market by building a short-range light transport named the Westland IV. This was first flown by Louis Paget on 22 February 1929, and following the exhibition of a second example at London's Olympia Aero Show in July of that year, it was decided to build two more of these aircraft. They were, in fact, given more powerful engines and completed under the name Wessex. Examples were acquired by the Belgian airline Sabena; Imperial Airways, which chartered them to the Great Western Railway; one special version was to serve with Portsmouth, Southsea and Isle of Wight Aviation; and subsequently three, ex-Sabena, were used by Sir Alan Cobham's Cobham Air Routes: two of these latter aircraft ended their days flying night publicity sorties with neon-light slogans beneath their

Right: **Wapiti IIA on floats** (*RAF Museum*)

wings. It cannot have been a very profitable operation for the company, and proved to be their last attempt to enter the civil transport market.

The efforts to gain new military contracts continued with the design of a single-seat fighter to meet the Air Ministry Specification F.20/27. This called for a high-speed interceptor which would offer performance superior to that of the new bomber aircraft which were beginning to enter service. As with the 26/27 Specification that led to the Wapiti, there was considerable competition to gain a production contract. Forsaking the biplane configuration, Westland's prototype for this competition was a low-wing monoplane which, despite having a radial engine power plant, succeeded in retaining very good lines. Apart from that it was plagued with troubles when first flown, suffering from instability problems, and low on power. A number of attempts were made to overcome the shortcomings, but before success was achieved the specification was changed, calling for the installation of a different engine. This was the last straw, and the company decided in this case to bring the project to an end and cut their losses. The only balance on the credit side came from the fact that the design office had gained new knowledge and confidence in dealing with some of the aerodynamic problems that had been involved.

Alongside the F.20/27 interceptor Westland developed the C.O.W. Gun fighter, designed to meet Air Ministry Specification F.29/27. Basically a larger version of the F.20/27, it incorporated a gun of 37 mm calibre that the Ministry wished to evaluate as a potential weapon for production fighter aircraft. When firing tests revealed that it was not a practical airborne weapon, the Ministry quickly lost interest in the aircraft that carried it, and again the company had followed the tortuous path of development for the sake of a single unwanted prototype.

Realising there was little future in many of the Ministry oddities, the company decided to proceed with the private venture design and construction of a light torpedo-bomber. It was to prove a significant decision for the P.V.3, as it was designated, was to become repowered by a supercharged Bristol Pegasus engine as the Houston-Westland and it, together with the Houston-Wallace, became the first aircraft in the world to fly over the peak of Mount Everest, on 3 April 1933. The Houston-Wallace had started life as a Wapiti Mk V, became a private venture prototype (P.V.6) as a stage in the development of an improved Wapiti, and had been

Westland Pterodactyl V uncovered

accepted for service trials as the Wapiti Mk VII, before its journey with the Everest expedition as the Houston-Wallace. After the holiday in the high skies over Nepal and Tibet, it was to come down to earth as the Wallace I, entering service with the RAF in late 1933.

At the time when the Wallace I had been known as the Wapiti V, it was taken on board ship to Buenos Aires, accompanied by Harald Penrose, who was to make demonstration flights with it in South America. Very shortly after his return, Louis Paget was demonstrating spins in a Widgeon, but failed to recover in time and was lucky to escape with nothing more serious than a badly damaged leg. Unfortunately, this took longer to mend than anticipated and, as a result, Paget decided the moment had come to retire. He was replaced by the appointment of Harald Penrose as chief test pilot, a position he was to retain for 25 years.

The P.V.6 demonstrated effectively that private venture gambles can sometimes pay off, for the Air Ministry contracted initially for 12 Wapiti to Wallace I conversions, and follow-on contracts were to bring the total conversions to 172 when the last of them was completed in late 1936. The massive P.V.7 which followed was designed to meet Specification G.4/31 for a general-purpose military aircraft. It

Westland advertisement of 1929

incorporated several innovations, and when first flown by Harald Penrose all seemed to be progressing well. Development continued without any serious problems, until expansion of the flight envelope was to show that the outer wing panels tended to twist with aileron application at high speed. This wing torsional problem was overcome by the introduction of strengthened wing bracing, and continued development, demonstration at the 1934 RAF Display, and the satisfactory progress of service trials, all seemed to suggest that this time the company had a winner. On 25 August 1934, Harald Penrose took off in the P.V.7 to carry out a constructors' test with the CG well aft. Without him being aware of the fact the aircraft had been overloaded, and when he nosed the aircraft down into the required dive test, watching his instruments carefully as the speed built up, there came a sudden irregularity in the smoothness of the dive. Before there was a chance to take any action, a muffled sound of tortured metal drew his attention to the port side, and to his horror the wing was torn away, followed by a dull thud as it carried the tail unit away with it. By little short of a miracle, Penrose escaped without serious

injury, the first pilot in Britain to make a successful parachute escape from an enclosed military aircraft. As he breathed a long sigh of relief at his escape, he probably pondered the thought that the life of a chief test pilot is not all beer and skittles.

The substitution of Penrose for Paget as the company's chief test pilot was not, by a long way, the only personnel change in 1934. After a long period of stability, with Robert Bruce as Managing Director, and Arthur Davenport as Chief Designer, the boat was rocked by an announcement that W.E.W. (Teddy) Petter, Sir Ernest's son, was to become a member of the Board. The internal repercussions that this would involve were not approved by Bruce, who had given so much to the company, and he decided to hand in his resignation. Geoffrey Hill, who had seemed likely to become the next Technical Director, also resigned. In the following year Westland Aircraft Works ceased to exist, replaced after 20 years by a new public company known as Westland Aircraft Ltd. Sir Ernest Petter was its Chairman and Managing Director, his son Teddy Petter Technical Director. P.D. Acland and Air Vice-Marshal N.D.K. MacEwen were also directors, the former a shrewd businessman who was to do much to help expansion of the company when Britain's rearmament programme demanded such action. Shortly after these changes, former test pilot Stuart Keep was to resign, being replaced by John Fearn as Works Manager.

While the P.V.7 prototype was taking shape, the company had been building at the same time a single-seat fighter prototype to meet the Air Ministry's F.7/30 Specification. This was first flown by Harald Penrose on 27 March 1934, not long after the maiden flight of the P.V.7., but despite lengthy development it failed to meet the specification required and was abandoned. Apart from Wapiti to Wallace conversions, Westland had little happening at that time, and was pleased to have the opportunity of submitting a design and tender to Air Ministry Specification A.39/34 which called for an army co-operation aircraft to replace the Hawker Audax then in service. It was the first design to be produced under the leadership of Teddy Petter, and no efforts were spared to ensure that the requirements would be met. The design team had even spent an enormous amount of time talking to pilots and leaders of army co-operation squadrons, trying to discover the real needs of the man at the controls, as well as those of the men on the ground with whom he was trying to co-operate. This good homework was to pay off, Westland receiving an order for two prototypes in June 1935. Very shortly afterwards the company was to receive a sub-contract from Hawker Aircraft for the production of the Hawker Hector which had been ordered from the company, also as an Audax replacement. Suddenly, Westland found that the pace was increasing, and it was not long before Peter Acland sought, and

Westland F.20/27 with tall fin and rudder

obtained, Board approval for the construction of a new main assembly building. Harald Penrose flew the first of the Hectors during February 1937, and a total of 178 were to be built by the company.

The first of the P8 prototypes to the A.39/34 requirement had been flown by Penrose some eight months earlier; within two years the first of the Lysanders, as they became known, had entered service with the RAF's No.16 Squadron at Old Sarum. It is unlikely that Westland, or any of the other contractors that had made a somewhat uninterested bid for the manufacture of a type that, traditionally, would be built in only small quantities, could have appreciated that production would eventually total more than 1,400.

Before Westland became involved in the Second World War, there was a further administrative change that was to give the company financial strength and first class managerial guidance at a moment when it was most needed. In July 1938 the well-known Clydeside shipbuilders, John Brown and Company, acquired a controlling interest in Westland Aircraft Ltd, as well as of Petters Ltd. That part of Petters' holding that was not taken up by John Brown was acquired subsequently by Associated Electrical Industries Ltd. Sir Ernest Petter was replaced by Lord Aberconway as Chairman, with Peter Acland and Eric Mensforth as Joint Managing Directors. Under this reshuffle, the functions of Teddy Petter, Arthur Davenport, and John Fearn were unchanged. This, then, was the team that was to guide the company's fortunes as it began six years of wartime production.

Overleaf: **Lysanders vie with contractors extending the work's hangar space, summer 1939** (*F. Ballam*)

Westland P.V.7 with pilot's enclosed cockpit

5. WAR AND PEACE

The story of Westland's wartime activities falls within two categories: the design, development and construction of their own products, and the sub-contract manufacture, repair, and servicing of aircraft built by both the British and American aircraft industries. Types within the first category include the Lysander, Whirlwind, and Welkin, with combined wartime production totalling some 1,200 aircraft. This was completely overshadowed by work carried out within the second category, for sub-contract manufacture of Supermarine Spitfire and Seafire aircraft alone reached almost 2,200, with a peak wartime production rate of aircraft within both categories climbing to a figure in excess of 20 per week. The number of personnel that was employed at the war's beginning was close on 3,000, but this was to more than double as the company's activities increased and, as can be imagined, work space was at a premium. This latter shortcoming was only relieved marginally by completion of the new main assembly shop, mentioned in the previous chapter, with the result that the company was to have small units spread around the Yeovil area, as well as facilities and sub-contractors far more distant. Some of this dispersal resulted from the desirability of making a greater concentration of manufacturing and production capacity at the main factory, and some sections were moved out to make this possible. For example, the design offices were established at Nether Compton, and other local offshoots included component works at Ilchester, Martock, and Sherborne; machine shops in Chard, and beneath Yeovil's Odeon cinema; and material stores in the old Nautilus Works, and at Preston Plucknett on the town's outskirts. All were within easy reach of the main factory, and only slightly more distant was a new hangar and facilities at Ilchester, built during 1939-40, where Lysander and Spitfire repairs were carried out. Far more distant was a factory site at Doncaster, Yorkshire, which had been taken over by the Ministry of Aircraft Production, and which was allocated to Westland for the repair of Lysanders and Vickers Wellingtons.

For the company, the Lysander represented the reward for so many past disappointments. Its distinctive shape, the almost unmistakeable note of its engine, and of course its exciting activities with the Special Duties Squadrons, surround this aircraft with a special aura that time is likely to enhance rather than dispel. So far as the factory was concerned, the Lysander was largely a routine production task which ended in early 1942. Its development was virtually completed before the war started, although some work continued during the war to develop special variants.

However, none of these were to enter production, for the only versions to enter service were conversions of earlier aircraft for clandestine operations and, when the type was withdrawn from first-line duties, to make them suitable for target towing. This was as well, for the Whirlwind and Welkin were to need a great deal of work.

Design of the aircraft that was to become named Whirlwind had originated in 1936 to meet the Air Ministry Specification F.37/35, which called for a single-seat heavily-armed fighter that must be equipped for both day and night operations. An attractive and original low-wing monoplane, it had been designed under the leadership of Teddy Petter, and was to be built under conditions of great secrecy. In fact, although it had been flown by Harald Penrose for the first time from Boscombe Down on 11 October 1938, it was not until late 1941 that existence of the Whirlwind was acknowledged officially. Early flight testing showed that this was in a very different category to any aircraft developed previously by the company, being fast and highly manoeuvrable. Problems were experienced with the cooling of its Rolls-Royce Peregrine engines, but these were overcome as development progressed, and Handley Page leading-edge slats, which had been incorporated in the wing to overcome any stall problems, were found to be superfluous and later eliminated. These two areas of the design were to hasten the demise of the Whirlwind, after only 112 had entered service with the RAF. The Rolls-Royce engine could not provide the required high-altitude performance at which wartime combats were being fought, and the Whirlwind's high landing speed limited the number of airfields from which it could operate. Any regrets over the short production run must have been offset to some extent by the knowledge that not only had it been the company's first fighter to enter RAF service, but also that it was the first twin-engine single-seat fighter to become operational with any service. Valuable experience had been gained and there would be other fighter contracts.

The next opportunity came when the company began the design of a high-altitude fighter to meet Air Ministry Specification F.7/41. This called for features that included a pressurised cabin for operation at a service ceiling of more than 12,800 m (42,000 ft), provision for the installation of A.I. radar, and armament comprising six 20 mm cannon. The Welkin retained a similarity to the Whirlwind that had preceded it, but was of mid-wing instead of low-wing configuration, and was powered by Rolls-Royce Merlin engines. The most difficult of the company's development problems in connection with this aircraft related to the

pressure cabin. This was an entirely new area of design so far as Westland was concerned, and great difficulty was experienced in arriving at a satisfactory and effective means of automatically controlling the pressure differential of the cabin. Eventually a small and compact valve was designed for this purpose, relieving the pilot from the task of having to monitor and manually adjust cabin pressure. This comparatively minor component of a complex fighter aircraft was to lay the foundation of the separate subsidiary of Normalair Limited. Known now as Normalair-Garrett, this company is also Yeovil-based, and in 1980 had a turnover of some £35.5 million. First flown on 1 November 1942, the Welkin was ordered into production with a contract for 100 examples. These were intended to intercept any attacks launched by German high-altitude aircraft: when such attacks failed to materialise there was no requirement for the Welkin, and production ended after about 80 had been built. None were issued to RAF squadrons, but they were to see considerable use for high-altitude research.

Sub-contract work began in the early days of the war, starting with the incorporation of minor modifications in Curtiss Mohawk, Tomahawk and Kittyhawk single-seat fighters which were acquired as a result of Direct Purchase Contracts, transferred from French purchases, or supplied under Lend-Lease. British radio installations were incorporated, and many of the aircraft which had been intended

Left: Lysander with de Lanne wing

Below: The 'Pregnant Perch' after its crash

Lysander with 20 mm cannons

for service with the French air force were given new instruments to replace those of metric notation. Far more important was an inquiry from the Ministry of Aircraft Production as to whether the company could undertake the large-scale production of Supermarine Spitfire fighters. This was the sort of task the company could carry out efficiently, and the workshops were soon filled with production lines of these superb aircraft. Spitfire IIAs, VBs and VCs were produced to a total of almost 700 aircraft and then, intermingled on the floor, came the first examples of another sub-contract for Fairey Barracuda torpedo-bomber/reconnaissance aircraft. Total production of Barracudas by Fairey and its sub-contractors was to exceed 2,500 aircraft, and Westland might well have had a large share of this total, but the company's efficient production of Spitfires was to lead to a continuing contract for the construction of Seafires, and the MAP regarded this to be of the greater importance. Barracuda production ended at Yeovil after only 18 examples had been built. One other sub-contract that should be mentioned involved the construction of a large number of wing centre-sections for Armstrong Whit-

worth Albemarles, an aircraft that was to see extensive service in a glider tug and transport role.

Westland's association with the Supermarine Seafire began with a sub-contract for the production of 110 Seafire IICs. While this work was under way, the company was involved with Supermarine in the design of a satisfactory manual wing-folding mechanism. On completion of the initial production batch, Westland was made prime contractor for all Seafire production, and this embraced IICs, IIICs, XVs, and XVIIs. When it was appreciated that the volume involved would clearly exceed the company's productive capacity, Westland appointed Cunliffe-Owen Aircraft as sub-contractor to them. Total production from these two companies was to exceed 2,400, with Westland responsible for just over 60 per cent of this total. With all these multiple activities, Westland was fortunate to escape serious attention from enemy attacks, and suffered nothing more serious than several hit-and-run strikes by individual intruders.

As the war progressed a number of changes occurred in executive appointments. One, regarded as something of an honour by the company, related to the selection of one of its Joint Managing Directors, Eric Mensforth, as Chief Production Adviser to Air Marshal Sir Wilfred Freeman, Chief Executive of the Ministry of Aircraft Production. His place

Top: **Whirlwind with alternative gun layout**

Above: **Westland Welkin I**

was filled on the Board by John Fearn, who became a Joint MD. Other changes involved the departure of Teddy Petter, in 1944, to become Chief Designer of the English Electric Company and, in the resulting re-shuffle, Arthur Davenport became Technical Director in his place, and John Digby filled the seat of Chief Designer that he had vacated.

Most of the senior executives of the company had clear memories of the immediate post-war difficulties that had followed the end of the First World War. While they could do nothing to overcome the sudden void in production that would come after the wartime manufacturing contracts were terminated, they were determined to do anything possible to ensure that redundancies within the company's workforce should be limited to the minimum. One of these moves involved the formation of Westland Engineers Ltd in 1944, a subsidiary company that would diversify into non-aviation activities so that it would be able to absorb some of the displaced workforce. This plan worked well, and the company was still in existence in 1981. In the previous year,

despite the recession in Britain's economy, more than 400 people were employed. Normalair Limited, mentioned earlier in this chapter, was not established as a separate company until 1946. It, too, continues to operate today on a worldwide basis, its labour force exceeding 2,000 people in 1980.

Before the war ended Westland was to become involved in the design of another aircraft of special interest. The Admiralty Specification N.11/44 called for the development of a single-seat ship-based strike aircraft. It was a demanding specification, requiring the initial installation of a Rolls-Royce 24-cylinder sleeve-valve engine, and the capability to accept turboprop power plant that was under development. Just how difficult was the problem of getting this aircraft into service can be appreciated by the fact that almost six and a half years separated the first flight of the prototype, and its entry into service with the Fleet Air Arm's No.813 Squadron in May 1953. This aircraft was the Westland Wyvern, first flown by Harald Penrose on 12 December 1946. Despite its long gestation period, only about 120 examples were to be built, and these saw a comparatively short span of first-line service. This, of course, was due to the fact that development of the Wyvern had been so extended, due to the introduction of a series of new and untried engines, that it was soon superseded by more advanced designs. This

Seafire and Welkin assembly, February 1944

aircraft is remembered with particular affection by Harald Penrose for, apart from the fact that it nearly killed him on one occasion in its early development stages, it was the last Westland production aircraft that he was to flight test. After 25 years as the company's Chief Test Pilot, he was promoted (Penrose would probably substitute the word demoted) to become Westland's sales manager.

D-Day and then VJ-Day passed and, as anticipated, a decision had to be made about the future direction that the company was to take. The Wyvern was under development, and might enter production, but the company had no long-term contract in existence, like that of the D.H.9A of the inter-wars years, to provide a steady fund of work and income. Neither was there Petters Ltd to fall back on. The Board must have taken a realistic view of the situation, appreciating that their hopes of gaining significant military contracts were rather remote, and that their chance of breaking into the civil market was virtually nil. Two major

fields were left: those of light general purpose aircraft, and the somewhat mysterious area of rotary-wing aircraft. Mysterious because their development to practicality was of fairly recent date, and no one could tell then the extent to which the market would develop.

Perhaps it should be mentioned that the latter was not a complete jump into the dark by Westland, for the company had worked unsuccessfully with a couple of autogiros, based on Juan de la Cierva's ideas, during the 1930s. Progress had been very limited, and when ground resonance problems with the C.29 could not be resolved, the aircraft was pushed into a hangar and left to gather dust. The aircraft that followed, the C.L.20, was test flown successfully just before the outbreak of war, but with the pressure of more serious activities lapsed into obscurity. Whether or not this brief episode in the company's history had any influence on future events, John Fearn was to head the team of Board members that visited the United States in 1946 to finalise licence-production agreements for the Sikorsky S-51. A satisfactory conclusion to this visit meant that the die was cast: Westland was to become a manufacturer of rotary-wing aircraft, and only the future would reveal whether the decision was sound or not.

6. ROTARY WINGS AND THE FUTURE

Westland's Board members had done their utmost to look into the future and select the most promising course for the company and its workforce. In making this decision, none of them had imagined that the path would be easy. There was little more than the Wyvern in the pipeline, and even with the best will in the world, and a modicum of luck, there would be a long period before helicopter production would reach a stage when it was producing any real income.

In the background, various moves had been taking place to strengthen the executive leadership, to provide a team that, hopefully, would guide the company into a strong industrial position. One of the first appointments after acquisition of the Sikorsky licence was that of O.L.L. Fitzwilliams as Helicopter Engineer; he had previously been in charge of the Rotary Wing Aircraft Section of the Airborne Forces Experimental Establishment at Beaulieu, Hampshire. Edward C. Wheeldon, who had joined the company as Planning Engineer in 1938, became Managing Director. With the support of Eric Mensforth, who was to become Chairman of the company in 1953, he added David Collins, Walter Oppenheimer, and David Hollis Williams to give added strength in production, financial, and technical areas respectively. Westland had girded its loins to become a specialist in the field of rotary wing aircraft.

It was hard going from the very first moment, probably far harder than anyone had expected. O.L.L. Fitzwilliams highlights the early problems, writing in *A History of British Rotorcraft 1865-1965*, that was produced by Westland. '. . . Due to a complete prohibition on dollar content, and the then wide differences between British and American materials and accessories, particularly bearings, the anglicising of the S-51 design was very extensive, every part of the helicopter being in some respects (and many parts in very major respects) different from the American original. The magnitude of this task was greatly underrated and it was carried out by a tiny staff – there being only 14 people, including the secretary and office boy, in the department when the first Westland S-51 flew at the beginning of October 1948 . . .' In principle each American drawing issued to the works was accompanied by an auxiliary Westland drawing or "Extract Sheet", containing instructions for anglicising the part. In practice, many of these "Extract Sheets" were as complex as the American originals and even for the basic aircraft many of the drawings issued were Westland originals . . .'.

The American drawings had been received from Sikorsky in May 1947, and having regard to the foregoing, added to the fact that everyone on the factory floor had a great deal to learn, it is not surprising that some 17 months were to pass before the first Westland-built S-51 was flown, during October 1948. And because the first batch of aircraft had been built by hand, there was a further delay of nearly 18 months before the first true production aircraft began to enter service with the Royal Navy and RAF. Although the Westland/Sikorsky S-51 was thus late into service, it nevertheless enabled the Navy's No.705 Squadron to gain the distinction of being the world's first helicopter squadron outside of the USA when it was formed in 1950. In mid-1951 the Dragonfly, as the type became named, gained a Certificate of Airworthiness, to become the first British-built civil helicopter, and the RAF's first squadron was formed during February 1953. A total of 133 Dragonflies were to be built for military and civil use, providing the company with a wealth of experience, and enabling them to develop an improved Widgeon by the installation of a more powerful engine. Only a small number of Widgeons were built, the market being attracted to the larger-capacity Whirlwind that became available, following the conclusion of licence negotiations during 1950 for the company to build the Sikorsky S-55.

At that time there was no great demand for helicopters. True, they could fulfil tasks that could be carried out by no other vehicle, but their capacity was very limited and they were expensive to operate. Beyond their use for roles covered loosely by the words rescue and reconnaissance, they seemed to have little real application in the aviation scene of the early 1950s. The Korean War, which began on 25 June 1950, was to change this thinking once and for all, for military commanders were soon to discover that the slow, noisy, costly, and humble helicopter was among the most valuable aircraft in their line-up. Within very little time the helicopter market was wide open, and the demand was to be enhanced still further when their importance was realised in connection with the exploration, operation, and maintenance of offshore natural gas and oil fields.

Westland was to build more than 400 of the Sikorsky S-55 under the name Whirlwind, and in the process gained considerable insight into the entire process of helicopter design and manufacture. Much of this experience came from the installation of a variety of engines, and the design and incorporation of innumerable special configurations to produce no less than 12 Whirlwind variants. Growing confidence led to the consideration of building a large transport helicopter, and with the agreement of Sikorsky to allow the company to utilise the dynamic system of the S-56, the Westland Westminster project was initiated. Under development simultaneously with the Wessex, only two

examples were built before, for a variety of reasons mentioned in the notes on the Westminster, development was abandoned.

The introduction of turboshaft engines on the Whirlwind had shown that, without any doubt, this was the helicopter power plant of the future. Negotiations were started with Sikorsky for a licence to build the much larger S-58, and from this was derived the Wessex. In this important helicopter, Westland was to introduce two innovations, the first relating to installation of a power plant comprising initially a single Napier Gazelle turboshaft. Some years later this was replaced by two Bristol Siddeley Gnome turboshaft engines, intercoupled so that in emergency either engine was able to drive the rotor system. This offered greater operational freedom, but of even greater significance was the introduction of an Automatic Flight Control System, developed as a co-operative effort between the company and Louis Newmark Ltd, that represented an enormous gain in operational capability. Providing fully automatic transition to and from the hover, coupled hover and turns to preselected headings, all in a fully duplicated system, this allowed all phases of the anti-submarine search and strike capability of the Navy's HAS.Mk 3s to be met automatically, from initial lift-off to positioning for landing. It was to result in fixed-wing carrier-based ASW aircraft disappearing rapidly from the Royal Navy's first-line inventory.

Almost simultaneously with the initiation of Wessex development, the British government issued its notorious Defence White Paper of 1957. Among a wealth of revolutionary ideas was the practical suggestion that the nation's

Left: **FAA Wyverns off Beachy Head**
(*RAF Museum/Charles Brown*)

Right: **Westminster G-APLE heavy lift helicopter**

Below: **Sycamore**

aviation industry should re-organise itself into a number of small groups. Westland's Board was to react fairly quickly to this suggestion, seeing an opportunity of becoming Britain's only – or at any rate leading – manufacturer of rotary wing aircraft. Thus, in 1959 the long-established company of Saunders-Roe Ltd was to be acquired, and including its facilities at Cowes, Isle of Wight, and at Eastleigh in Hampshire. In 1960, the procurement of the Helicopter Division of Bristol Aircraft Ltd from the Bristol Aeroplane Company was followed, less than a couple of months later, by the purchase of the UK aviation interests of Fairey Aviation Ltd. Additional facilities gained by these acquisitions included the Fairey works at Hayes, Middlesex, but far more important were those of Bristol's Helicopter Division, at Weston-super-Mare, Somerset, for they added

Left: **Fairey Rotodyne**

Below: **Westland Sea King Mk 1 of the Royal Navy**

Below right: **Westland Sea King Mk 5 of the Royal Navy with dunking sonar**

to the company's design, research and production capability. Initially these companies were adopted as divisions of the parent company, known as Bristol Helicopter, Fairey Aviation, and Saunders-Roe, with the operation at Yeovil identified as the Yeovil Division. Their coming was to build up an enormous fund of technical expertise, adding the capabilities of personalities such as Raoul Hafner from Bristol, and Dr Hislop of Fairey.

And, of course, these companies brought new products that were already in production or under development. From Bristol came the Belvedere short-range twin-rotor tactical transport helicopter, then under development, and although this continued, only 24 production examples were to be built for the RAF. Fairey added the fixed-wing Gannet, the majority of 44 AEW.Mk 3s being completed after the acquisition, plus some conversions to AS.Mk 6 and AS.Mk 7. Potentially far more important from this source was the Fairey Rotodyne, a VTOL airliner intended to carry up to 60 passengers between city centres. Despite strenuous attempts to bring this project to fruition, it eventually had to be abandoned when the cost of continued development was more than the company could finance without government support, and this was not forthcoming. Saunders-Roe added

the P.531 project for a five-seat general-purpose helicopter derived from the Skeeter. Development of this was continued, becoming produced as the Westland Scout, and the first of these entered service in 1963. Of those that were built, more than 100 remained in British Army Aviation service in 1981. From the Scout, the company developed the navalised Wasp, and more than 60 of these remained in Royal Navy service in 1981. The acquisition of Saunders-Roe gave Westland control of that company's Hovercraft programme, and subsequently a subsidiary company named British Hovercraft was formed to control and continue development of a potentially important vehicle. In 1980 this company recorded sales totalling almost £23.9 million, at which time British Hovercraft had just over 2,000 employees. Also gained from Saunders-Roe was the Black Knight ballistic test vehicle, development of which was cancelled in 1964 after one two-stage and 19 single-stage firings had been carried out at the Woomera test-range in Australia. Development continued of a small three-stage satellite launch vehicle known as Black Arrow, derived from Black Knight, but cancellation of this programme came in 1971.

Since that time, the company's operations have become rationalised by the formation of separate subsidiary companies to handle activities that do not relate directly to the design, development, and manufacture of rotary wing aircraft. In addition to British Hovercraft, Normalair-Garrett, and Westland Engineers, which have already been mentioned, there are also FPT Industries at Portsmouth, Hampshire, and Saunders-Roe Developments at Hayes, Middlesex. FPT Industries, which in 1980 employed almost 400 and had a turnover of approximately £3.3 million, is concerned with the manufacture of advanced rubber products, including flexible fuel tanks. Saunders-Roe Developments, with some 250 employees, is developing and marketing a line of advanced electro-luminescent products. All of the foregoing, together with Westland Helicopters Ltd, form the

Left: **RN Lynx landing on HMS *Sheffield***

Above: **The first Lynx for the Royal Danish Navy, at the Pool of London**

Right: **Lynx landing on HMS *Birmingham***

principal component members of the Westland Aircraft Group.

As already related, Westland's entry into the field of rotary wing aircraft resulted from the Sikorsky licence agreement of 1946, and international relationships have continued to be very much a part of the company's activities in helicopter manufacture. When the Bell Model 47 was selected as standard equipment for the British Army, Westland built 250 47G-3B-4s under licence from Agusta in Italy. Far more important however, was the agreement concluded in 1968 with Aérospatiale in France, covering the collaborative production of three different helicopters. The first two to come out of this co-operation were the Puma and Gazelle. For the Puma, Westland activity has been confined to component manufacture, and the assembly and com-

pletion of 40 Puma HC.Mk 1s, now in service with the RAF, followed by eight more with composite rotor blades that were assembled during 1980-81. In 1981 the company was continuing the manufacture of Puma components for the Aérospatiale production line. Very much more volume has come from the Gazelle co-operation, and with well over 800 helicopters ordered, Gazelle construction was being continued energetically in 1981.

Chronologically, the next of the company's helicopters is the Sea King, which derives from a licence agreement concluded with Sikorsky in 1959, and relating to that company's S-61 which has amphibious capability. From this basic design Westland retained the dynamic system and a similar fuselage structure for the first HAS.Mk 1 version, but since that time has developed no fewer than 19 variants with progressively increasing capability.

The agreement with Aérospatiale covering the third helicopter, identified originally as the WG.13, was very different to that relating to the Puma and Gazelle, for it gave Westland design leadership. With its backlog of experience, enhanced by the expertise gained from company acquisitions, this presented a golden opportunity to demonstrate that the company could design and develop a first class product. This has proved to be the case, with sales for the helicopter, which became named Lynx, comfortably exceeding the 300 mark in 1981. More recently, however, the

company has initiated the private venture design and development of an enlarged version of the Lynx, which retains the basic dynamic system of that helicopter, with increased rotor diameter. Designated the WG.30 for military use, and Westland 30 as a civil transport, these helicopters were under development in 1981. Two examples of the Westland 30 have been ordered by British Airways Helicopters, and these are scheduled to enter service in 1982.

Today, the Westland Group has as its President Sir Eric Mensforth, who for so long has had the company's interests very close to his heart. The Chairman of the Board is Lord Aldington, and his Deputy Chairman Lord Aberconway. Vice-Chairman and Chief Executive is Mr B.D. Blackwell, who is also Chairman and Managing Director of Westland Helicopters Ltd. Together, these men and their fellow directors and other executives have the difficult task of continuing to maintain the profitability of the company. Difficult, not because the product is inferior to that of other manufacturers in any part of the world, but because of tightening defence budgets, and the relationship of the pound sterling to the currencies of other nations. There is no doubt that the company has excellent products to sell, and to give them the best possible opportunity to hold their position in world markets, Westland has recently undergone a major internal reorganisation. This aims to provide a better service to existing customers, and to make the

company more responsive to potential new customers. The company organisation now includes a Civil Division, with Tom Brennan as its Director, to cater for the needs of the civil and commercial customer; the HMG Business Group, headed by Frank Stanton, to focus all company activities associated with the UK government; and a Military Export Business Group, with Don Berrington as Divisional Director, which is concerned particularly with the military export market. Backing these business groups are Product Groups, concerned with build standard, quality, reliability, and cost of the company's products; together with Support Groups and Site Management.

There is one other potentially important activity, namely the partnership with Agusta of Italy, which has led to the establishment of E.H. Industries Ltd, to develop and manufacture a Sea King replacement under the initial designation of EH.101. Westland has never been more active, or more vitally aware of the need to keep ahead in the development of the advanced equipment required by new-generation rotary-wing aircraft, both civil and military. The company has the strength around it to do just this, particularly having regard to the technological muscle that was gained as a result of the groupings that have occurred during the last 20 odd years.

The foundations established in Northover Fields in 1915 have so far stood the test of time most admirably. There is every reason to believe that the townsfolk of Yeovil will continue to have pride in their major industry for many more years to come!

Left: **W.G.30 picks up Army Milan anti-tank missile teams**

Below: **Artist's impression of EH.101**

AIRCRAFT SECTION

WESTLAND-BUILT (Sub-contract)

SHORT SEAPLANE, ADMIRALTY TYPE 184

TYPE: Two-seat multi-role seaplane.

NOTES: Designed by Short Brothers at Rochester, Kent, and intended to serve as a torpedo-carrier, the Short 184 was to prove unsuitable for this task, but was to be built extensively for service during World War I, primarily in bomber and reconnaissance roles. Total production exceeded 650 aircraft, by Shorts and nine sub-contractors, and Westland Aircraft Works was one of this latter number. First aircraft to be built by the company, it was powered by a 168 kW (225 hp) engine, resulting in it being known by Westland as The Short 225. With this engine, irrespective of manufacturer, it acquired the nickname 'Two-Two-Five'. Having no prior experience of aircraft construction, a group of the company's executives spent two weeks at Short Brothers' works to receive instruction. Westland built 12 of these 'Short 225s', work on the first starting in August 1915. Due to lack of experience, and having especial problems in mastering the technique of achieving taut doped fabric surfaces, the first was not completed until December of that year. It was despatched in January 1916, disassembled and crated, and the first stage of the journey was by horse-drawn vehicle to Yeovil Junction. From there these seaplanes were delivered by rail to Short Brothers for reassembly and testing.

STRUCTURE: Braced three-bay biplane, mainly of wooden construction, with fabric covering. Wings fold for stowage. Inflated wingtip floats. Fuselage of wooden construction, fabric-covered. Braced tail unit, of similar construction to wings, fabric-covered. Float landing gear comprising two main floats, and tail float with water rudder.

ACCOMMODATION: Two open cockpits for pilot, forward, and observer, aft.

DATA (Westland/Short 225):

POWER PLANT: One 168 kW (225 hp) Sunbeam inline piston-engine. Standard fuel capacity 341 litres (75 Imp gallons). Oil capacity 34 litres (7.5 Imp gallons).

Wing span	19.36 m (63 ft 6¼ in)
Wing area	63.92 m² (688 sq ft)
Length overall	12.38 m (40 ft 7½ in)
Height overall	4.11 m (13 ft 6 in)
Weight empty	approx 1,588 kg (3,500 lb)
Max T-O weight	2,313 kg (5,100 lb)
Max level speed at 610 m (2,000 ft)	
	65 knots (121 km/h; 75 mph)

ARMAMENT: One Lewis gun on movable mount for observer. One 14-in torpedo or bomb load of approx 181 kg (400 lb).

Short 184/Westland 225

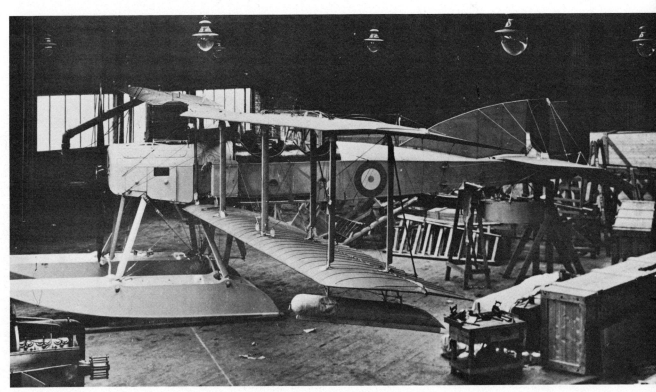

WESTLAND-BUILT (Sub-contract)

SHORT SEAPLANE, ADMIRALTY TYPE 166

TYPE: Torpedo-carrying or bombing/reconnaissance seaplane.

NOTES: Designed by Shorts as a torpedo-carrying seaplane, it was chronologically of earlier origin than the Type 184. Only six were built by Shorts, but Westland constructed an additional 20 under subcontract from 1916. Early experience with the Shorts-built aircraft had shown them to be of little use as torpedo-carriers, and no records exist to confirm that any of these six aircraft launched a torpedo operationally. The first real work of Westland's embryo drawing office was to modify the float mounting so that there was no provision for a torpedo, but to allow instead for the carriage of three 112-lb bombs. Additionally, as they were provided with very few working drawings, they had to create their own in collaboration with Shorts. Powered by a 149 kW (200 hp) Salmson (Canton Unné) engine, this aircraft was identified by Westland as the Short 220 Canton Unné. As they were completed they were crated and sent by rail to Hamble, Hampshire for assembly and flight testing, the first of them delivered in July 1916.

STRUCTURE: Braced unequal-span two-bay biplane wings of wooden construction with fabric covering. Wings folded for stowage. Inflated wingtip floats. Fuselage of wooden structure, fabric-covered. Braced tail unit of similar construction to wings, fabric-covered. Float landing gear, comprising two main floats, and tail float with water rudder.

ACCOMMODATION: Two open cockpits for pilot, forward, and observer, aft.

DATA (Westland/Short 220):

POWER PLANT: One 149 kW (200 hp) Salmson (Canton Unné) radial piston-engine. Standard fuel capacity 395 litres (87 Imp gallons). Oil capacity 30 litres (6.5 Imp gallons).

Wing span (upper)	17.45 m (57 ft 3 in)
Wing span (lower)	12.80 m (42 ft 0 in)
Wing area	53.23 m² (573 sq ft)
Length overall	12.37 m (40 ft 7 in)
Height overall	4.29 m (14 ft 0¾ in)
Weight empty	1,588 kg (3,500 lb)
Max T-O weight	2,077 kg (4,580 lb)
Max level speed	approx 56 knots (105 km/h; 65 mph)
Endurance	about 4 h

ARMAMENT: Lewis gun on movable mount in aft cockpit, with six drums of ammunition. Three 112-lb bombs.

Short 166/Westland 220 on the slipway

WESTLAND-BUILT (Sub-contract)

SOPWITH 1½-STRUTTERS

TYPE: Two-seat fighter/reconnaissance/bomber aircraft, single-seat bomber.

NOTES: Designed by the Sopwith Aviation Company to meet an Admiralty requirement for a two-seat fighter for service with the RNAS, it was designated Sopwith Type 9700. By the RFC it was known originally as the Sopwith Two-Seater. However, its unofficial title of Sopwith 1½-Strutter, most likely derived from the short outer bracing struts of the upper wing centre-section, was eventually adopted generally. Westland Aircraft Works received an initial contract for 50 two-seaters to follow on after completion of the Short 220s. A later contract for an additional 25 aircraft comprised 20 two-seaters and five single-seat bombers. All 75 aircraft were completed between the Autumn of 1916 and Spring 1917, but because the company had no flying field at that period all of these aircraft, like the Shorts aircraft that had preceded them, were crated for delivery by rail.

STRUCTURE: Braced equal-span single-bay biplane with ailerons on both wings. Two-spar wooden wing structure with fabric covering. Wooden fuselage structure with plywood decking fore and aft of cockpits. The single-seat version had continuous plywood decking from front cockpit to tail; remainder of structure fabric-covered. Braced tail unit of wooden construction with fabric covering, variable-incidence tailplane. Landing gear comprising two mainwheels, each on half-axle with rubber bungee shock-absorption, and tail skid.

ACCOMMODATION: Two-seat version with two open cockpits, pilot forward, observer/gunner aft. Single-seat version with forward cockpit for pilot only.

DATA (Westland/Sopwith 1½-Strutter): A: two-seat version; B: single-seat bomber.

POWER PLANT: Both Westland-built versions had one 97 kW (130 hp) Clerget rotary piston engine. Standard fuel capacity (A) 182 litres (40 Imp gallons); (B) 273 litres (60 Imp gallons).

Wing span	10.21 m (33 ft 6 in)
Wing area	32.52 m² (350 sq ft)
Length overall	7.70 m (25 ft 3 in)
Height overall	3.12 m (10 ft 3 in)
Weight empty:	
A	592 kg (1,305 lb)
B	597 kg (1,316 lb)
Max T-O weight:	
A	975 kg (2,150 lb)
B	1,062 kg (2,342 lb)
Max speed at 1,980 m (6,500 ft):	
A	87 knots (161 km/h; 100 mph)
B	89 knots (164 km/h; 102 mph)
Service ceiling:	
A	4,725 m (15,500 ft)
B	3,960 m (13,000 ft)

ARMAMENT: (A) Fixed forward-firing synchronised Vickers machine-gun with 500 rounds ammunition, Lewis gun on movable mounting in rear cockpit with 5 drums ammunition, and 12 le Pecq bombs; two 65-lb bombs for anti-submarine patrol. (B) Forward-firing machine-gun as A, plus four 56-lb bombs or lighter bombs to equivalent weight.

Sopwith 1½-Strutter, two-seater

D.H.4 with 220 hp Puma

WESTLAND-BUILT (Sub-contract)

AIRCO (DE HAVILLAND) D.H.4

TYPE: Two-seat day bomber, but used also in anti-submarine, anti-Zeppelin, fighter-reconnaissance, and photographic roles.

NOTES: Designed by Captain Geoffrey de Havilland to meet a requirement for a day bomber, the D.H.4 was one of the classic aircraft of World War I. More than 1,400 were built in Britain by the Aircraft Manufacturing Company and three sub-contractors, one of which was Westland. Construction of D.H.4s began before the last of the Sopwith 1½-Strutters was completed, so that in early 1917 the Yeovil works must have presented a busy scene. A total of 150 were contracted, but there is doubt as to whether more than about 140 were completed. Built for both the RFC and RNAS, there were some differences from standard armament, and two different power plants were involved. Early aircraft had 186 kW (250 hp) Rolls-Royce Eagle IIIs; later machines were to have been powered by the 172 kW (230 hp) B.H.P. (Beardmore-Halford-Pullinger) engine built by the Siddeley-Deasy Motor Car Company, but instead had the similar 172 kW (230 hp) Siddeley Puma. This, however, had slightly different engine mountings, causing some delay in production while Westland carried out modifications to accept the Puma. Of the total of about 100 delivered in May and June 1917, the standard single forward-firing synchronised machine-gun was replaced by twin Vickers guns, and the ring mounting for the observer's Lewis gun raised.

STRUCTURE: Equal-span two-bay braced biplane wings of wooden construction with fabric covering. Ailerons on both wings. Fuselage of wood, forward section plywood-covered, rear fuselage fabric-covered. Braced tail unit of similar construction to wings, with fabric covering. Variable-incidence tailplane. V-type main landing gear units with through-axle; tail skid at rear.

ACCOMMODATION: Two open cockpits; pilot forward between wings, observer aft.

DATA (A: with Rolls-Royce Eagle III; B: with Siddeley Puma engine):

POWER PLANT: One 186 kW (250 hp) Rolls-Royce Eagle III inline piston-engine, or one 172 kW (230 hp) Siddeley Puma inline piston-engine. Standard fuel capacity 300 litres (66 Imp gallons). Oil capacity 29.5 litres (6.5 Imp gallons).

Wing span	12.92 m (42 ft 4⅝ in)
Wing area	40.32 m² (434 sq ft)
Length overall	9.35 m (30 ft 8 in)
Height overall:	
A	3.17 m (10 ft 5 in)
B	3.07 m (10 ft 1 in)
Weight empty:	
A	1,045 kg (2,303 lb)
B	1,012 kg (2,230 lb)
Max T-O weight:	
A	1,572 kg (3,466 lb)
B	1,465 kg (3,230 lb)
Max level speed:	
A at 915 m (3,000 ft)	103 knots (192 km/h; 119 mph)
B at 1,980 m (6,500 ft)	92 knots (171 km/h; 106 mph)
Service ceiling:	
A	4,875 m (16,000 ft)
B	5,305 m (17,400 ft)
Endurance:	
A	3.5 h

ARMAMENT: Twin fixed forward-firing synchronised Vickers machine-guns with 1,000 rounds ammunition. Lewis gun on Scarff ring, or single pillar mounting, with six double drums of ammunition. Bombs or depth charges could be carried to a maximum load of 209 kg (460 lb).

WESTLAND-BUILT (Sub-contract)

AIRCO (DE HAVILLAND) D.H.9

TYPE: Two-seat bomber; used also for reconnaissance and anti-submarine patrol.

NOTES: An urgent need in mid-1917 to supplement the D.H.4 by a longer-range aircraft in the same class resulted in the very similar D.H.9. It was planned to power it with the Siddeley Puma at a promised rating of 224 kW (300 hp), but the engine proved completely unreliable at this power output; and as a result it was derated to 172 kW (230 hp). With this reduction of almost 24 per cent in power, the performance of the D.H.9 was inferior to that of the D.H.4. This was known before the D.H.9 entered service, but despite the strongest possible protest from Major-General Hugh Trenchard, it was decided that plans were too advanced to be cancelled. More than 3,200 were built by the Aircraft Manufacturing Company and 12 sub-contractors, including Westland. In attempts to improve performance, Westland had the task of producing prototype installations of the D.H.9 with a 186 kW (250 hp) Fiat A-12 inline engine, and also with a 298 kW (400 hp) American-designed Liberty engine.

STRUCTURE: Generally similar to that of D.H.4, with wings and tail unit being identical. Major differences included resiting the pilot's cockpit further aft, and the provision of a retractable radiator for engine cooling beneath the forward fuselage. A clear-view cut-out was incorporated in the wing root of the starboard lower wing to improve the pilot's downward view.

ACCOMMODATION: Two open cockpits, pilot forward, observer aft. Pilot's position, aft of wings, improved crew communication but reduced his view.

DATA:

POWER PLANT: One 172 kW (230 hp) Siddeley Puma inline piston-engine. Standard fuel capacity 336 litres (74 Imp gallons). Oil capacity 36 litres (8 Imp gallons).

Wing span	12.92 m (42 ft 4⅝ in)
Wing area	40.32 m² (434 sq ft)
Length overall	9.30 m (30 ft 6 in)
Height overall	3.40 m (11 ft 2 in)
Weight empty	1,012 kg (2,230 lb)
Max T-O weight	1,508 kg (3,325 lb)
Max level speed at 3,050 m (10,000 ft)	
	96 knots (177 km/h; 110 mph)
Service ceiling	4,725 m (15,500 ft)
Endurance	4.5 h

ARMAMENT: One fixed forward-firing synchronised Vickers machine-gun. One or two Lewis guns on Scarff ring mounting in aft cockpit. Bombs could be carried to a maximum load of 209 kg (460 lb).

D.H.9 two-seat bomber

WESTLAND-BUILT (Sub-contract)

AIRCO (DE HAVILLAND) D.H.9A

TYPE: Two-seat day bomber.

NOTES: As mentioned in the notes relating to the D.H.9, Westland had been responsible for the prototype installation of a Liberty engine in this airframe. Subsequent testing was to show that this power plant gave much improved performance, and it was decided to build a version with this engine as standard. Arrangements were made to obtain 3,000 Liberties from the USA, but production did not match up with expectations and when deliveries to Britain ended in July 1918, only 1,050 had been received. Deeply involved with development of the D.H.10, the Aircraft Manufacturing Company could not cope with another programme involving the D.H.9, and Westland was made prime contractor for this aircraft. In addition to finalising the engine installation, Westland carried out some redesign of the airframe: this involved the provision of increased chord wings of greater span, and changes in the fuselage construction with wire cross-bracing replacing the plywood bulkheads of the D.H.9. The retractable radiator was replaced by one forward of the engine, as in the D.H.4, and the resulting D.H.9A looked far more like a D.H.4 than its immediate predecessor. The prototype (B7664) was flown with a 280 kW (375 hp) Rolls-Royce Eagle VIII engine, presumably because no Liberty engine was available. Of the total of 885 D.H.9As built (some 390 by Westland, the remainder sub-contracted), a fair number were powered by Rolls-Royce engines. The first Liberty-engined aircraft (C6122) was flown shortly after the prototype, and by the end of June 1918, the first 18 examples had been delivered to the RAF. Modifications, which resulted from in-service use of the Liberty-engined aircraft, were initiated by Westland to overcome nose-heaviness. These included a change in the neutral setting of the variable-incidence tailplane, and an increase in wing stagger which was achieved as a result of moving the upper wing 0.10 m (4 in) further forward.

Known as the 'Nine-Ack' – for like most enduring aircraft the D.H.9A acquired a service nickname – it proved to be an important aeroplane in establishing Westland as a permanency in Britain's aircraft industry. Not only were the wartime contracts of significant volume, but during the difficult post-war decade the company was kept busy building, repairing, and refurbishing Nine-Acks. During this period of time, a number of aircraft had Napier Lion engines installed. It should be stressed also that the D.H.9A was an important aircraft for the RAF, examples remaining in service until 1931.

STRUCTURE: Generally similar to that of D.H.9, except wing span and area increased. Retractable radiator replaced by one mounted forward of engine.

D.H.9A with 350 hp Eagle

ACCOMMODATION: Two open cockpits, pilot forward and observer aft, sited similarly to those of D.H.9.

DATA (A: Rolls-Royce Eagle; B: Liberty; and C: Napier Lion engine):

POWER PLANT: One 280 kW (375 hp) Rolls-Royce Eagle VIII, or 298 kW (400 hp) Liberty 12, or 336 kW (450 hp) Napier Lion inline piston-engine. Standard fuel capacity 491 litres (108 Imp gallons). Oil capacity 59 litres (13 Imp gallons).

Wing span	13.97 m (45 ft 10 in)
Wing area	46.17 m² (497 sq ft)
Length overall	9.09 m (29 ft 10 in)
Height overall:	
A	3.51 m (11 ft 6 in)
B	3.56 m (11 ft 8 in)
Weight empty:	
A	1,227 kg (2,705 lb)
B	1,256 kg (2,770 lb)
C	1,160 kg (2,557 lb)

Max T-O weight:	
A	2,184 kg (4,815 lb)
B	2,107 kg (4,645 lb)
C	2,114 kg (4,660 lb)
Max level speed at 3,050 m (10,000 ft):	
A	109 knots (201 km/h; 125 mph)
B	104 knots (193 km/h; 120 mph)
C	116 knots (216 km/h; 134 mph)
Max rate of climb at S/L:	
B	181 m (595 ft) min
Service ceiling:	
A	6,100 m (20,000 ft)
B	5,790 m (19,000 ft)
C	6,490 m (21,300 ft)
Endurance:	
A	4.5 h
B	5.75 h

ARMAMENT: One fixed forward-firing synchronised Vickers machine-gun with 750 rounds ammunition, one or two Lewis guns on Scarff ring mounting in aft cockpit with six drums of ammunition, and up to a maximum load of 299 kg (660 lb) bombs.

WESTLAND-BUILT (Sub-contract)

VICKERS F.B.27 VIMY

TYPE: Three-seat heavy bomber.

NOTES: Increasing bombing activity by German aircraft during 1917, in which London, the Home Counties and East coastal towns and military installations were favoured targets, resulted in the provision of a new generation of bomber aircraft for the RFC. By the time they were ready for operational use the RFC had become the RAF, and the de Havilland D.H.10 Amiens, Handley Page V/1500, and Vickers Vimy all materialised too late to see action during World War I. In fact, only the Vimy was to enjoy a lengthy period of service with the RAF, its standard heavy bomber until displaced by Vickers Virginias from late 1924, but continuing to serve in a variety of training roles until 1931.

Westland received in August 1918 a sub-contract to build 75 of these aircraft, and it was specified originally that they should be powered by Liberty engines. Only 25 of this total were completed, the end of the war bringing contract cancellations. So far as is known these Westland Vimys were quite standard, but because of the non-availability of Liberty engines were completed as Vimy Mk IVs with Rolls-Royce Eagle VIII engines.

STRUCTURE: Braced biplane wings of wooden construction with fabric covering. Ailerons on both wings. Forward fuselage of steel tube, aft fuselage of wood, with fabric covering. Braced biplane tail unit of wood with fabric covering; elevator on each horizontal surface, and with twin fins and rudders. Fixed tailskid type landing gear, each main unit carrying two wheels on a through axle. Strut-mounted skid beneath forward fuselage to reduce possibility of nosing-over.

ACCOMMODATION: Three open cockpits, with gunner in nose, pilot just forward of wing leading-edge, and rear gunner just aft of wing trailing-edge.

DATA (Mk IV):

POWER PLANT: Two 268 kW (360 hp) Rolls-Royce Eagle VIII inline piston engines, each mounted in a nacelle outboard of the fuselage and mid-set between the wings. Standard fuel capacity 2,055 litres (452 Imp gallons). Oil capacity 82 litres (18 Imp gallons).

Wing span	20.73 m (68 ft 0 in)
Wing area	123.56 m^2 (1,330 sq ft)
Length overall	13.27 m (43 ft 6½ in)
Height overall	4.76 m (15 ft 7½ in)
Weight empty	3,221 kg (7,101 lb)
Max T-O weight	5,670 kg (12,500 lb)
Max level speed	89 knots (166 km/h; 103 mph)
Service ceiling	2,135 m (7,000 ft)
Endurance	11 h

ARMAMENT: One or two Lewis guns in each gunner's cockpit, mounted on Scarff ring, and with six drums ammunition in each cockpit. Maximum bomb load 1,123 kg (2,476 lb), and comprising 18 112-lb and two 230-lb bombs.

Vickers Vimy

WESTLAND N.1B SCOUT SEAPLANE

First flown: Autumn 1917

TYPE: Single-seat scout seaplane.

NOTES: To meet an Admiralty requirement for a single-seat scout seaplane which could operate from ships at sea, Westland initiated the design of an aircraft within the Admiralty category N.1B. The Sopwith Schneider, and the Sopwith Baby developed from it, had made the Royal Navy appreciate the value of 'eyes' that could see beyond the horizon as viewed from deck height. Westland's design, emanating from Robert Bruce and Arthur Davenport, was very similar to the Baby in appearance. Two prototypes were built, N 16 and N 17, the first incorporating a variable wing camber device for which Bruce had filed a patent application in December 1916: today we would call this a wing trailing-edge flap. N 16 had Sopwith floats, comprising two main strut-mounted pontoon like floats, plus a smaller float at the tail which was provided with a water rudder. N 17 was generally similar, except that the variable camber device was not included in the wing structure, and had much longer upturned floats of Westland design, making it possible to dispense with the tail float. These may not have been entirely satisfactory, for N 17 was later seen with Sopwith floats. Both forms of main floats could mount two wheels with a through axle so that these aircraft could take off from the deck of a suitable vessel, jettisoning the wheels once airborne and landing on the sea after their mission was completed, to be recovered by crane. According to records, both these prototypes performed well in official trials, held during October 1917, but their development came too late. By that time both take-offs and a landing had been demonstrated on ships at sea, and clearly all emphasis needed to be given to this new capability. The most important aspect

Westland N.1B, with Sopwith floats

Westland N.1B, Westland floats

was that it would then dispense with the need for a seaplane carrier to heave to and recover its 'bird', making the vessel an interesting and vulnerable target for a suitably placed U-boat. As a result, no further examples of Westland's N.1B type were built.

STRUCTURE: Braced equal-span biplane. Two-spar structure of wood with fabric covering. Ailerons on both wings. Trailing-edge flaps. Wings fold for shipboard stowage. Fuselage of wood, fabric-covered. Braced tail unit with wooden structure and fabric covering. Float plus wheel landing gear as described above.

ACCOMMODATION: Open cockpit for pilot. Cut-out in trailing-edge of upper wing centre-section to provide some upward view.

DATA (A: N 16 with Sopwith floats; B: N 17 with Westland floats):

POWER PLANT (both): One 112 kW (150 hp) Bentley B.R.1 rotary piston-engine. Standard fuel capacity 136 litres (30 Imp gallons). Oil capacity 23 litres (5 Imp gallons).

Wing span	9.54 m (31 ft 3½ in)
Wing area	25.83 m² (278 sq ft)
Length overall	7.76 m (25 ft 5½ in)
Height overall	3.40 m (11 ft 2 in)
Weight empty:	
A	682 kg (1,504 lb)
B	686 kg (1,513 lb)
Max T-O weight:	
A	897 kg (1,978 lb)
B	901 kg (1,987 lb)
Max level speed:	
A at 1,145 m (3,750 ft)	
	94 knots (174 km/h; 108 mph)
B at 625 m (2,050 ft)	
	93 knots (172 km/h; 107 mph)
Service ceiling:	
A	3,870 m (12,700 ft)
B	3,170 m (10,400 ft)
Endurance	2.75 h

ARMAMENT: One fixed forward-firing synchronised Vickers machine-gun, with 250 rounds of ammunition; one Lewis gun on mounting above the upper-wing centre section, with three drums of ammunition; and two 65-lb bombs on under-fuselage rack.

Westland Wagtail

WESTLAND WAGTAIL

First flown: April 1918

TYPE: Single-seat fighter.

NOTES: Although disappointed at the failure of the N.1B Scout to win a production order, the official trials of these two seaplane prototypes had been encouraging to Westland's management, which was soon involved in the design of a single-seat fighter to meet the requirements of the RFC's Specification A1a. This called for a manoeuvrable fighter with a good rate of climb, and in late 1917 Bruce and Davenport put their ideas together in the hopes of creating a high-performance aircraft that would win a worthwhile production contract. Identified initially as the Westland Wasp, because of the chosen power plant of an A.B.C. Wasp I radial engine, a mock-up had been built for inspection by January 1918, and as a result three prototypes were ordered. Required for competitive evaluation against the B.A.T.Bantam, designed by Frederick Koolhoven, and the Sopwith Snail, all three companies had elected to use the same power plant. By the time that Westland's first prototype airframe was complete it had been given the company name of Wagtail. This was in early April, and there was some delay before the Wasp engine was received and installed. A few days later, about mid-April 1918, it was flown for the first time by test pilot Captain Alexander. It proved to be highly manoeuvrable, but early modification showed that there was a shortcoming which needed improvement. As first flown, both wings had a dihedral of 2° 30'; they were rerigged so that the lower wing had no dihedral and the upper wing 5°. This resulted in lowering the upper wing centre-section and restricting the pilot's view. It was remedied by eliminating the centre-section trailing-edge, and by providing a large cut-out in the centre-section, between the spars, to increase the field of view. In addition, the area of the tailplane, elevators, and fin were reduced, and that of the rudder increased. It was in this form that the prototypes were evaluated by the RAF, flown in mock combat against a captured Fokker D.VIII. In competition with the submissions of the British Aerial Transport Company and Sopwith, the Wagtail proved to be the best all-rounder. However, the Bantam, both fast and manoeuvrable, won a small production contract, but this came to an end after only nine had been built, due to the unreliability of the Wasp I engine. Once again Westland was unfortunate, and only two more Wagtails were to be built post-war to serve as flying testbeds for the improved 149 kW (200 hp) A.B.C. Wasp II radial engine. Of the five prototypes, one was later converted for experimental purposes. Provided with strengthened landing gear, and with the fuselage nose shortened slightly, it was powered by a 119 kW (160 hp) Armstrong Siddeley Lynx radial engine.

STRUCTURE: Braced single-bay equal-span biplane wings. Two-spar wooden structure with fabric covering. Ailerons on both wings. Fuselage of wooden construction, fabric-covered. Braced tail unit of similar construction to wings, fabric-covered. Tail-skid landing gear, with main units of divided axle type carried on braced V-struts and with rubber bungee shock-absorption.

ACCOMMODATION: Open cockpit for pilot. As the Wagtail was intended as a high-altitude fighter, there was provision for the installation of oxygen equipment.

DATA (original prototypes):

POWER PLANT: One 127 kW (170 hp) A.B.C. Wasp I radial piston-engine. Standard fuel capacity 118 litres (26 Imp gallons). Oil capacity 13.5 litres (3 Imp gallons).

Wing span	7.06 m (23 ft 2 in)
Wing area	17.65 m² (190 sq ft)
Length overall	5.77 m (18 ft 11 in)
Height overall	2.44 m (8 ft 0 in)
Weight empty	338 kg (746 lb)
Max T-O weight	603 kg (1,330 lb)
Max level speed at 3,050 m (10,000 ft)	
	109 knots (201 km/h; 125 mph)
Service ceiling	5,180 m (17,000 ft)
Endurance at 4,570 m (15,000 ft)	2.5 h

ARMAMENT: Two fixed forward-firing synchronised Vickers machine-guns, with 1,000 rounds of ammunition.

WESTLAND WEASEL

First flown: late 1918

TYPE: Two-seat fighter/reconnaissance aircraft.

NOTES: The Bristol F.2B fighter had entered service on the Western Front in April 1917, but despite the excellence of this aircraft the speed of progress was such that little time was lost in seeking for a successor of even higher performance. Specification Type III(A) was drawn up for a two-seat fighter-reconnaissance aircraft of improved capability, and the competing Austin Greyhound, Bristol Badger, and Westland Weasel were all based on a new A.B.C. radial engine, the Dragonfly, which the manufacturers claimed would have a power output of 254 kW (340 hp). Westland's Weasel, of which three prototypes were ordered originally, was very much a larger scale version of the Wagtail. Almost identical in configuration, its span was greater by 3.76 m (12 ft 4 in) and length by 1.80 m (5 ft 11 in). The pilot's cockpit was sited in much the same place as that of the Wagtail, requiring a large cut-out between the spars of the upper wing centre-section to give an adequate view above. The observer/gunner's cockpit was close behind that of the pilot, but was deep enough to give him rather more than average protection from the slipstream. First flown in late 1918 the Weasel, like the other aircraft against which it was contending, suffered from the failure of the Dragonfly engine. Developing less than the estimated power, overweight and suffering from serious vibration, at its best it could not be relied upon to operate for much over three hours without failure. Not surprisingly, none of the contending aircraft were to enter production. After service trials, Westland's three prototypes (F.2912-14) were used later by the RAE as flying testbeds for differing engines. The latter of these three is known to have flown with a 261 kW (350 hp) Armstrong Siddeley Jaguar II radial engine. The fourth prototype (J6577), ordered in August 1919, had a 298 kW (400 hp) Bristol Jupiter II engine installed and this, too, was used by the RAE.

STRUCTURE: Braced two-bay equal-span biplane wings. Two-spar wooden structure with fabric covering. Ailerons on both wings. Fuselage of wooden basic structure with internal wire bracing, plywood-covered forward and fabric-covered aft. Braced tail unit of similar construction to wings with fabric covering. Modifications made to some of the RAE's aircraft included an increase in fin area, and the provision of a horn-balanced rudder and/or horn-balanced ailerons on one or two aircraft. Landing gear of tailskid type with main units comprising braced V-struts.

ACCOMMODATION: Two open cockpits, pilot forward, observer/gunner aft. Oxygen equipment and electrical heating provided for both cockpits.

DATA (original prototypes as flown in service trials):

POWER PLANT: One 239 kW (320 hp) A.B.C. Dragonfly radial piston-engine. Standard fuel capacity 277 litres (61 Imp gallons). Oil capacity 30 litres (6.5 Imp gallons).

Wing span	10.82 m (35 ft 6 in)
Wing area	34.19 m² (368 sq ft)
Length overall	7.57 m (24 ft 10 in)
Height overall	3.07 m (10 ft 1 in)
Weight empty	847 kg (1,867 lb)
Max T-O weight	1,393 kg (3,071 lb)
Max level speed at 1,980 m (6,500 ft)	
	113 knots (209 km/h; 130 mph)
Service ceiling	6,310 m (20,700 ft)

ARMAMENT: Two fixed forward-firing synchronised Vickers machine-guns, with 1,200 rounds of ammunition; one Lewis gun on Scarff ring in rear cockpit, with five double drums of ammunition.

Westland Weasel

WESTLAND LIMOUSINE I & II

First flight (I): July 1919
First flight (II): October 1919

TYPE: Short-range light passenger transport.
NOTES: During World War I aero-engines had grown in terms of power output and reliability, making possible larger, more robust airframes than those with which the combatant nations went to war in the Summer of 1914. Thus, at the war's end, there were enthusiastic attempts to initiate civil air services. For hardware, would be operators had to rely initially upon hasty conversions of ex-military aircraft: while cheap to buy from the government disposal source, they offered little comfort to the comparatively small number of civilians that were prepared to sample the 'delights' of air travel. Westland's Limousine, designed by Arthur Davenport, was one of the first serious attempts to provide comfortable accommodation for the passenger. This was implied by the name 'Limousine', and suggesting the kind of amenities that we would now associate with an executive transport. The prototype Limousine I, providing accommodation for a pilot and three passengers, was flown for the first time during July 1919 by Captain A.S. Keep. Identified initially as K.126, and later becoming registered as G-EAFO, it was powered by a Rolls-Royce Falcon engine, as was the Limousine II (G-EAJL) flown in October 1919. It differed by having modifications that included a slight reduction in wing span, increased fin and rudder area, a larger rectangular radiator replacing the circular radiator of the prototype, and consequently having changed engine cowlings. A series of demonstrations during 1919-20 resulted in some interest, and a second Limousine II was built (G-EAMV) to evaluate a 306 kW (410 hp) Cosmos Jupiter radial engine. First flown in April 1920, it presumably had inferior performance, for it was re-engined subsequently to standard. It was planned to build four more II's, but available evidence suggests that only three were completed. Of these, one (G-EARG) had the standard power plant, but G-EARE and G-EARF differed by having 224 kW (300 hp) Hispano-Suiza eight-cylinder Vee inline engines. In addition, on these two latter aircraft the standard fuel tank, which was mounted aft of the engine and separated from the cabin by an asbestos-filled double wooden bulkhead, was replaced by two external tanks. Of streamline shape, these were mounted beneath the lower wing, one each side, and provided an increase of 16 per cent in fuel capacity.

Westland Limousine II

Removal of the fuselage tank made it possible to increase slightly the cabin volume, and the opportunity was taken to install a light alloy/asbestos fireproof bulkhead between the cabin and engine bay.

STRUCTURE: Equal-span braced biplane. Two-spar structure of wood. Engine cowled; cabin area free of internal bracing and plywood covered; rear fuselage with internal wire bracing and fabric covering. Strut- and wire-braced tail unit of wood with fabric covering. Tailskid landing gear, mainwheels mounted on through axle on V-struts.

ACCOMMODATION: Pilot and three passengers in an unusual seating arrangement. Pilot on aft port seat, mounted on 0.76 m (2 ft 6 in) pedestal so that his head projected through an opening in the cabin roof. Rear passenger seat facing forward, the two front passenger seats with one facing forward, one aft.

DATA (A: Limousine I; B: standard Limousine II):

POWER PLANT: One 205 kW (275 hp) Rolls-Royce Falcon III inline piston-engine standard fuel capacity 227 litres (50 Imp gallons); G-EARE/RF 264 litres (58 Imp gallons). Oil capacity 18 litres (4 Imp gallons).

Wing span:
A   11.63 m (38 ft 2 in)
B   11.51 m (37 ft 9 in)
Wing area:
A   40.88 m² (440 sq ft)
Length overall   8.46 m (27 ft 9 in)
Height overall   3.28 m (10 ft 9 in)
Weight empty:
A   990 kg (2,183 lb)
B   912 kg (2,010 lb)
Max T-O weight:
A   1,535 kg (3,383 lb)
B   1,724 kg (3,800 lb)
Max level speed   87 knots (161 km/h; 100 mph)
Cruising speed:
A   74 knots (137 km/h; 85 mph)
B   78 knots (145 km/h; 90 mph)
Max rate of climb at S/L:
A   183 m (600 ft)/min
B   198 m (650 ft)/min
Service ceiling   5,180 m (17,000 ft)
Range:
A   252 nm (467 km; 290 miles)
B   347 nm (644 km; 400 miles)

VARIANT: Limousine III, described separately.

WESTLAND LIMOUSINE III

First flight: early 1920

TYPE: Short-range light passenger transport.

NOTES: The Air Ministry, anxious to foster the development of purpose-built civil aircraft, gave advance details of a Commercial Aeroplane Competition that was to be held during 1920. Westland's directors considered that they should participate, and it was decided to enter a scaled-up version of the Limousine in the 'small Aeroplane' class. Work began on the design and construction of what was to become designated as the Limousine III and which, in general configuration, was similar to the Limousine I and II. Of increased span and length, however, it had a cabin to accommodate the pilot and five passengers, and was provided with a more powerful Napier Lion engine. In addition to the increased capacity, another requirement of the Air Ministry's competition was short-field landing capability. As a result, wheel brakes were fitted, and twin nosewheels on a single axle were strut-mounted beneath the engine, braced back to the main gear. These were introduced to prevent the aircraft from nosing-over if heavy application of the brakes was necessary during the short-landing tests. The underwing fuel tanks, which had been introduced on the Hispano-Suiza-engined Limousine IIs, were included on the Limousine III prototype (G-EARV). First flown by Stuart Keep in early 1920, it was he who piloted the aircraft in the competition which was held at Martlesham Heath. There it achieved a narrow victory over the competing Sopwith Antelope, winning the Air Ministry's first prize of £7,500 for the particular class. Despite this success, only one other example of the Limousine III was built, G-EAWF, and in April 1921 this was acquired by the Air Council. Once again Westland was unfortunate, this time developing an efficient short-range civil transport that was not technically ahead of the state of the art, but certainly far too premature for the anticipated, but non-existent, demand for commercial aircraft.

STRUCTURE: Equal-span three-bay braced biplane. Two spar structure generally as for Limousine I/II. Braced tail unit of wood with fabric covering. Landing gear basically of tailskid type, but with the addition of anti-noseover wheels forward of the main landing gear.

ACCOMMODATION: Pilot and five passengers. As with Limousine I/II pilot seated at rear on port side with head projecting through an opening in the cabin roof, but all passengers on forward-facing seats.

DATA:

POWER PLANT: One 336 kW (450 hp) Napier Lion inline piston-engine.

Wing span	16.46 m (54 ft 0 in)
Wing area	67.45 m² (726 sq ft)
Length overall	10.21 m (33 ft 6 in)
Height overall	3.81 m (12 ft 6 in)
Weight empty	1,734 kg (3,823 lb)
Max T-O weight	2,654 kg (5,850 lb)
Max level speed	102 knots (190 km/h; 118 mph)
Cruising speed	78 knots (145 km/h; 90 mph)
Service ceiling	3,750 m (12,300 ft)
Range	452 nm (837 km; 520 miles)

Westland Limousine III

Westland Walrus

WESTLAND WALRUS

First flown: 1920

TYPE: Three-seat carrier-based spotter-reconnaissance aircraft.

NOTES: During 1919, when Britain's armed forces were trying to effect the best possible transition from war to peace, it soon became apparent to the RAF that there were a number of lean years ahead. With no money available to procure new aircraft, it meant that existing equipment would have to be adequate for whatever tasks might arise, and would also have to last as long as possible. From 1 April 1918, when despite the Royal Navy's protests the RNAS and RFC had been unified as the Royal Air Force, all the Navy's requirements in terms of aviation equipment were controlled by the RAF. When, in 1919, the Navy needed a three-seat spotter-reconnaissance aircraft for service that could include operation from an aircraft carrier, the most economical solution appeared to be a conversion of the de Havilland D.H.9A, of which a large number were in service.

For reasons which are now obscure, it seems that Armstrong Whitworth was contracted to develop a prototype conversion. Perhaps it was considered that they could look rather more objectively than Westland at the conversion of what was fundamentally a production aircraft of the latter company. This resulted in D.H.9A E8522 retaining its original 298 kW (400 hp) Liberty engine, but with accommodation provided for a third crew member aft of the standard gunner's position. This meant that the clean line of the fuselage upper surface acquired a dorsal hump to give increased internal volume. At the same time, a ventral bulge with windows was added, so that the observer could adopt a prone position to view the scene below. With the new service serial J6585 this prototype, which Armstrong Whitworth named the Tadpole, flew for the first time in 1920. It was Westland, however, which was awarded a contract for 36 aircraft, but there were a number of differences between the Tadpole and Westland's Walrus.

Externally visible changes included replacement of the Liberty engine by a British built Napier Lion; the introduction of jettisonable main landing gear with a hydrovane forward of this, so that in emergency a landing could be made on water; the provision of flotation bags beneath each lower wing root, which could be inflated in flight from an onboard compressed air cylinder if an emergency landing seemed imminent; and an arrangement of jaws on the main landing gear spreader bar, provided to engage the fore and aft arrester wires then standard on the Navy's aircraft carriers. Other changes made it possible for the wings to be detached easily for stowage, the elimination of virtually all of the wing stagger of the D.H.9A; and the introduction of a fuel jettison system that enabled the main fuel tanks to double as emergency flotation chambers, automatically sealed off as soon as the fuel had gone.

Walrus aircraft entered service first with No. 3 Squadron at RAF Leuchars, serving subsequently with Nos. 420 and 421 Fleet Spotter Flights from 1923 until 1925, when they were withdrawn from service.

STRUCTURE: Generally as for D.H.9A (which see), except as detailed above.

ACCOMMODATION: Two open cockpits for pilot (forward) and gunner, with observer accommodated in aft fuselage.

DATA:

POWER PLANT: One 336 kW (450 hp) Napier Lion II inline piston-engine.

Wing span	13.97 m (45 ft 10 in)
Wing area	46.08 m^2 (496 sq ft)
Length overall	9.14 m (30 ft 0 in)
Height overall	3.53 m (11 ft 7 in)
Max T-O weight	2,265 kg (4,994 lb)
Max level speed	108 knots (200 km/h; 124 mph)

ARMAMENT: One forward-firing synchronised Vickers machine-gun; one or two Lewis guns on Scarff ring mounting in aft cockpit.

The futuristic-appearing Westland Dreadnought

WESTLAND DREADNOUGHT

First flown: 9 May 1924

TYPE: Experimental mail/passenger civil transport.
NOTES: The majority of early aircraft, despite the role they had to fulfil, were of biplane configuration. It was not because this method of construction was considered to be more efficient, but the two wing surfaces with interplane struts, and internal and external wire bracing, provided a lightweight but robust structure that could not be improved upon at the time. There was little doubt that a 'clean' cantilever monoplane wing would be more efficient, not having to suffer the drag-producing penalties of struts and wires, however well these were streamlined. But the method of building such a wing, one that would be able to withstand the complex stresses imposed upon such a structure, had not then been developed. A number of early designers had suggested the use of a very deep, or thick, aerofoil section, which would allow the use of adequate internal bracing, so dispensing entirely with external struts and wires. From there it was a comparatively short step to the idea of a wing root that was thick enough to provide accommodation for flying crew and passengers or cargo.

Among the advocates of such a configuration was the Russian inventor Woyevodsky. His proposals for what in later years became regarded as 'flying-wing' designs, were of sufficient interest to attract the attention of Britain's Air Ministry. Following the design and wind tunnel testing of several different proposals based on this concept the most promising, with twin engines and retractable landing gear, was offered to Westland for design development, and construction in prototype form. Intended for operation as a mail carrier, Westland changed the design to incorporate fixed landing gear and only a single engine, but in other respects Westland's Dreadnought Postal Monoplane followed closely the Air Ministry's selected model, and a contract for its construction was issued on 13 January 1923. As it began to take shape in Westland's Vimy shop, the complex metal structure dominated even this large area. The wing-section was a variation on the standard T.64, with a chord of 5.49 m (18 ft) at the root. Basic construction was of steel tube, incorporating six spars, and it was intended that in a production configuration each wing root would be able to accommodate five passengers. This multi-spar wing of metal basic construction was the first of its type to be built in Britain. Ailerons were of early Frise type, and the metal wing structure was fabric-covered. The remainder of the airframe was largely of wood, the large tail unit incorporating elevators and rudder with inset balances.

When the finished aircraft was rolled out in late April of 1924, it gave an immediate impression of futurism. The large cantilever wing, blending into the fuselage and completely free from struts and wires, seemed to suggest new standards of efficiency and performance. Unfortunately, this was not to be, for following successful taxi tests on 8 May, the Dreadnought stalled shortly after take-off on 9 May, crashing on Westland's airfield and seriously injuring test pilot Stuart Keep. The design had stepped into an area of unknown aerodynamic problems and, when the wreckage had been cleared away, was not to be resurrected by the company.
STRUCTURE: Cantilever monoplane wing blending into the fuselage structure; basic construction of metal with fabric covering. Fuselage and tail unit of wood, with wood and fabric covering. Tailskid landing gear.
ACCOMMODATION: Open cockpit for crew of two in upper fuselage, forward of wing. There was space within the blended wing root/fuselage for eight to ten passengers.
DATA:
POWER PLANT: One 336 kW (450 hp) Napier Lion II inline piston-engine.

Wing span	21.18 m (69 ft 6 in)
Wing area	78.04 m² (840 sq ft)
Length overall	17.07 m (56 ft 0 in)

Westland Woodpigeon prototype

WESTLAND WOODPIGEON I/II

First flown: G-EBIY Summer 1924
G-EBJV 17 September 1924

TYPE: Two-seat light biplane.
NOTES: In 1923 the *Daily Mail*, which almost from the first days of powered flight had actively encouraged the development of aviation by awarding worthwhile prizes for specific achievements, offered a number of money prizes (including a first prize of £1,000) for a series of Motor Glider Competitions. Staged at Lympne airfield, Kent, during the week beginning 8 October 1923, these were intended to encourage the development of light aircraft that would speed the growth of the private flying movement.

A rather more ambitious attempt to achieve a similar result was launched early in 1924, by the Air Ministry, which announced that Two-Seat Light Aeroplane Trials would be held from 29 September to 4 October, with Lympne again the venue. The rules for competing aircraft were rather more stringent, including the requirement that the wings could be folded easily to facilitate storage, that the engine capacity should not exceed 1,000 cc, and that a minimum control speed below 72 km/h (45 mph) should be complemented by a maximum speed of more than 96.5 km/h (60 mph).

Uncertain whether biplane or monoplane configurations would be most successful, Westland placed an each-way bet, building Woodpigeon biplane and Widgeon (which see) monoplane designs for entry in the competition. A small but conventional biplane, two examples of the Woodpigeon were built (G-EBIY and G-EBJV), each powered originally by a Bristol Cherub III piston-engine. Although unsuccessful in the Air Ministry trials G-EBJV, flown by Flying Officer S.H. Gaskell, gained second place in the Grosvenor Challenge Cup 161 km (100 mile) air race which was held at Lympne on the last day of the trials.

In an attempt to improve performance, the second of these Woodpigeon Is (G-EBJV) was re-engined with an ABC Scorpion engine in 1926. Both were to be given Anzani radial engines in 1927, and G-EBIY had its wing span increased by 1.30 m (4 ft 3 in). In this form they were designated Woodpigeon II and remained in private use until 1930 (G-EBIY) and 1932 (G-EBJV).
STRUCTURE: Single-bay braced biplane of wooden construction with fabric covering. Wings folded. Fuselage and braced tail unit of similar construction. Fixed tailskid type landing gear; mainwheels, mounted on Vee struts with through axle, had friction-damped spring shock-absorbers.

ACCOMMODATION: Two open cockpits for pilot and passenger, pilot seated aft.
DATA (A: Woodpigeon I with Bristol Cherub III; B: Woodpigeon II with Anzani engine):
POWER PLANT: One 24 kW (32 hp) Bristol Cherub III horizontally-opposed, or one 22 kW (30 hp) ABC Scorpion, or 45 kW (60 hp) Anzani radial piston-engine.

Wing span:

A	6.93 m (22 ft 9 in)
B (G-EBIY)	8.23 m (27 ft 0 in)

Wing area:

A	14.40 m² (155 sq ft)
B (G-EBIY)	18.58 m² (200 sq ft)

Length overall:

A	5.94 m (19 ft 6 in)
B	6.32 m (20 ft 9 in)

Height overall:

A	2.13 m (7 ft 0 in)
B	2.16 m (7 ft 1 in)

Weight empty:

A	204 kg (450 lb)
B	247 kg (545 lb)

Max T-O weight:

A	363 kg (800 lb)
B	401 kg (885 lb)

Max level speed:

A	62.5 knots (116 km/h; 72 mph)
B	61 knots (113 km/h; 70 mph)

Westland Widgeon G-EBRQ

WESTLAND WIDGEON I/II

First flown: 22 September 1924

TYPE: Two-seat light monoplane.

NOTES: As mentioned in the Woodpigeon entry, the Widgeon I was Westland's monoplane entry for the Air Ministry's Two-Seat Light Aeroplane Trials of 1924. Fuselage, tail unit, and landing gear of the Woodpigeon and Widgeon I were generally similar in both configuration and construction. The wing, of course, was very different, being a monoplane attached to the fuselage as a parasol wing, with centre-section struts, and large Vee bracing struts each side. Arthur Davenport was the protagonist of monoplane configuration, as opposed to Robert Bruce's biplane layout for the Woodpigeon. Davenport had given a great deal of thought to the development of a wing that would be both efficient and, at the same time, limit the pilot's vision as little as possible. The resulting dual-tapered wing had its maximum chord and thickness at about two-fifths semi-span, with built-up H-section spars of spruce and plywood. As with the Woodpigeon, the wings had to be capable of manual folding to comply with the rules of the competition, and when one adds full-span trailing-edge surfaces which could serve differentially as ailerons, or collectively as flaps, one can see that this was then an advanced wing design. These dual purpose wing control surfaces were a development of those which had been introduced on Westland's N 16 and N 17 during World War I.

Unfortunately, while being flown on a qualifying circuit of the Lympne trials course, only five days after its first flight, the Widgeon I prototype (G-EBJT) sideslipped and was badly damaged when it hit the ground, eliminating it from the trials. Its pilot, Captain Winstanley, escaped without injury, and was able to confirm that the Widgeon was very much underpowered. It was then rebuilt, and at which time the area of its rudder was reduced, and its 26 kW (35 hp) Blackburne Thrush three-cylinder radial piston-engine replaced by an Armstrong Siddeley Genet five-cylinder radial of increased power. Redesignated Widgeon II, but retaining the registration G-EBJT, this little two-seater was flown by Westland in competitive evaluation against the Woodpigeon II biplane, proving conclusively the superiority of the monoplane configuration. G-EBJT was later sold to a private buyer, who lost his life in this aircraft when attempting a forced landing at dusk, near Detling, Kent, in October 1930. Long before then, however, G-EBJT had pointed the way to the Widgeon III (which see), built by Westland in modest numbers until production ended in 1929.

STRUCTURE: Parasol-wing monoplane with folding wings of wooden construction, fabric-covered. Fuselage and braced tail unit of similar construction. Fixed tailskid type landing gear; main wheels, mounted on Vee struts with through axle, had friction-damped spring shock-absorbers.

ACCOMMODATION: Two open cockpits for pilot and passenger, pilot seated aft.

DATA (A: Widgeon I with Blackburne Thrush; B: Widgeon II with Armstrong Siddeley Genet):

POWER PLANT: One 26 kW (35 hp) Blackburne Thrush, or 45 kW (60 hp) Armstrong Siddeley Genet radial piston-engine.

Wing span:
A, B   9.35 m (30 ft 8 in)
Wing area:
A, B   13.47 m² (145 sq ft)
Length overall:
A, B   6.40 m (21 ft 0 in)
Height overall:
A, B   2.21 m (7 ft 3 in)
Weight empty:
A   215 kg (475 lb)
Max T-O weight:
A   370 kg (815 lb)
B   522 kg (1,150 lb)
Max level speed:
A   62.5 knots (116 km/h; 72 mph)
B   95.5 knots (177 km/h; 110 mph)
Max rate of climb at S/L:
A   91 m (300 ft)/min

VARIANTS: See Widgeon III.

Westland Widgeon IIIA, G-AAGH

WESTLAND WIDGEON III

First flown: March 1927

TYPE: Two-seat light monoplane.

NOTES: The decision to put the Widgeon III into production resulted in the introduction of some changes in construction. These were intended not only to improve the product, but also to make it easier and quicker to build. First candidate for simplification was the parasol wing, which on the Widgeon I/II tapered in chord both inboard and outboard of a point at about two-fifths semi-span, and at which position the upper ends of the Vee bracing struts were attached to each wing. In addition, the wing tapered in thickness both inboard and outboard of this same datum point, so it was no simple structure to build. It was replaced by a constant-chord wing of greater span, increasing wing area by almost 40 per cent, and retaining the dual-purpose full-span trailing-edge surfaces which had obviously proved effective. The other airframe structural change involved the fuselage, thin plywood skinning replacing the fabric covering of the earlier aircraft.

It was an age when those who could afford to acquire and operate a private aircraft usually had sufficient money to ensure that, for example, it incorporated individual features of their own choice. And this ability to exercise personal options meant that Widgeon IIIs were flown with a variety of power plants. These included the 56 kW (75 hp) Armstrong Siddeley Genet II, 63 kW (85 hp) A.B.C. Hornet, and A.D.C. Cirrus II, 67 kW (90 hp) A.D.C. Cirrus III, and 75 kW (100 hp) de Havilland Gipsy I.

After an initial batch of Widgeon IIIs had been built, an improved IIIA appeared which introduced two significant changes in airframe construction. The fuselage was provided with a basic structure of square-section duralumin tube, its components united by flat plates and tubular steel rivets. This was covered by plywood decking forward of the pilot's cockpit, removable metal decking aft, duralumin sheet beneath the cockpits, and the remainder of the exposed surfaces with fabric covering. The other change deleted the narrow-track rather solid main landing gear, replacing it by a much wider-track layout of the split type, with crossed axles. Shock-absorbers were again of the spring type, with Ferodo friction dampers. Of this landing gear C.G. Grey commented in the 1929 edition of *Jane's All the World's Aircraft* that: 'The undercarriage is extremely strong, and the machine can be landed completely stalled. The wide track makes it very steady when taxying and prevents any tendency to blow over in a cross-wind.'

The Widgeon IIIA was also to appear with a variety of engines, adding to those already mentioned for the III the 78 kW (105 hp) Cirrus Hermes I and 89 kW (120 hp) Hermes II. There are no accurate records of just how many were built, but it would seem the total was about 30 when, in 1929, the productive capacity was needed for potentially far more important and profitable military aircraft.

DATA (Widgeon III, A: Cirrus II; B: Cirrus III; C: Gipsy I; D: Genet II. Widgeon IIIA, E: Cirrus III; F: Gipsy I):

POWER PLANT: One inline or radial piston-engine as detailed in notes. Standard fuel capacity 91 litres (20 Imp gallons).

Wing span	11.09 m (36 ft 4½ in)
Wing area	18.58 m² (200 sq ft)
Length overall	7.14 m (23 ft 5¼ in)
Height overall	2.57 m (8 ft 5 in)
Weight empty:	
A	386 kg (852 lb)
D	352 kg (775 lb)
E	424 kg (935 lb)
Max T-O weight:	
A	635 kg (1,400 lb)
B	726 kg (1,600 lb)
C, E, F	748 kg (1,650 lb)
D	600 kg (1,323 lb)
Max level speed:	
A	87 knots (161 km/h; 100 mph)
B	91 knots (169 km/h; 105 mph)
C, F	94 knots (174 km/h; 108 mph)
E	90 knots (167 km/h; 104 mph)
Cruising speed:	
A	74 knots (137 km/h; 85 mph)
E	75 knots (138 km/h; 86 mph)
Max rate of climb at S/L:	
A	171 m (560 ft)/min
E	195 m (640 ft)/min
Service ceiling:	
A	4,265 m (14,000 ft)
B, C, F	4,875 m (16,000 ft)
E	4,570 m (15,000 ft)
Range with standard fuel:	
F	274 nm (507 km; 315 miles)

Westland Yeovil

WESTLAND YEOVIL

First flown: June 1925

TYPE: Two-seat long-range day bomber.
NOTES: Westland was one of the British manufacturers which, in August 1923, received a copy of Air Ministry Specification 26/23, calling for a two-seat long-range day bomber for the RAF. It was considered to be important by Westland, representing the company's first post-war opportunity to design and tender for a new military aircraft, a field of manufacture in which they were anxious to become established. The resulting design, which had to be based around a single Rolls-Royce Condor III engine, was of sufficient interest for three prototypes to be contracted. This, however, represented only a first minor victory, for designs which the Air Ministry received from the Bristol, Handley Page, and Hawker companies were also selected for prototype construction and subsequent competitive evaluation. These resulted respectively in the Bristol Berkeley, Handley Page H.P.28 Handcross, and Hawker Horsley.

The Westland Yeovil, as the company named their contender, was a large biplane with a narrow-chord lower wing, conventional braced tailplane, and non-retractable tailskid landing gear. The prototypes differed, the first two (J7508 and J7509) being of composite metal/wood construction and having the designation Yeovil I. The third prototype (Yeovil II, J7510) was basically of metal construction, and differed also by having a Leitner-Watts metal propeller, and by changes to the main landing gear, tail unit, and in the fairings over the fuel tanks that were mounted on the top surface of the upper wing. Special features included the introduction of a lightweight gas starter engine which had been developed by the Bristol company's Aero-Engine Department, and intended to simplify the starting of the Condor engine, which at that moment in time was the most powerful being produced in Britain. The Condor turned via reduction gearing a two-blade propeller that was 4.42 m (14 ft 6 in) in diameter, and from which it can be judged that this was quite an impressive aeroplane. Equipment included radio, and an oxygen system.

Flown for the first time by Captain Frank Courtney in June 1925, J7508 performed satisfactorily. The Yeovil was not, however, selected for production, for although it was able to meet the Air Ministry's specification the Hawker Horsley was considered more suitable and ordered into production. Westland had gained nothing but experience, and was compelled to wait for a new opportunity to win a military production contract for an aircraft of its own design.

STRUCTURE: Two-bay biplane with ailerons on upper wing only. Lower wing of reduced chord. Fuel tanks mounted on top surface of upper wing, one each side of centre-section. Braced tail unit of conventional design. Tailskid landing gear with main wheels carried on shock-absorber struts, with N-type struts beneath the fuselage to mount and brace the axle frame. Third (Yeovil II) prototype had a different fin and rudder profile, simplified landing gear mounting/support struts, and modified fairings for the wing-mounted fuel tanks.
ACCOMMODATION: Two open cockpits in close proximity, pilot forward, gunner/observer aft.
DATA:
POWER PLANT: One 485 kW (650 hp) Rolls-Royce Condor III inline piston-engine.

Wing span	18.14 m (59 ft 6 in)
Length overall	11.23 m (36 ft 10 in)
Max T-0 weight	3,425 kg (7,550 lb)
Max level speed	104 knots (193 km/h; 120 mph)

ARMAMENT: One forward-firing synchronised Vickers machine-gun, one Lewis gun on Scarff ring mounting in aft cockpit, and up to 236 kg (520 lb) bombs.

Westland Westbury, first prototype

WESTLAND WESTBURY

First flown: 1927

TYPE: Three-seat twin-engine biplane fighter.
NOTES: Air Ministry thinking on fighter aircraft with greater fire power was to result in Specification 4/24, which called for a heavily armed twin-engined fighter. The two engines were considered necessary to cater for a pilot who could concentrate on control of the aircraft, plus two gunners, each armed with an automatic weapon of larger-than-average calibre. Only the two West Country manufacturers showed interest in this project, with Westland receiving a contract in June 1925 for two examples of their design submission, which was identified as the Westbury. The competitive element was to be supplied by the Bristol Bagshot which, of similar twin-engine configuration, was a shoulder-wing monoplane.

Westland's Westbury was a conventional three-bay biplane, the engines mounted in nacelles on the upper surface of the lower wing. The landing gear was of wide-track tailskid type, with the main units mounted beneath the wing, just outboard of the engines. The first prototype (J7765) was of wooden construction with fabric covering, except for the fuselage which was of composite metal, wood, and fabric; the second prototype (J7766) differed in its basic structure by having duralumin wing spars, a more rounded nose to the fuselage, and the engine nacelles extended aft of the lower wing to improve streamlining.

The Air Ministry's specification had not stated the armament that was to be carried, and when the manufacturers first learned that two 37 mm cannon and a Lewis gun had been chosen, it must have come as something of a shock. Bristol's Bagshot was not of sufficiently heavy construction to cater for the 37 mm C.O.W. (Coventry Ordnance Works) guns, but Westland's big biplane took these in its stride. J7765 was flown for the first time during 1927 by Captain Frank Courtney, the initial flight made at Andover, which offered more space in the event of problems than did the somewhat confined company airfield. All went well however, and on the following day Laurence Openshaw flew the aircraft back to Yeovil from where subsequent tests, and those of the second prototype, were flown.

One of the C.O.W. guns was mounted on a rotating ring in the nose cockpit; the rear gunner had the second cannon mounted to fire forwards and upwards, and was also provided with a Lewis gun, that could be discharged through an aperture in the floor of his cockpit, to deter attacks from below. The 37 mm gun was a formidable weapon for its day,

firing 1.5 lb shells at a rate of 100 per minute, but it was demonstrated successfully from both the fore and aft gun positions of the Westbury. Its 907 kg (2,000 lb) recoil presented no problems to this big aircraft, even when fired broadside, but it was found necessary to add a metal shield for the upper wing centre-section to protect it from damage by muzzle blast of the aft gun.

Neither of the contenders in this competition were successful: although the Westbury performed well it failed to secure a production order, and Bristol's Bagshot did not get to the starting post because of major structural problems with its monoplane wing. Yet again, Westland was to be disappointed in its efforts to gain a worthwhile military contract.
STRUCTURE: Two-bay biplane of divergent gap; the first prototype of all wooden structure, the second introducing duralumin spars. Ailerons on both wings. Fuselage of composite steel and wood construction. Braced tail unit with large fin and rudder. Wide-track fixed tailskid type landing gear.
ACCOMMODATION: Crew of three in open cockpits; one gunner in nose, pilot just forward of upper wing, second gunner amidships. Access to pilot's cockpit within fuselage from aft gun position, or via fuselage footholds and walkway over wing centre-section.
DATA:
POWER PLANT: Two 336 kW (450 hp) Bristol Jupiter VI radial piston-engines.

Wing span	20.73 m (68 ft 0 in)
Wing area	79.89 m² (860 sq ft)
Length overall	13.23 m (43 ft 5 in)
Height overall	4.19 m (13 ft 9 in)
Weight empty	2,198 kg (4,845 lb)
Max T-O weight	3,573 kg (7,877 lb)
Max level speed	109 knots (201 km/h; 125 mph)
Service ceiling	6,400 m (21,000 ft)

ARMAMENT: Two 37 mm C.O.W. guns, one on rotating mount in nose position, the other on mounting in aft position. The fuselage decking of this aft position could be removed to accept a Scarff ring mounting for Lewis gun. Standard armament included a Lewis gun mounted in the floor of the fuselage.

Westland Wizard II

WESTLAND WIZARD

First flight: November 1926

TYPE: Single-seat monoplane fighter.

NOTES: Originating as a private design exercise by enthusiasts in Westland's drawing office, this project, of monoplane configuration, gained the approval of Arthur Davenport. When R.A. Bruce saw the drawings he liked the basic design, and having suggested some improvements it was decided to build a single prototype as a private venture. The resulting aircraft was basically of wooden construction, with the introduction of a plywood monocoque for the forward portion of the clean oval-section fuselage, and the remainder fabric-covered. To keep initial costs to a minimum, the 205 kW (275 hp) Rolls-Royce Falcon III, which had earlier powered the prototype Limousine, was installed in the airframe of this new fighter, soon to be named Wizard.

First flown by Laurence Openshaw in November 1926, early testing demonstrated exciting performance, but this was halted suddenly when an air-lock in the fuel system stalled the engine immediately after take-off. In the resulting forced landing, not far from the company airfield, Openshaw made a successful touch down in limited space but the Wizard nosed-over after hitting a small hedge. The wooden structure was badly damaged, but after showing such performance it was decided to rebuild the aircraft. The resulting Wizard I had a metal tube structure of Westland design, and was powered by a newly-developed Rolls-Royce F.XI unsupercharged engine. First flown by Louis Paget in November 1927 it really gave 'wizard' performance with the far more powerful engine, and with Air Ministry interest having been demonstrated practically by modest financial support, the Wizard I was to take part in the 1928 RAF Display at Hendon. There its superb rate of climb was to bring the accolade from one journalist of 'the star turn of the fighters', and winning from the Air Ministry a contract for a modified prototype to meet Specification F.20/27.

In the process of developing the Wizard to satisfy the official requirement, it gained an increased span reduced-chord all-metal wing, with a very thin centre-section and large trailing-edge cut-out to improve the pilot's forward and upward view. Power plant was changed to a supercharged Rolls-Royce F.XIS, but testing was to show that the 'improvements' had reduced the performance of this Wizard II by comparison with the unmodified prototype. Yet again Westland's hopes for a military contract were dashed, for the drop in performance and the continuing official prejudice against the monoplane configuration brought this project to an end.

STRUCTURE (Wizard II): Parasol-wing monoplane with bracing struts each side. All-metal wing structure with inset Frise-type ailerons. Fuselage basic structure of metal, enclosed from the pilot's cockpit forward by detachable metal panels, the aft section fabric-covered. Braced tail unit of all-metal construction. Fixed tailskid landing gear, main wheels carried on Vee struts with oleo-pneumatic shock-absorption.

ACCOMMODATION: Open cockpit for pilot just aft of wing centre-section trailing-edge. Seat height adjustable, and high-pressure oxygen installation.

DATA (A: Wizard I; B: Wizard II):

POWER PLANT: A: one 365 kW (490 hp) Rolls-Royce F.XI, or B: one 373 kW (500 hp) Rolls-Royce F.XIS, inline piston-engine. Standard fuel capacity 250 litres (55 Imp gallons).

Wing span:

A	12.04 m (39 ft 6 in)
B	12.19 m (40 ft 0 in)

Wing area:

A	22.11 m² (238 sq ft)
B	21.74 m² (234 sq ft)

Length overall:

A, B	8.18 m (26 ft 10 in)

Height overall:

A, B	2.84 m (9 ft 4 in)

Wheel track:

A, B	1.68 m (5 ft 6 in)

Weight empty:

A	1,067 kg (2,352 lb)

Max T-O weight:

A	1,486 kg (3,275 lb)

Max level speed at 3,050 m (10,000 ft):

A	163 knots (303 km/h; 188 mph)

Max rate of climb at 3,050 m (10,000 ft):

A	610 m (2,000 ft)/min

ARMAMENT: Two fixed forward-firing synchronised Vickers machine-guns, one in each side of fuselage.

VARIANTS: *Wizard.* Original prototype, wooden structure, Rolls-Royce Falcon III engine.

Wizard I. Prototype, rebuilt from Wizard, with metal structure fuselage, Rolls-Royce F.XI engine.

Wizard II. Prototype, converted from Wizard I, with metal wings and tail unit added, armament, and Rolls-Royce F.XIS engine.

WESTLAND WAPITI

First flight: March 1927

TYPE: Two-seat general-purpose military biplane.
NOTES: As the first post-World War I decade was drawing to a close, it was clear to the Air Ministry that the RAF had as its equipment a motley collection of ageing aircraft. The time had come to begin modest re-equipment, with priority allocated to a general-purpose aircraft that could be adapted to fulfil a variety of tasks. This lead to Specification 26/27, to initiate design and development of a D.H.9A replacement with improved performance and load-carrying capability. A requirement was that, for economical reasons, the new aircraft should incorporate as many D.H.9A components as possible, for large quantities were held in service stores around the world. An all-metal airframe was considered to be desirable, as was use of the Napier Lion engine, for large stocks of these power plants existed.

As the D.H.9A 'experts', Westland was in a strong position to meet this requirement, and the new design used wings, interplane struts, ailerons, and tail unit from the earlier aircraft. The landing gear was slightly different in design to the standard D.H.9A, being of an improved form that had been developed for, but not used on, that aircraft. The fuselage was entirely new, deeper and wider: its construction was composite, the forward section of duralumin tube with metal panels, the aft fuselage of wood with internal wire bracing. Wisely, West-land ignored the Lion as a power plant, selecting instead a direct-drive 313 kW (420 hp) Bristol Jupiter VI engine. The prototype (J8495) was first flown in March 1927, by Laurence Openshaw, who was to discover on the maiden flight that the rudder was totally ineffective. Subsequent investigation was to reveal that a complete fuselage bay had been omitted from the final drawing, and the short-term remedy was a progressive increase in fin/rudder area until adequate yaw control was gained.

With all aviation manufacturers desperately short of work, many were anxious to try and win this contract. Westland must have wondered whether, once again, they were to be left at the post when confronted by competing prototypes that included the Armstrong Whitworth Atlas GP, Bristol Beaver, de Havilland D.H.9AJ Stag, Fairey IIIF, Gloster Goral, and Vickers Valiant, and Vixen VI (with Condor engine). Strongest competition came from the Valiant which, like Westland's prototype, was powered by a Jupiter VI; it failed primarily because it made far less use of D.H.9A components. Westland was victorious, gaining an initial contract for 25 examples of their submission under the designation Wapiti I. It was to be built extensively for the 'between wars' years, with a total of 517 supplied to Air Ministry contracts, 38 for Australia, four for South Africa, and four for China. An additional 27 examples were licence-built in South Africa for service with the South African Air Force, and in 1935 the Royal Canadian Air Force acquired 25 from the RAF, and four more RAF machines were sold to the Hejaz. This aircraft represented a turning point in the company's fortunes.

Westland Wapiti prototype

Wapiti IIA, K1132

STRUCTURE: Wapiti I was conventional two-bay braced biplane. Wings and tail unit of wooden construction, fabric-covered. Composite fuselage, forward section of light alloy tube with metal covering, and aft fuselage of wood, fabric-covered. Fixed tailskid landing gear.

ACCOMMODATION: Pilot's cockpit just aft of trailing-edge of upper wing, observer/gunner's cockpit immediately behind. Wireless and oxygen equipment standard. Provisions for mounting camera in bay behind rear cockpit. Prone bomb-aiming position for observer.

DATA (Wapiti IIA; A: with Jupiter VIIF engine; B: Jupiter XFA):

POWER PLANT: Generally one 358 kW (480 hp) Bristol Jupiter VIII or VIIIF, or 373 kW (500 hp) Jupiter XFA radial piston-engine. Standard fuel capacity 491 litres (108 US gallons).

Wing span	14.15 m (46 ft 5 in)
Wing area	43.48 m² (468 sq ft)
Length overall	9.65 m (31 ft 8 in)
Height overall	3.61 m (11 ft 10 in)
Weight empty:	
A	1,728 kg (3,810 lb)
B	1,506 kg (3,320 lb)
Max T-O weight:	
A, B	2,449 kg (5,400 lb)
Max level speed:	
A at 1,525 m (5,000 ft)	
	122 knots (225 km/h; 140 mph)
B at 3,660 m (12,000 ft)	
	139 knots (257 km/h; 160 mph)
Cruising speed:	
A	96 knots (177 km/h; 110 mph)
B	108 knots (200 km/h; 124 mph)

Initial rate of climb at S/L:	
A	430 m (1,410 ft)/min
B	369 m (1,210 ft)/min
Service ceiling:	
A	6,280 m (20,600 ft)
B	8,230 m (27,000 ft)
Range with standard fuel:	
A	460 nm (853 km; 530 miles)
B	269 nm (499 km; 310 miles)

ARMAMENT: One fixed forward-firing synchronised Vickers machine-gun; one Lewis gun on Scarff ring mounting in rear cockpit; bomb load up to 263 kg (580 lb).

VARIANTS: *Wapiti IA*. Version with 358 kW (480 hp) Jupiter VIIIF engine. Handley Page leading-edge slots introduced on IA, and standard on all subsequent variants. This version was supplied to the RAAF.

Wapiti IB. Version of the IA with divided axle landing gear and Jupiter VIIIF engine, supplied to South Africa. During service the Jupiter engines were replaced by 410 kW (550 hp) Armstrong Siddeley Panther radials.

Wapiti II. Interim development to AM Specification 16/31 similar to IA, but with fuselage basic structure of all duralumin tube and metal-structure fabric-covered wings. Examples of the Wapiti II were flown with float landing gear and with the 410 kW (550 hp) Bristol Jupiter IXF radial and 444 kW (595 hp) Hispano-Suiza 12b inline engine.

Wapiti IIA. Major production version with all-metal basic airframe structure. Metal frame wings designed and built initially by the Steel Wing Company, a subsidiary of Gloster Aircraft, which were fabric-covered by Westland. At a late stage of production the wing was built completely by Westland. An experimental IIA had a 410 kW (550 hp) Bristol Jupiter XIF engine installed. IIAs could use

Wapiti IIA, on floats

the divided axle type of landing gear, and float or ski installations.

Wapiti III. Version of the IIA with divided landing gear of which 27 licence-built in South Africa, with 365 kW (490 hp) Armstrong Siddeley Jaguar VI engines.

Wapiti IV. Projected version, with extended fuselage to replace missing bay, and power plant of one 485 kW (650 hp) Hispano-Suiza 12N*bis* inline engine. Not completed, but influenced development of Mk V.

Wapiti V. Extended fuselage version, with strengthened landing gear, wheel brakes, tailwheel, and rudder of increased chord. Small number built for RAF with 410 kW (550 hp) Bristol Jupiter VIIIF. One was powered experimentally for a short period by a Bristol Draco direct fuel-injection engine, driving a four-blade light alloy propeller.

Wapiti VI. Dual control trainer version to AM Specification 17/31, built in 1932. Total of 16 supplied with Jupiter IXF engine and no armament.

Wapiti VII. Interim designation of experimental version with one 488 kW (655 hp) Bristol Pegasus IV engine. This aircraft was originally the second production Mk V, which with a 410 kW (550 hp) Panther II engine had been demonstrated in South America. It was to become known subsequently as the Houston-Wallace, or P.V.6 (which see), before becoming designated Wapiti VII.

Wapiti VIII. Developed from the uncompleted Mk IV, this had a 382 kW (512 hp) Armstrong Siddeley Jaguar VI radial engine installed and was demonstrated to the Central Chinese Government. Four were ordered with split-axle landing gear, and powered by Armstrong Siddeley Panther IIA engines.

SPECIAL VARIANTS: A Wapiti I airframe served as testbed for a 362 kW (485 hp) Bristol Phoenix I compression-ignition diesel engine. After successful testing, a moderately supercharged Phoenix II was installed, and this aircraft was flown to a record height of 8,535 m (28,000 ft) by Harald Penrose. The Wapiti I prototype (J8495) was also used as a testbed for the 447 kW (600 hp) Bristol Pegasus IM engine. One Wapiti IIA was equipped as a receiver aircraft for early flight refuelling experiments involving a Vickers Virginia tanker. One special Wapiti I, powered by a 313 kW (420 hp) Bristol Jupiter I, and of similar configuration to the Mk VI trainer, was built for HRH The Prince of Wales (later the Duke of Windsor).

WESTLAND WITCH

First flight: 30 January 1928

TYPE: Two-seat short-range day bomber.

NOTES: Air Ministry Specification 23/25 was drawn up to detail the requirement for a two-seat day bomber, with proposed use of Bristol's new Orion supercharged engine. Gloster, Handley Page, Hawker, and Westland all built prototypes, under the respective designations G.25 Goring, H.P.34 Hare, Hawker Harrier Mk.I, and Witch. All were biplanes except Arthur Davenport's design, which followed his favoured monoplane configuration and utilised the parasol wing layout that had been used earlier in the Widgeon and Wizard. As had been proposed in the specification, the Witch was designed to be powered by the Bristol Orion, developed from the Jupiter. This was expected to be available at a take-off rating of 369 kW (495 hp), but had not progressed far enough along the development trail, and failed to materialise. Instead, a 313 kW (420 hp) Jupiter VI was installed in this prototype (J8596), with which it was flown for the first time by Louis Paget at Andover, on 30 January 1928. This maiden flight showed the Witch to be very unstable longitudinally, with the CG well aft, which was overcome by extending the engine mounting some distance forward.

An advanced feature was the inclusion of a bomb bay, so that these weapons could be carried internally, the bay enclosed by doors. These could be opened mechanically by the observer/bomb aimer, and were also spring loaded so that, in the event of accidental release, the bombs would fall clear of the aircraft. Wide-track landing gear would have made the Witch suitable also as a torpedo carrier.

The Orion engine still failing to materialise, it was decided to get rather nearer to the power output for which the aircraft was designed, and resulting in the installation of a Jupiter VIIIF. Although performance of the Witch with this power plant was superior to its competitors, it did not succeed in winning a production contract, reportedly because the Air Ministry decided subsequently that it did not really require an aircraft of this category.

STRUCTURE: Braced parasol-wing monoplane. Composite structure of wood and steel tube, with plywood and fabric covering. Tapering horn-balanced ailerons. Fuselage of metal construction, braced tail unit of composite construction. Tailskid fixed landing gear, with wide-track divided main units incorporating oleo-pneumatic shock-absorbers. ers.

ACCOMMODATION: Pilot in open cockpit, just aft of trailing-edge of wing; observer's cockpit immediately aft. Prone position for bombing operations. Oxygen system and wireless equipment standard.

DATA:

POWER PLANT: One 358 kW (480 hp) Bristol Jupiter VIIIF radial piston-engine.

Wing span	18.59 m (61 ft 0 in)
Wing area	49.61 m² (534 sq ft)
Length overall	11.48 m (37 ft 8 in)
Height overall	3.51 m (11 ft 6 in)
Weight empty	1,533 kg (3,380 lb)
Max T-O weight	2,744 kg (6,050 lb)
Max level speed	122 knots (225 km/h; 140 mph)

ARMAMENT: One fixed forward-firing synchronised Vickers machine-gun, one Lewis gun on Scarff ring mounting in aft cockpit, and up to 236 kg (520 lb) bombs.

Westland Witch

Westland Pterodactyl IB

WESTLAND PTERODACTYL IA

First flight: June 1928

TYPE: Two-seat tailless research monoplane.

NOTES: In an attempt to create an inherently-stable aircraft that would offer new standards of safety in flight and, in particular, to overcome the dangers of the stalled wing, Captain Geoffrey Hill (later Professor) built in the early 1920s a glider based on the earlier work of John W. Dunne at Farnborough. Dunne had arrived at a swept wing tailless configuration, appreciating that if the centre of pressure of the wing was distributed over a V-shape that extended fore and aft of a normal CG position, the wing should be self-balancing over the aircraft's speed range without requiring a horizontal tail surface. Hill added wingtip controls, to serve collectively as elevators or differentially as ailerons: these would now be dubbed 'elevons'. Immediately inboard of these surfaces, each of which had a span of 2.29 m (7 ft 6 in), Hill mounted a rudder from the undersurface of each wing. These rudders did not operate precisely in unison, for to provide yaw in a turn the inner one needed to move sufficiently to induce drag, and the outer one just enough to inhibit drag. A simple two-wheel undercarriage was provided below the pilot's central and open seat, completed by a longish tailskid. In this form the glider was flown for the first time on 13 December 1924.

Several tests were made, with results that were sufficiently encouraging to obtain some Air Ministry sponsorship. This led to the installation of a 24 kW (32 hp) Bristol Cherub III engine with pusher propeller, which was mounted on the aft airframe bulkhead; the fuselage was enclosed by a nacelle of plywood-balsa-plywood sandwich; and a small tailwheel replaced the tailskid. The first powered flight of what became known as the Pterodactyl I was made from RAE Farnborough on 2 November 1925. The Air Ministry decided that this adaptation of the glider was most promising, and Westland was chosen to build an improved powered version, with Geoffrey Hill joining the company to mastermind the development of his creation. Progress was comparatively slow, due to the small number of people involved in this project, and it was almost three years before the new Westland-Hill Mk IA Pterodactyl was ready for testing. In the interim period the Pterodactyl I (J8067) had been used for a certain amount of development work, and had been provided with elevons of reduced span. While flying this during 1927 Laurence Openshaw crashed it in a stalled condition after a premature and low-speed take-off!

The Mk IA was of superior construction to its predecessor, sporting a very 'clean' streamlined nacelle to accommodate two people side by side, and with a Cherub III engine mounted at the rear. The wings appeared to be much 'cleaner', having lost the underwing rudders. These were replaced by what were then termed 'electroscopic' rudders but were, in fact, trailing-edge flaps inboard of the elevons. They could be operated differentially for directional control, or collectively as air brakes. The landing gear consisted of a single main wheel, with a faired balancing wheel carried on trailing struts beneath each wing.

First flown from Andover during June 1928, the Pterodactyl IA (J9251) was found to be reasonably pleasant to fly once the pilot had become accustomed to certain idiosyncrasies that were imposed by its configuration. Testing and development led to the designation of Pterodactyl IB after the installation of a 52 kW (70 hp) Armstrong Siddeley Genet engine driving a Watts two-blade propeller. A subsequent collapse of the single-wheel undercarriage resulted in the design and construction of a new tandem-wheel central landing gear, of which the forward wheel was steerable. In this form the Pterodactyl was redesignated IC, and this tandem-wheel gear was to become standard on future developments.

STRUCTURE: Braced high-wing monoplane with sweptback wings, constructed primarily of wood with fabric covering. Central nacelle of oval section, with maximum dimension horizontal, and consisting of ash formers with a diagonally laid spruce skin. Fixed tricycle landing gear with, initially, a single main wheel forward and two trailing balancer wheels. Tandem-wheel main unit introduced on the IC.

ACCOMMODATION: Open cockpit seating two, side by side, in central nacelle.

DATA (A: Pterodactyl IA; B: Pterodactyl IB/IC):

POWER PLANT: (A) One 24 kW (32 hp) Bristol Cherub III two-cylinder horizontally-opposed piston-engine. (B) One 52 kW (70 hp) Armstrong Siddeley Genet five-cylinder radial piston-engine.

Wing span	13.87 m (45 ft 6 in)
Length overall	5.18 m (17 ft 0 in)
Max T-O weight:	
A	408 kg (900 lb)
B	590 kg (1,300 lb)
Max level speed:	
A	61 knots (113 km/h; 70 mph)

WESTLAND IV

First flight: 22 February 1929

TYPE: Short-range light passenger transport.

NOTES: Designed during 1928, and named occasionally as the Limousine IV, the Westland IV was intended as a small taxi, or feederline passenger transport. A three-engine configuration was chosen to ensure greater in-service reliability, providing the capability to maintain height with full load on the power of any two engines. The prototype (G-EBXK, construction number WA.1771) was powered originally by three 71 kW (95 hp) ADC Cirrus Mk III inline piston-engines, and was flown for the first time from the Yeovil airfield by the company's chief test pilot of that period, Louis Paget. A second example was built (G-AAGW, c/n WA.1867) with more powerful Cirrus Hermes I engines, and was exhibited at the Olympia Aero Show in London during July 1929. Construction of two more Westland IVs was started, but these were modified and completed under the name Wessex (which see).

STRUCTURE: Braced high-wing monoplane. Two-spar wings of wood with fabric covering. Prototype fuselage of all-wood construction, fabric-covered; second aircraft had forward section to aft of main cabin of wood, and rear fuselage of square-section duralumin tubing, all fabric-covered. Braced tail unit of composite construction, fabric-covered. Landing gear non-retractable, with divided wide-track main units, and tailskid.

ACCOMMODATION: Enclosed flight deck, for crew of two, with dual controls, forward of the wing. Separate cabin for four passengers, with large baggage compartment at rear.

DATA (Westland IV G-AAGW):

POWER PLANT: Three 78 kW (105 hp) ADC Cirrus Hermes I inline piston-engines. Standard fuel capacity 436 litres (96 Imp gallons).

Wing span	17.53 m (57 ft 6 in)
Wing area	45.52 m² (490.0 sq ft)
Length overall	11.43 m (37 ft 6 in)
Height overall	2.90 m (9 ft 6 in)
Weight empty	1,429 kg (3,150 lb)
Max T-O weight	2,495 kg (5,500 lb)
Max level speed	94 knots (174 km/h; 108 mph)
Cruising speed	87 knots (161 km/h; 100 mph)
Max rate of climb at S/L	158 m (520 ft)/min
Service ceiling	4,265 m (14,000 ft)
Range at econ cruising speed	
	456 nm (845 km; 525 miles)

VARIANTS: See Wessex.

Westland IV, G-AAGW

WESSEX

First flight: May 1930

TYPE: Short-range light passenger transport.

NOTES: As mentioned in the Westland IV entry, construction of two more examples of this aircraft was initiated. Intended for overseas buyers, and allocated the registrations G-AAJI and G-AULF, subsequent cancellation of these orders resulted initially in G-AAJI (c/n WA.1897) being completed with three 78 kW (105 hp) Armstrong Siddeley Genet Major radial engines. This served as the prototype of a small family of transports which was given the name Wessex, and was re-registered as G-ABAJ before flying for the first time. The original Westland IV prototype (G-EBXK) was converted similarly, as was the second of the cancelled Westland IVs, and two new aircraft were built to this standard. At a later date the second Westland IV (G-AAGW), serving with Imperial Airways, was modified to Wessex configuration. Four new aircraft were built with more powerful Genet Major IA engines. Of these, one ordered by Portsmouth, Southsea, and Isle of Wight Aviation Ltd (G-ABVB, c/n WA.2156) differed by having a composite wing structure incorporating duralumin tubes, strengthened landing gear, an increase in fin and rudder area, and accommodation provided for six passengers by reducing the available baggage space. This aircraft also had a slightly raised flight deck, and all four late production machines had metal skins on the forward fuselage.

STRUCTURE: Braced high-wing monoplane. Two-spar wings of wood with fabric covering, but c/n WA.2156 also incorporated square-section duralumin tube in the wing structure. Forward section of fuselage, to aft of main cabin, of wood; rear section of square-section duralumin tubing. Four converted Westland IV and first two Wessex had fuselage all fabric-covered; last four Wessex had metal skinned forward fuselage. Braced tail unit of composite construction, fabric-covered. Landing gear non-retractable, with divided wide-track main units, and tailwheel.

ACCOMMODATION: Enclosed flight deck, for crew of two, with dual controls, forward of the wing. Separate cabin for four passengers, with large baggage compartment at rear. Wessex c/n WA.2156 had cabin for six passengers and reduced baggage stowage.

DATA (A: with Genet Major I engines; B: with Genet Major IA engines; C: Wessex G-ABVB c/n WA.2156).

POWER PLANT: Three Armstrong Siddeley Genet Major I or Genet Major IA engines, of 78 kW (105 hp) and 104 kW (140 hp) respectively. Standard fuel capacity 455 litres (100 Imp gallons).

Westland Wessex, G-ABEG

Wing span	17.53 m (57 ft 6 in)	**Westland Wessex, G-ABVB**
Wing area	45.52 m² (490 sq ft)	
Length overall:		
A, B	11.43 m (37 ft 6 in)	
C	11.58 m (38 ft 0 in)	
Height overall	2.90 m (9 ft 6 in)	
Weight empty:		
A	1,728 kg (3,810 lb)	
B	1,765 kg (3,891 lb)	
C	1,783 kg (3,930 lb)	
Max T-O weight:		
A	2,608 kg (5,750 lb)	
B, C	2,858 kg (6,300 lb)	
Max level speed:		
A	102 knots (190 km/h; 118 mph)	
B, C	106 knots (196 km/h; 122 mph)	
Cruising speed:		
A, B	87 knots (161 km/h; 100 mph)	
C	91 knots (169 km/h; 105 mph)	
Max rate of climb at S/L:		
A	183 m (600 ft)/min	
B	207 m (680 ft)/min	
C	186 m (610 ft)/min	
Service ceiling:		
A	3,750 m (12,300 ft)	
B	4,540 m (14,900 ft)	
C	4,175 m (13,700 ft)	
Range at econ cruising speed:		
A	452 nm (837 km; 520 miles)	
B	365 nm (676 km; 420 miles)	
C	295 nm (547 km; 340 miles)	

WESTLAND F.20/27 INTERCEPTOR

First flight: 1929

TYPE: Single-seat fighter prototype.

NOTES: By the mid-1920s, Air Ministry specifications were leading to the development of bomber aircraft with performance capabilities comparable to, and in isolated cases better than, the fighters/interceptors that could be ranged against them in training exercises. If this trend was general, then it was to be assumed that possible enemies could have bombers with the same potential, or very soon develop them. The Air Ministry's Specification F.20/27 was drawn up in an attempt to redress this situation, calling for an advanced single-seat high-altitude interceptor, powered by an air-cooled radial engine, and with an armament of two machine-guns. It was required to be able to overtake, in the shortest possible time, an enemy passing overhead at 6,100 m (20,000 ft) at a speed of 130 knots (241 km/h; 150 mph).

Britain's aviation industry was having a fairly lean time at that period, with something like 15 airframe manufacturers competing for contracts that were for 'penny packet' numbers of aircraft. F.20/27 seemed to offer the prospect of a worthwhile order for the winning contender, and no fewer than four biplane and three monoplane prototypes were built to take part in the competition for a production contract. The biplanes comprised the Bristol Type 107 Bullpup, Fairey Firefly II, Gloster SS.19B, and Hawker F.20/27; the monoplanes were the de Havilland D.H.77, Vickers Type 151 Jockey, and Westland's F.20/27 Interceptor. It is interesting to record, though somewhat out of context, that no production aircraft were built to this specification. Fairey's Firefly II was to be manufactured by Avions Fairey in Belgium for service with that nation's air force, Gloster's SS.19B was to be developed into the very successful Gauntlet, and Hawker's prototype was to lead, via the Hornet prototype, to the renowned Fury I, the RAF's first operational fighter capable of a speed in excess of 174 knots (322 km/h; 200 mph) in level flight.

With the Wapiti, Westland had achieved success with a biplane configuration. To meet the requirements of F.20/27 a low-wing layout was chosen by Arthur Davenport: it was wire-braced to both the upper fuselage and landing gear. This method of

Westland F.20/27, with shortened fin and rudder

construction was to receive some criticism, particularly from pilots, who considered that damage to the landing gear structure could hazard the stability of the wing. This was, perhaps, a little unlikely in view of the massive oleo-pneumatic shock struts and bracing struts provided for the through-axle main landing gear units. In most other respects the design was forward looking, the well-streamlined fuselage seeming to minimise the large-diameter of the 328 kW (440 hp) Bristol Mercury IIA radial engine with which it was first flown. Features of the design included large cut-outs in the wing trailing-edges, to improve the pilot's view; a door, to simplify access to the cockpit; an adjustable seat and rudder pedals; wheel brakes; an oxygen system; and heating for the machine-guns provided from the engine exhaust system.

Registered J9124, the prototype F.20/27 Interceptor was flown for the first time by Louis Paget from Westland's airfield. It could hardly be described as a successful flight, for not only was the Mercury engine low on power output, then being in an early development stage, but there was also aircraft handling problems. In addition to instability in turns, the tail unit vibrated badly at high angles of attack, affecting longitudinal control. Investigation showed that turbulence was being generated at the wing roots and, as an interim measure, automatic slots were installed in the leading-edge, adjacent to the fuselage. When this failed, new wind tunnel and flight tests led to the provision of redesigned wing fillets. To overcome the problems being experienced with the Mercury IIA, a Jupiter VII was installed so that the flight/development tests could continue while the Mercury was getting over its teething troubles. Flight testing was resumed, only to discover that J9124 was reluctant to come out of a spin. There was another delay while the tail unit was redesigned, emerging from the works with taller, narrow-chord vertical surfaces. Unfortunately the troubles were not ended: when, at a later date, Louis Paget landed after completing dive tests with the new tail unit, it was discovered that the fuselage attachments of the forward tailplane struts had failed.

By that time the performance of Westland's prototype was known to be inferior to that of some other contenders and, in any event, the F.20/27 specification had been amended to require the installation of a Rolls-Royce Kestrel engine: further development of Westland's F.20/27 Interceptor ended. The foregoing details sound rather more than depressing, but there was also a balance on the credit side. Before the failure of the forward tailplane strut attachments, flight tests had shown that Westland had developed a fighter that was light on the controls and a pleasure to fly. The resolution of the turbulence problems came from the company's own efforts, involving some original research that was to give the design office greater confidence in dealing with the quest for ever higher performance.

STRUCTURE: Braced low-wing monoplane with a basic all-metal structure, fabric-covered. Frise type ailerons. Rectangular-section fuselage structure of duralumin tube, faired to an oval section. Forward fuselage covered by detachable metal panels, aft fuselage fabric-covered. Conventional braced tail unit of metal structure, fabric-covered. Tailplane incidence ground adjustable. Non-retractable tail-skid landing gear. Wheel brakes standard.

ACCOMMODATION: Pilot only in open cockpit.

DATA:

POWER PLANT (as last flown): One 313 kW (420 hp) Bristol Jupiter VII radial piston-engine. Fuel contained in main and gravity fuselage tanks with combined capacity of 291 litres (64 Imp gallons).

Wing span	11.58 m (38 ft 0 in)
Wing area, gross	18.95 m² (204 sq ft)
Length overall	7.73 m (25 ft 4¼ in)
Height overall	2.95 m (9 ft 8 in)
Wheel track	2.04 m (6 ft 8½ in)
Weight empty	1,066 kg (2,350 lb)
Max T-O weight	1,508 kg (3,325 lb)

ARMAMENT: Two synchronised forward-firing Vickers machine-guns.

WESTLAND PTERODACTYL IV

First flight: March 1931

TYPE: Three-seat tailless research monoplane.
NOTES: In 1930, Stanley T. A. Richards, who was nicknamed 'Star' for fairly obvious reasons, joined the Westland company to work as Geoffrey Hill's chief draughtsman. Both were soon busily engaged in the design of a new three-seat Pterodactyl that was to become the Mk IV. The designation gap between this and the Pterodactyl Is, is explained by two unbuilt fighter projects that failed to progress beyond the drawing board. Both had a gull-wing configuration, but differed in power plant install-ation: the Pterodactyl II had a pusher layout similar to the Is, the III with a forward-mounted engine and tractor propeller. Both were considered by the Air Ministry to represent too big a step into an uncertain future, and leading to the Pterodactyl IV.

The original Pterodactyl I prototype had incor-porated an innovative idea by using a plywood-balsa-plywood sandwich in the construction of its nacelle. The new three-seater was not to be out-done, its high-set monoplane wing including vari-able-geometry that allowed for 5° adjustment in wing sweep to cater for solo or passenger-carrying flight. Other changes from the earlier research versions included a very thin streamlined fairing for the struts of the underwing-mounted balancer wheels, and the tandem main-wheel unit of the Pterodactyl IC was retained. The open cockpit had given place to an enclosed cabin, and considerably more power was provided by the installation of a de Havilland Gipsy III engine, driving a pusher propeller. The variable-geometry feature was not the only change in wing design, for while the 'electroscopic' rudders were retained, the wingtip controllers were replaced by true elevons, inset in the trailing-edge between the wingtip and the 'electroscopic' rudders.

In this form the aircraft (K1947) was first flown from Andover by Louis Paget during March 1931; it was immediately found to be a considerable im-provement over its predecessors, but lacking in yaw control. Subsequently, the differentially or collectively actuated trailing-edge flaps (electro-scopic rudders) were deleted, being replaced by a rudder mounted at, and mostly above, each wingtip. Unlike the somewhat complicated underwing rud-der system of the Pterodactyl I prototype, each rudder of the Mk IV could be actuated individually for control in yaw, but could also be used collec-tively to serve as airbrakes.

In this developed form the Pterodactyl IV was flown extensively for some years. Not surprisingly, its flight characteristics were somewhat different from those of a conventionally-configured aircraft, but having gained experience with this machine pilot's had every confidence in it. They soon dis-covered that however unconventional it appeared to be, it could be flown like any other aeroplane, and was capable of being used for aerobatics. Tested extensively at RAE Farnborough by Flt Lt George Stainforth, who had established in 1931 the first world speed record exceeding 347 knots (644 km/h; 400 mph) in the Supermarine S.6B seaplane, it was to be flown by him during more than one RAF Display at Hendon. In 1932 it delighted the crowd when, looking more grotesque than usual with a new paint scheme that included shark's teeth, George Stainforth launched repeated attacks against balloons of hippopotamus shape.

Such manoeuvrability did not go un-noticed, and Westland was soon involved in the creation of a new fighter aircraft based upon the Pterodactyl con-figuration.

STRUCTURE: Braced high-wing monoplane with sweptback wings, and with provision for variation of wing sweep through 5°. Ventral nacelle construc-ted of wood, with conventional use made of form-ers, stringers, and plywood skins. Fixed tricycle landing gear, but with the forward main unit incor-porating two wheels in tandem, the forward wheel steerable, and underwing strut-mounted balancer wheels.

ACCOMMODATION: Enclosed cabin for pilot and two passengers.

DATA:

POWER PLANT: One 89 kW (120 hp) de Havilland Gipsy III inline piston-engine.

Wing span	13.51 m (44 ft 4 in)
Wing area	24.06 m² (259 sq ft)
Length overall	5.94 m (19 ft 6 in)
Height overall	2.29 m (7 ft 6 in)
Max T-O weight	953 kg (2,100 lb)
Max level speed	98 knots (182 km/h; 113 mph)
Service ceiling	5,180 m (17,000 ft)

Westland Pterodactyl IV as first flown

Westland C.O.W. Gun Fighter with upward firing
37-mm cannon

WESTLAND C.O.W. GUN FIGHTER

First flight: Not known

TYPE: Single-seat fighter.

NOTES: In the mid to late-1920s the armament of fighter aircraft was little changed from that of a decade earlier. There had, of course, been no such thing as a fighter aircraft at the beginning of World War I; only observation/reconnaissance types. When the need, or desirability, of arming these aircraft arose, the small-bore weapons that had been developed for infantry use were adopted for aircraft as well. Automatic weapons used by the Royal Flying Corps, the Royal Naval Air Services, and subsequently the Royal Air Force, were primarily the Lewis and Vickers machine-guns. The latter, in fact, was an extensively used weapon, serving the armed forces of many nations.

From the mid-1920s, there was growing interest to increase the fire-power of fighter aircraft, and one of the weapons which held great interest for the Air Ministry had the somewhat unwarlike name of C.O.W. Gun. These initials stood for the Coventry Ordnance Works which had designed and developed this weapon, a quick-firing gun using shells of 37 mm calibre. In order to settle once and for all the potential of this gun for installation in a fighter aircraft, the Ministry drew up Specification F.29/27 covering the requirement for a single-seat fighter with a C.O.W. Gun.

There were only three interested companies: Bristol, Vickers, and Westland. Bristol's Type 112 monoplane to the F.29/27 specification would have had a Mercury III power plant, but was purely a project without an example being built. Vickers' Type 161 was a quite unique design of biplane configuration, the power plant installed in the rear of a central nacelle, and driving a pusher propeller that rotated within an open frame structure. An odd-looking feature was the spinner, a tapered tubular fairing, mounted astern of the propeller and within the frame structure.

Westland's C.O.W. Gun fighter was derived directly from the F.20/27 Interceptor which had been the subject of so much development, being basically a larger version of that aircraft. The overall length was increased by just over 1.22 m (4 ft), this being sufficient to make the new fighter look far more attractive and better proportioned. The fact that the F.20/27 and F.29/27 fighters were being worked on almost simultaneously is reflected in the tail unit of the latter which, as first flown, had the low aspect-ratio fin and rudder that had been seen initially on the Interceptor. The power plant was a Bristol Mercury IIIA, driving a four-blade propeller.

Following the maiden flight, the F.29/27 had to follow the same pattern of development as its predecessor. In due course it was flown with the increased-height fin and rudder and, although it retained the Mercury IIIA engine, the four-blade propeller was replaced by one with two blades. In due course the C.O.W. gun and its prismatic gun sight was installed. The gun, which had an overall length of 2.44 m (8 ft), was mounted in the starboard side of the cockpit so that it was easily accessible to the pilot. It was set at an angle of 55°, so that it would fire upward and forward, the prismatic sight providing an aiming point along this line of fire. The intention was to attack formations of bombers from below and behind, then a notorious blind spot, and a method of attack that was tried by the Luftwaffe during World War II, but using different weapons. Following official trials with the Vickers and Westland prototypes, the Air Ministry lost interest in the project and the C.O.W. Gun failed to emerge as an aircraft weapon. Testing had shown that its rate of fire was inadequate, and because of the heavy weight of the shells that it fired, very few could be carried.

STRUCTURE AND ACCOMMODATION: As described for F.20/27 Interceptor, but dimensions increased.

DATA:

POWER PLANT: One 362 kW (485 hp) Bristol Mercury IIIA radial piston-engine. Fuel contained in main and gravity fuselage tanks with combined capacity of 291 litres (64 Imp gallons).

Wing span	12.45 m (40 ft 10 in)
Wing area, gross	20.62 m² (222 sq ft)
Length overall	9.09 m (29 ft 10 in)
Height overall	3.22 m (10 ft 6¾ in)
Wheel track	2.06 m (6 ft 9 in)
Propeller diameter	3.25 m (10 ft 8 in)
Weight empty	1,186 kg (2,615 lb)
Max T-O weight	1,762 kg (3,885 lb)
Max level speed	160 knots (296 km/h; 184 mph)
Climb to 3,050 m (10,000 ft)	6.1 min
Climb to 6,100 m (20,000 ft)	14.3 min
Service ceiling	8,900 m (29,200 ft)

ARMAMENT: One Coventry Ordnance Works 37 mm quick-firing cannon, mounted at an angle of 55° in the starboard side of the cockpit, and provided with prismatic sight.

WESTLAND P.V.3

First flights:
P3 (P.V.3) prototype: early 1931
Houston-Westland (G-ACAZ): 21 January 1933

TYPE: Designed as a light torpedo-bomber.
NOTES: With work tailing off on the C.O.W. Gun fighter, it was decided that, in the absence of any urgent work, the design of a light torpedo-bomber should begin. This was a private venture, allocated the designation P.V.3, which followed fairly closely the design of the successful Wapiti and, in fact, incorporated many of its components. It was slightly larger than early versions of the Wapiti, and because it was intended for shipboard use the wings could be folded to simplify stowage. Ailerons on both wings, and upper wing leading-edge Handley Page automatic slots, were retained from the earlier design; the only conspicuous change in wing configuration was the replacement on each wing of the inner pair of parallel interplane struts by N-type struts. The fuselage and tail unit was generally similar to that of the Wapiti, but split main landing gear units were introduced to provide accommodation for a 454 kg (1,000 lb) torpedo: neat spats enclosed the main wheels to reduce drag, and a tailwheel replaced the Wapiti's tailskid. Power plant comprised an uncowled 429 kW (575 hp) Bristol Jupiter XFA radial engine, driving a two-blade wooden propeller.

Flown by Louis Paget in early 1931, the P.V.3 was able to demonstrate excellent overall performance, including a ceiling of 7,925 m (26,000 ft). This was to prove of importance at a slightly later date, but was to be of no help in selling the P.V.3 to the Fleet Air Arm. By the time it had flown, the torpedo which it had been designed to carry was no longer in Navy use, replaced by a larger weapon which was too heavy for the P.V.3. Once again it appeared that Westland was too late.

The story of the P.V.3 might well have ended at this point. However, in March 1932 Major L.V.S. Blacker submitted to the Royal Geographical Society a proposal for a flight over Mount Everest. Its purpose was two-fold: to wave the flag for Britain's aviation industry, and to carry out a photographic

Houston-Westland G-ACAZ

survey that might help mountaineers to conquer this peak; the world's highest, towering some 8,848 m (29,030 ft). In June 1932 it was decided that the Bristol Pegasus supercharged engine would be suitable for this task, a choice that was endorsed emphatically on 16 September 1932, when the Vickers Type 210 Vespa Mk VII, powered by a Pegasus S3, and piloted by Cyril Uwins, achieved a new world altitude record of 13,404 m (43,976 ft). The choice of a suitable airframe in which to install the engine needed the satisfaction of five major points: a deep and broad fuselage to allow room for an observer to move around, and have adequate storage space for cameras and equipment; large wing area, for good high altitude performance; one designed for the installation of a radial engine, to save time and conversion cost; tall landing gear, to permit the use of a large diameter propeller; and, of course, two-seat accommodation. Not many aircraft could satisfy all of these requirements, and in October 1932 Westland's P.V.3 had been selected as the most suitable, needing a minimum of modification.

With availability of the 391 kW (525 hp) Bristol Pegasus IS3 supercharged engine, it was calculated that the P.V.3 would be able to attain a height of some 10,670 m (35,000 ft). Modifications included the conversion of the rear cockpit into an enclosed cabin for the observer, removal of the wheel spats, replacement of the tailwheel by a tailskid, removal of all surplus military equipment to reduce weight as much as possible, and installation of the Pegasus engine, complete with a Townend ring. Given the civil registration G-ACAZ, the aircraft was renamed as the Houston-Westland, to honour Lady Houston who was financing this expedition. A back-up aircraft, the P.V.6 (which see), was registered G-ACBR and named the Houston-Wallace.

In early January 1933 the modified P.V.3 flew for the first time, and on 25 January Harald Penrose climbed the aircraft to a height of about 10,670 m (35,000 ft) with Air Commodore P.F.M. Fellowes, chief executive officer for the expedition, as his passenger. Just over a fortnight later the two aircraft were en route to Karachi, aboard the SS *Dalgoma*, and on 3 April 1933 became the first aircraft to fly over Everest.

STRUCTURE (P.V.3): Two-bay biplane with wings of equal span. Basic wing structure of metal, fabric-covered. Frise type ailerons on both wings. Handley Page slots in leading-edge of upper wing. Fuselage basic structure of metal with light alloy cowlings forward and fabric covering aft. Conventional braced tail unit of metal with fabric covering. Non-retractable tailwheel landing gear.

ACCOMMODATION (P.V.3): Pilot and observer/gunner in open cockpits.
DATA (P.V.3):
POWER PLANT: One 429 kW (575 hp) Bristol Jupiter XFA radial piston-engine.

Wing span	14.17 m (46 ft 6 in)
Wing area, gross	46.36 m² (499 sq ft)
Length overall	10.41 m (34 ft 2 in)
Height overall	3.56 m (11 ft 8 in)
Wheel track	4.04 m (13 ft 3 in)
Max T-O weight	2,540 kg (5,600 lb)
Max level speed at S/L	142 knots (262 km/h; 163 mph)
Service ceiling	7,925 m (26,000 ft)

ARMAMENT (P.V.3): One fixed forward-firing Vickers machine-gun for the pilot, one Lewis Mk III for the observer, mounted on a Scarff ring in the rear cockpit. One 454 kg (1,000 lb) torpedo, or bombs up to a maximum of 499 kg (1,100 lb).

WESTLAND P.V.6/WALLACE

First flight:
P.V.6 (P6): 30 October 1931

TYPE: Two-seat general-purpose military biplane.
NOTES: The initial prototype of the Westland Wapiti (which see) was deficient of a complete fuselage bay, due to a drawing office error, and it was not until the Mk V version of this aircraft was built that the fuselage was restored to the length intended originally. It also incorporated other improvements, including strengthened landing gear, wheel brakes, a tailwheel, and a rudder of increased chord. At that time the company was in need of a demonstrator aircraft, to participate in the British Empire Exhibition being staged at Buenos Aires in 1931, and so the second production Mk V aircraft was completed for this purpose. In place of the Bristol Jupiter engine which was then standard in most versions of the Wapiti, a 410 kW (550 hp) Armstrong Siddeley Panther II radial was installed, also uncowled, and in this form, with the registration G-AAWA, the Wapiti Mk V took the long sea voyage to Argentina. It was accompanied by Harald Penrose as pilot, who flew it with both wheel and float landing gear, demonstrating it also in Chile, Peru, and Uruguay before voyaging home.

On its return to Yeovil, G-AAWA was used for a new private venture project, under the designation P.V.6, to further develop the successful Wapiti. The landing gear was provided with spats for the main wheels, and the Panther II engine was replaced by a 488 kW (655 hp) Bristol Pegasus IV radial in a neat cowling. When flown by Harald Penrose in October 1931 it was found that the new venture, then with the class B registration P6, was a decided improvement on earlier Wapitis. Not only were its handling qualities much better, but the combination of reduced drag and more power gave a top speed that was some 17 knots (32 km/h; 20 mph) faster than its predecessors. With the temporary designation Wapiti Mk VII it was accepted by the Air Ministry for service trials. While these were under way, arrangements were being concluded for the P.V.3 to be used for the Everest project. Upon return of the Mk VII from Martlesham Heath, where the trials had been conducted, and leading to production of the Wallace, it was prepared as the back-up aircraft to the P.V.3 under the name Houston-Wallace, acquiring the civil registration G-ACBR. It was then modified in the same way as the P.V.3, with an enclosed cabin for the observer and, similarly, losing its wheel spats to save weight.

Both of these Westland aircraft completed the Everest expedition with flying colours, and on the return home G-ACBR was converted back to military configuration. With the designation Wallace I and registration K3488, it entered service with the RAF in December 1933. Prior to that, however, while G-ACBR was gallivanting around the Himalayas, the Air Ministry had issued Specification 19/32 covering the conversion of 12 Wapitis to Wallace Mk I

P.V.6 prototype

Westland Wallace II

configuration. They differed from the prototype by having a 425 kW (570 hp) Bristol Pegasus IIM3 radial engine; improved easily-detachable metal fuselage panels, with the standard rear fuselage fabric covering replaced by fabric sections united by zipp fasteners, to permit easy inspection of the airframe structure; and detail improvements. They were used to equip No.501 (City of Bristol) Squadron in early 1933. Subsequent Specifications 7/33 and 9/33 covered an additional 56 Wapiti to Wallace I conversions before the much-designated K3488 was returned to Yeovil to serve as the prototype of an improved Wallace II. Increased power was provided by the installation of a Pegasus IV engine, but the major recognition feature of this new version was the provision of a glazed canopy for both cockpits. The pilot's portion could be pushed forward to provide access, but the observer/gunner's section was of lobster-shell configuration, with three curved sections telescoping into a fourth outer cover. Wallace IIs were built as new production aircraft to Specification G.31/35, the last of 104 being delivered in late 1936, and serving with Royal Auxiliary Air Force squadrons, and with the Anti-Aircraft Co-operation Flight. When they became obsolete for general-purpose duties in squadrons, many were converted to serve as target tugs, with some remaining in service in this role until 1943.
STRUCTURE: Two-bay biplane with wings of equal span. Basic wing structure of metal, fabric-covered. Frise type ailerons on both wings. Handley Page slots in leading-edge of upper wing. All-metal basic fuselage structure, the forward section covered by removable metal panels, the aft section by removable fabric covering. Conventional braced tail unit of metal with fabric covering. Non-retractable tail-wheel landing gear. Float or ski installation optional.
ACCOMMODATION: Pilot and observer/gunner in open (Wallace I) or enclosed (Wallace II) cockpits. Prone bombing position for observer, and provisions for installation of camera.
DATA (Wallace II):
POWER PLANT: One 507 kW (680 hp) Bristol Pegasus IV radial piston-engine. Fuel contained in three tanks with a combined maximum capacity of 596 litres (131 Imp gallons).

Wing span	14.15 m (46 ft 5 in)
Wing area, gross	45.34 m² (488 sq ft)
Length overall	10.41 m (34 ft 2 in)
Height overall	3.51 m (11 ft 6 in)
Wheel track	2.08 m (6 ft 10 in)
Propeller diameter	3.76 m (12 ft 4 in)
Weight empty, equipped	1,742 kg (3,840 lb)
Max T-O weight	2,608 kg (5,750 lb)
Max level speed at 1,525 m (5,000 ft)	
	137 knots (254 km/h; 158 mph)
Speed at 4,750 m (15,000 ft)	
	131 knots (243 km/h; 151 mph)
Service ceiling	7,345 m (24,100 ft)
Range at cruising speed with max standard fuel	
	408 nm (756 km; 470 miles)

ARMAMENT: One fixed forward-firing Vickers machine-gun in port side of fuselage, Lewis gun for observer in aft cockpit, and up to 263 kg (580 lb) bombs.

Westland P.V.7

WESTLAND P.V.7

First flight: 3 October 1933

TYPE: Two-seat general-purpose military aircraft.
NOTES: Air Ministry Specification G.4/31, issued initially in July 1931, and amended three months later, sought the development of a general-purpose military aircraft that could combine a wide range of roles. These included army co-operation, casualty evacuation, dive bombing, light bombing by day or night, photography, reconnaissance over the coast or land, and torpedo bombing. One could be excused for thinking that the problems raised in providing such widespread capability would very much limit manufacturers' interest. Perhaps, without one other piece of information, this would have been true. But when it is appreciated that this was to be a replacement for the Fairey Gordon and Westland Wapiti, of which a combined total of about 700 had entered service, there seemed every likelihood that there was a significant contract to be won.

As a result, no fewer than nine manufacturers showed interest. These included Armstrong Whitworth (A.W.19); Blackburn (B-7); Bristol (4 biplane and 2 monoplane projects, none built); Fairey (G.4/31 Mk I and II); Handley Page (H.P.47); Hawker (P.V.4); Parnall (G.4/31); Vickers (Type 253); and Westland (P.V.7). Excluding the Bristol projects, all were biplanes except for the prototypes built by Handley Page and Westland, the latter flying for the first time in October 1933.

Westland's P.V.7 (Class B registration P7) was an attractive gull-wing monoplane with two large bracing struts on each side. These struts were of wide chord, and had an aerofoil section so that they would contribute to total lift. The root end of the gull wings tapered in thickness to improve the pilot's view, for his cockpit was situated between the wing roots, his head just forward of the wing leading-edge. Other features of the wing included Handley Page leading-edge slots and, on the trailing-edge, split flaps of Westland design mounted inboard of the ailerons. These were provided to function as air brakes in the dive-bombing role. The observer/gunner was accommodated in an enclosed cockpit just aft of the wing trailing-edge, his segmented canopy designed so that it could fold forward to provide a clear rearward field of fire for his Lewis gun.

The P.V.7 was a big aeroplane, everything about it looking massive and robust, but initial flight testing by Harald Penrose showed that all was not well. Early modifications included the introduction of an enclosure for the pilot's cockpit for the complicated airflow, resulting from the propeller wash in close proximity to the roots of the gull wings, was providing rather more than ventilation. Fin and rudder area were also increased, allowing expansion of the flight envelope, and permitting dive tests that showed the outer wing panels were twisting if any aileron load was imposed simultaneously. This was cured by strengthened wing bracing, and from that time the P.V.7 became a high-performance machine that was pleasant to fly. Power plant consisted of a Bristol Pegasus IIM3 radial engine that gave it a maximum speed of 150 knots (278 km/h; 173 mph) at 1,525 m (5,000 ft). Not surprisingly, Westland hopes were high when, after almost a year of company development and testing, the P.V.7 was delivered to Martlesham Heath. It was not to be. During dive tests under overload conditions a port wing bracing strut failed: before Harald Penrose could take any action the wing was torn from the aircraft, carrying away the tail unit. As the wreck plummeted to the ground Penrose managed to escape by parachute, landing without any serious injury: in so doing he had achieved one of the first successful escapes by parachute from the enclosed cockpit of a military aircraft.

The P.V.7 project ended there and then, and despite the flurry of activity by the nation's manufacturers no production aircraft were built to the G.4/31 specification. The Vickers Type 253 was the competition winner, gaining an initial contract for 150 production aircraft. However, this was cancelled soon after at Vickers' suggestion, the company offering instead a more advanced design that was to be built eventually under the name Wellesley.
STRUCTURE: Braced gull-wing monoplane with constant chord wing. Basic structure of metal with fabric covering, and incorporating Handley Page leading-edge slots, ailerons, and split trailing-edge flaps. Fuselage and braced tail unit of conventional metal structure with fabric covering. Non-retractable tailwheel landing gear, with single wheel on each unit.
ACCOMMODATION: Pilot and observer/gunner in enclosed cockpits, forward and aft of the wing respectively.
DATA:
POWER PLANT: One 538 kW (722 hp) Bristol Pegasus IIM3 radial piston-engine.

Wing span	18.36 m (60 ft 3 in)
Length overall	11.79 m (38 ft 8 in)
Weight empty	2,048 kg (4,515 lb)
Max T-O weight	3,253 kg (7,172 lb)
Max level speed at 1,525 m (5,000 ft)	
	150 knots (278 km/h; 173 mph)

ARMAMENT: Fixed forward-firing Vickers machine-gun for the pilot, a Lewis gun in the rear cockpit, one 454 kg (1,000 lb) torpedo beneath the fuselage, or an equivalent weight of bombs.

WESTLAND PTERODACTYL V

First flight: May 1934

TYPE: Two-seat tailless sesquiplane fighter.
NOTES: The Pterodactyl IV had carried research of Geoffrey Hill's unconventional designs as far forward as economically possible: the next step was to design an aircraft that, hopefully, would lead to a production contract. It took the form of a two-seat fighter that, while recognisably of the Pterodactyl family, incorporated many changes which resulted from experience with the earlier aircraft: other variations were made specifically to satisfy the fighter role.

Initial design led to the Air Ministry Specification F3/32, calling for a prototype of what was to become designated as the Pterodactyl V. It differed very considerably from the Mk IV of only two years earlier. The central nacelle mounted a 447 kW (600 hp) Rolls-Royce Goshawk engine at its forward end, this driving a two-blade fixed-pitch tractor propeller. At the rear of the nacelle, the pilot was accommodated in an open cockpit, with a gunner immediately behind him in a tail cockpit that could carry an electrically-actuated gun turret with one or two Lewis guns. Faired into the lower surface of this nacelle was the tandem wheel main landing gear unit, with little more than the wheel tyres exposed. The forward wheel was steerable, and the aft wheel incorporated brakes.

At the lower surface of the nacelle a short span conventional wing was mounted. Beneath this wing, and adjacent to the tips, the trailing skids of the landing gear were mounted. Above were struts which, together with cabane struts and wire bracing, supported the upper swept wing. This differed in planform from earlier designs, having a wide unswept centre-section, and outer panels swept at 42.5° on the leading-edge. In its original form this upper wing incorporated wingtip rudders with elevons immediately inboard, and automatic leading-edge slats adjacent to the wingtips.

Little time had been lost in building this new aircraft, and it was in early February of 1933 when it was wheeled out at Yeovil for engine running and first taxi trials, before being dismantled for transport to Andover for the first flight. The first taxying test proved to be something of an anti-climax, for within minutes of the chocks being waved away the port outer wing collapsed. Apparently the interplane struts were inadequately stressed, and failed from an unexpected load imposed by the struts of the port balancing skids.

It was not until fifteen months later, during May 1934, that Harald Penrose was able to take the controls at Andover. Five taxying runs preceded the take-off, followed by a promising first flight of about 20 minutes. However, there were many problems to be faced, involving not only the airframe, but also the Goshawk engine. This introduced a steam (more accurately evaporative) cooling system that proved to be unreliable, and which was responsible for the termination of Goshawk production after only a small number of examples had been built. Additionally, the torque of this engine raised ground handling problems that had not been completely overcome

Westland Pterodactyl V, rear

Westland Pterodactyl V, front

even after the tandem main wheels had been slightly offset, and small wheels added to the balancing skids. Airframe modifications were to include the leading-edge slats being moved further inboard, the addition of underwing fins just inboard of the elevons, and the wingtip rudders increased in size to become combined fins and rudders. At a later stage the area of the underwing fins and of the wingtip rudder/fins was increased, and to improve directional stability the wingtip vertical surfaces were canted outward.

Development of the Pterodactyl V lost some impetus after Geoffrey Hill left Westland Aircraft in late 1934, accepting the Kennedy Chair of Engineering at University College, London. With most of its bugs ironed out, however, and with the Class B registration P8 (later registered K2770), it was duly handed over to Farnborough for testing. It was to be abandoned later, after evaluation had led to the conclusion that it was not sufficiently advanced by comparison with contemporary conventional fighters in service or under development.

STRUCTURE: Braced sesquiplane structure, lower narrow-chord wing mounted at base of and towards aft end of central nacelle, upper swept supported by interplane and cabane struts. Basic structure of aerofoil surfaces of metal, fabric-covered. Central nacelle basically an all-metal structure. Fixed tricycle-type landing gear, the forward main unit with two wheels in tandem and, ultimately, two balancer wheels strut mounted from beneath the lower wing.

ACCOMMODATION: Open cockpit for pilot, directly above lower wing. Open cockpit for gunner in aft end of central nacelle.

DATA:

POWER PLANT: One 447 kW (600 hp) Rolls-Royce Goshawk inline piston-engine.

Wing span, upper	14.22 m (46 ft 8 in)
Wing span, lower	6.96 m (22 ft 10 in)
Wing area, upper	31.77 m² (342 sq ft)
Wing area, lower	5.02 m² (54 sq ft)
Length overall	6.40 m (21 ft 0 in)
Height overall	3.15 m (10 ft 4 in)
Balancer wheel track	5.94 m (19 ft 6 in)
Max T-O weight	2,313 kg (5,100 lb)
Max level speed	165 knots (306 km/h; 190 mph)
Service ceiling	9,145 m (30,000 ft)

AVIONICS: Com transceiver.

ARMAMENT: Two forward-firing synchronised Vickers machine-guns under pilot's control. Electrically-powered turret in aft cockpit with one or two Lewis guns. Provisions to carry light bombs.

VARIANTS (projected): *Pterodactyl VI.* Generally similar to Pterodactyl V, but with power plant installation/accommodation reversed. Thus gunner would have bow cockpit with gun-turret, and pilot immediately aft would have forward-firing guns. Power plant aft in pusher configuration. It was envisaged that Mk VI and Mk V aircraft would act respectively as fore and aft escorts for a bomber force.

Pterodactyl VII. Flying-boat version, designed to Air Ministry Specification R1/33, with conventional single-step hull. Sponsons of aerofoil section on each side of hull to provide balance on water and lift in flight. Upper wing carried on struts from sponsons and upper surface of hull. Power plant was to comprise four Gipsy Six engines, in tandem pairs, to drive tractor and pusher propellers, and mounted in underwing nacelles, one at each centre-section/outer wing panel junction. Wing span 19.25 m (63 ft 2 in); sponson span 6.96 m (22 ft 10 in); length overall 10.82 m (35 ft 6 in).

Pterodactyl VIII. Airliner version, intended to carry passengers within the wing, but of which no details have been found.

WESTLAND C.29 AUTOGIRO

First flight: Not flown

TYPE: Five-seat cabin autogyro.

NOTES: Westland's first involvement in rotary wing aircraft came in 1934, some 12 years before the company made a bold decision to specialise in the design and construction of helicopters. The autogyro represented an interim phase in the development of rotary wing aircraft, being brought to practicality in the early 1920s by the Spaniard, Juan de la Cierva. His C4 Autogiro, flown successfully at Getafe, Spain, on 9 January 1923, made the first recorded flight of an aircraft of this type. The Cierva Autogiro Company was formed in Britain on 24 March 1926, to develop and manufacture autogyros of de la Cierva's design, and resulting in a growth in the appreciation and experience of the problems relating to this type of aircraft. Unlike the helicopter, its rotor is unpowered, deriving lift during autorotation, when forward movement of the aircraft is provided by a conventionally mounted engine and propeller.

Westland's C.29 represented an attempt to take a major step forward in the development of a safe passenger-carrying aircraft that would embody a rotary wing. Agreement was reached with the Cierva Company to co-operate in the task with Westland being responsible for the airframe, and Cierva for its three-blade rotor and controls. The C.29 was very much bigger than any earlier project, and design effort was concentrated to produce a strong, lightweight structure. This was realised by creating a basic metal airframe that was wholly fabric-covered. The tail unit comprised dorsal and ventral fins; a rudder; a tailplane which had its aerofoil section inverted on the port side, to help offset propeller torque; and endplate fins on the tailplane, with the upper portion outward canted. Powerplant consisted of a 447 kW (600 hp) Armstrong Siddeley Panther engine.

Early ground testing, carried out during 1934, revealed serious ground resonance problems. These were thought to be caused by rotor vibration, but very little was then understood about this phenomenon. Since then it has been established that landing gear design is critical, if it is to prevent amplification of rotor induced vibration. In 1934 no corrective measure could be discovered, and it was decided to shelve the project until further research in the rotary wing field of activities could find a solution. The death of Juan de la Cierva, in 1936, also contributed to bring the C.29 programme to a close.

STRUCTURE: Three-blade autorotating rotor. Fuselage and tail unit basic structure of light alloy, fabric-covered. Non-retractable tailwheel landing gear, with single wheel on each unit.

ACCOMMODATION: Pilot and four passengers in an enclosed cabin.

DATA:

POWER PLANT: One 447 kW (600 hp) Armstrong Siddeley Panther II radial piston-engine, mounted in a pronounced nose-down attitude to provide propeller wash over the rotor.

Rotor diameter	15.24 m (50 ft 0 in)
Rotor disc area	182.41 m² (1,963.5 sq ft)
Length overall	11.58 m (38 ft 0 in)
Weight empty	1,461 kg (3,221 lb)
Max T-O weight	2,268 kg (5,000 lb)
Max level speed (estimated)	
	139 knots (257 km/h; 160 mph)
Max rate of climb (estimated)	457 m (1,500 ft)/min

Westland C.29 autogiro

WESTLAND F.7/30

First flight:
F.7/30 (K2891): 27 March 1934

TYPE: Single-seat fighter.

NOTES: The Air Ministry Specification F.7/30 was drawn up to spur the development of a high-performance single-seat fighter, one that would be far superior to the Armstrong Whitworth Siskin IIIA that was then used extensively by the RAF's fighter squadrons, and even the superb Hawker Fury that was on the point of replacing them in service. It was required to be suitable for operation by day or night; to have a maximum speed of more than 217 knots (402 km/h; 250 mph) and, in terms of performance, to have corresponding improvements in ceiling, manoeuvrability, and rate of climb; and was to carry an armament of four machine-guns. This latter item was indeed forward-looking, showing a growing appreciation of the fact that higher speeds would need greater fire-power to cope with more fleeting targets. The manufacturer would need to resolve for himself the pros and cons of monoplane versus biplane configuration, made difficult by the night fighter requirement which, at the 1930 state of the art, needed a speed range that would allow of well controlled low speed landings. Favoured power plant was the evaporatively-cooled Rolls-Royce Goshawk, but as this was suffering serious development problems there was no hard and fast requirement.

This specification presented a formidable challenge to designers, but brought a large response because of the production potential that, clearly, could result for an outstanding design. The biplane/monoplane uncertainty is reflected by the submission of biplane layouts by Armstrong Whitworth, Blackburn, Bristol, Gloster, Hawker, and Westland. Monoplanes came from Bristol (an each way bet), Supermarine, and Vickers.

It would be difficult to decide which of the two aircraft designed by Blackburn and Westland was the most unorthodox. Clearly, both had adopted unusual configurations in an attempt to resolve the problems posed by the night fighter requirement. Arthur Davenport had concentrated first on providing the pilot with a good fore and aft view, retaining the gull-wing of the P.V.7 monoplane to serve as the upper wing: this gave the necessary aft view. He then mounted the Goshawk engine within the fuselage, more or less on the C/G, driving the propeller via an extended shaft and gearing. This allowed the pilot to be accommodated high on the fuselage, forward of the upper wing, and so providing an optimum forward view. It also allowed the fuselage nose to make an excellent mounting for the four

Westland F.7/30, K2891

forward-firing synchronised machine-guns. In other respects the fuselage and tail unit were similar to the P.V.7, but with the lower wing level with the bottom of the fuselage. This change from the P.V.7's monoplane configuration to the F.7/30 biplane lay-out had been adopted by Arthur Davenport, perhaps reluctantly, to ensure the low-speed controllability that was needed for the night fighter landing capability.

First flown by Harald Penrose in 1934, the F.7/30 proved quite pleasant to fly, but in common with most Westland aircraft up to that period, required an addition to the area of both the fin and rudder. During subsequent testing, Penrose was somewhat disconcerted when the excellent rear view disclosed the fact that the fabric down one side of the fuselage and that of the tailplane was disappearing in flames. Modification to the fuel system was considered the appropriate remedy, until it happened again immediately after. This time the exhaust ejectors were changed, and the problem was solved.

However pleasant to fly, however controllable, official testing at Martlesham Heath was to show that this biplane just did not have anything like the required performance, and further tests were abandoned. K2891 was to be retained only for experimental flying and no further examples were built.

STRUCTURE: Braced single-bay biplane with wings of unequal span, upper wing of gull-wing configuration. Basic structure of metal with fabric covering. Handley Page slots on leading-edge of upper wing. Ailerons on upper wing only. Fuselage and braced tailplane had basic structure of metal, with fabric covering, except for forward fuselage and in area of engine bay. Non-retractable tailwheel landing gear, with single spatted wheel on each unit.

ACCOMMODATION: Pilot only in enclosed cockpit. Radio transceiver, oxygen, blind flying instrumentation, and night flying equipment standard.

DATA:

POWER PLANT: One 447 kW (600 hp) Rolls-Royce Goshawk VIII evaporatively-cooled inline piston-engine.

Wing span	11.73 m (38 ft 6 in)
Length overall	8.99 m (29 ft 6 in)
Height overall	3.28 m (10 ft 9 in)
Wheel track	1.98 m (6 ft 6 in)
Weight empty	1,672 kg (3,687 lb)
Max T-O weight	2,359 kg (5,200 lb)
Max rate of climb at S/L	443 m (1,455 ft)/min
Max level speed	161 knots (298 km/h; 185 mph)

ARMAMENT: Four fixed forward-firing synchronised Vickers machine-guns.

WESTLAND-BUILT (Sub-contract)

HAWKER AUDAX

TYPE: Two-seat army co-operation aircraft.

NOTES: H.G. Hawker Engineering Ltd designed the Audax, a Hart derivative, to meet Air Ministry Specification 7/31 for an army co-operation aircraft required to replace the Armstrong-Whitworth Atlas. Evaluation of this during the Summer of 1931 led to an initial production order for 40 aircraft, first of these (K1995) being flown for the first time on 29 December 1931. Orders began to flow in, not only for the RAF, but also from overseas customers. Because of Hawker's limited production capacity, related to the number of military aircraft that were being marketed, construction of the Audax under sub-contract (in common with all Hart variants) was arranged with Bristol, Gloster, A.V. Roe, and Westland.

Westland's initial contract was negotiated by Hawker Aircraft Ltd (the name adopted in 1933), and covered 18 aircraft. This, and a second contract for an additional 25 aircraft, was dated 1935. Two aircraft from the second contract were supplied to the South African Air Force in 1937.

STRUCTURE: Single-bay biplane of unequal span. Basic structure of metal with fabric covering. Handley Page leading-edge slots, and ailerons on upper wing only. Fuselage and braced tail unit of metal with fabric covering. Non-retractable tailskid landing gear.

ACCOMMODATION: Pilot and observer/gunner in open cockpits.

DATA:

POWER PLANT: One 395 kW (530 hp) Rolls-Royce Kestrel IB inline piston-engine.

Wing span	11.35 m (37 ft 3 in)
Wing area, gross	32.33 m² (348 sq ft)
Length overall	9.02 m (29 ft 7 in)
Height overall	3.17 m (10 ft 5 in)
Weight empty	1,333 kg (2,938 lb)
Max T-O weight	1,989 kg (4,386 lb)
Max level speed at 730 m (2,400 ft)	
	147 knots (274 km/h; 170 mph)
Service ceiling	6,555 m (21,500 ft)
Endurance	3.5 h

ARMAMENT: One fixed forward-firing Vickers machine-gun, one Lewis gun on mounting in rear cockpit; four 20 lb practice bombs, or two 112 lb supply containers beneath lower wings.

Hawker Audax license-built by Westland
(Michael J.H. Taylor)

WESTLAND LYSANDER

First flights:
First prototype (K6127): 15 June 1936
Second prototype (K6128): 11 December 1936

TYPE: Two-seat army co-operation aircraft.
NOTES: The Lysander was almost certainly the first product of the company to make the name of Westland known to almost every man, woman, and child in wartime Britain, its distinctive configuration leaving little doubt that it was 'one of ours'. Even the least talented amateur spotters could point with confidence and say 'Look, a Westland Lysander', or, more frequently as the war years progressed, 'Look, there's a Lizzie', adopting the affectionate nickname bestowed by pilots upon an aircraft which they had tried in battle, and learned to trust.

The P.8, as it was identified initially by Westland, was the company's submission to meet Air Ministry Specification A.39/34, drawn up to find a successor to the Hawker Audax which entered service in 1932. This specification had little appeal to the industry: it may have been considered there would be only limited production of a type that was then beginning to be outdated, or perhaps they had more important commitments. It is most unlikely that any manufacturer, Westland included, could have believed that approximately 1,400 examples of the winning design would be built, and the only contender to vie with Westland for this contract was the Bristol Type 148 low-wing monoplane.

The P.8 was the first design to enter production that originated from a team headed by the brilliant W.E.W. ('Teddy') Petter. No effort had been spared to arrive at a configuration that would meet the requirements of wide speed range, good low-speed control, short field take-off and landing capability, and suitability for the general-purpose duties that fell to the lot of an army co-operation aircraft. To heighten their appreciation of exactly what was needed, the design team spent a considerable amount of time with pilots of the RAF's army co-operation squadrons before finalising their ideas. Their design proposal won a contract for two prototypes in June 1935, and within 12 months the first of them (K6127) was ready for taxying tests, rolled out at Yeovil on 10 June 1936. During the next five days it was moved to RAF Boscombe Down where, on 15 June, it was flown for the first time by Harald Penrose, who landed it back at Westland's airfield.

The most unusual, and easily recognisable, feature of the design was the braced high-set monoplane wing. This had an all-metal basic struc-

Westland Lysander II

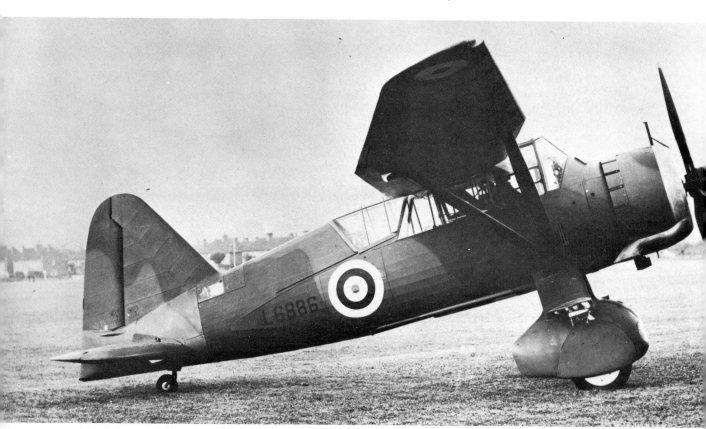

ture, metal skinned from leading-edge to main spar, with fabric covering aft, and in planform had an inner panel with a swept-forward leading-edge, and an outer panel of which almost the whole of the trailing-edge was swept forward. The necessary short-field performance was provided by full-span leading-edge slats, in two sections, and wide span trailing-edge flaps which extended from the fuselage to just outboard of the inner wing panels: the remainder of the wing trailing-edge was occupied by wide-span ailerons. A V-strut on each side braced the wing to the main landing gear structure. Power plant selected for the two prototypes, and used also for the initial production version, was the 664 kW (890 hp) Bristol Mercury XII radial engine.

As first flown, the prototype was without engine cowling gills and armament, the landing gear was only partially faired, and a two-blade fixed-pitch wood propeller substituted for the three-blade variable-pitch propeller that was standard on production aircraft. Expanded flight testing revealed some longitudinal instability, unresolved by the first attempted 'fix' of an increase in tailplane area. It was to be overcome by the introduction of a variable-incidence tailplane, and a change in handling techniques, but did not deter the Air Ministry from awarding an initial contract for 144 Lysander Is in September 1936. The first of these entered service with No.16 Squadron in June 1938. They were among the first British aircraft to be based in France at the beginning of World War II, and Lysanders of No.4 Squadron were the last of the British Air Component to see action in France during the evacuation from Dunkirk.

Westland Lysander IIISCW (*F. Ballam*)

Subsequently, Lysanders were to serve in Burma, Egypt, Greece, India, and Palestine, before being superseded by Curtiss Tomahawks, and after withdrawal from front-line squadrons continued to render valuable service with Special Duties units, and for air-sea rescue and target towing. A total of 19 Lysander I's, plus one Mk III, was supplied to the Royal Egyptian Air Force.

STRUCTURE: Braced high-wing monoplane, basic wing structure of light alloy with metal-skinned leading-edges and fabric covering. Wing incorporated full-span leading-edge slats, wide-span trailing-edge flaps, and ailerons. Fuselage and tail unit of metal basic structure, fuselage covered by metal panels forward and fabric aft: tailplane all-metal, other tail unit surfaces fabric-covered. Non-retractable tailwheel landing gear with streamlined fairings for main wheels. Provisions for attachment of small stub-wings to main wheel struts, just above streamlined fairings, to carry weapons and stores. Message hook below fuselage.

ACCOMMODATION: Pilot in enclosed cockpit forward of wing. Continuous transparent canopy aft to observer/gunner's position at rear of wing. Equipment included radio, oxygen, full blind-flying instrumentation, night flying equipment, and camera.

DATA (Lysander I):

POWER PLANT: One 664 kW (890 hp) Bristol Mercury XII radial piston-engine. Fuselage fuel tank with capacity of 432 litres (95 Imp gallons).

Wing span	15.24 m (50 ft 0 in)
Wing area, gross	24.15 m² (260 sq ft)
Length overall	9.30 m (30 ft 6 in)
Height overall	3.35 m (11 ft 0 in)
Tailplane span	3.81 m (12 ft 6 in)
Wheel track	2.74 m (9 ft 0 in)
Propeller diameter	3.35 m (11 ft 0 in)
Weight empty	1,844 kg (4,065 lb)
Max T-O weight	2,685 kg (5,920 lb)

Max level speed at 3,050 m (10,000 ft)
 199 knots (369 km/h; 229 mph)
Cruising speed at optimum altitude
 130 knots (241 km/h; 150 mph)
Min control speed 48 knots (89 km/h; 55 mph)
Max rate of climb at S/L 503 m (1,650 ft)/min
Service ceiling 7,925 m (26,000 ft)
Range at cruising speed, allowances for T-O and climb
 521 nm (966 km; 600 miles)

ARMAMENT: Two fixed forward-firing Browning machine-guns in wheel fairings, under pilot's control; one Lewis gun on Fairey mounting in rear cockpit. With bomb carriers on stub-wings and beneath the fuselage a max of 227 kg (500 lb) of weapons could be carried.

VARIANTS: *Lysander II.* Generally similar to Mk I, but powered by a 675 kW (905 hp) Bristol Perseus XII radial sleeve-valve piston-engine. Supplied also to l'Armée de l'Air (1), Irish Air Corps (6), and Turkish Air Force (36). About 20 were transferred from the RAF to serve with the Free French Air Force. One

Westland Lysander with de Lanne wing and tail turret mock-up

aircraft supplied to Canada as a pattern for licence construction by National Steel Car Corporation (later Victory Aircraft) at Malton, Ontario, which built 75 with Perseus XII engines. Max T-O weight 2,728 kg (6,015 lb).

Lysander III. Generally similar to Mk I, but powered by a 649 kW (870 hp) Bristol Mercury XX radial piston-engine. Yeovil factory built 250, Westland's Doncaster, Yorkshire, factory 17. One supplied to Royal Egyptian Air Force. A total of 150 licence-built in Canada, powered by 649 kW (870 hp) Bristol Mercury 30 radial piston-engine. Max T-O weight 2,866 kg (6,318 lb).

Lysander IIIA. Generally similar to Mk III, but with Mercury 30 engine, and twin Browning guns replacing single Lewis gun in rear cockpit. Total of 347 built by Westland. One supplied to Free French Forces, eight to Portugal, and two to USAAF.

Lysander III SCW. Conversion of Mk III or IIIA aircraft for clandestine operations, carrying agents or VIPs to and from enemy occupied territory. Long-range fuel tanks beneath fuselage, access ladder to aft cockpit mounted on port side of fuselage, guns removed from aft cockpit, and special equipment added. Served with No.138 and 161 Squadrons, and carrying out more than 400 operations. Max T-O weight 4,536 kg (10,000 lb); max endurance eight hours.

Lysander TT.Mk I. Designation of 14 Lysander Is after conversion for target-towing duties.

Lysander TT.Mk II. Designation of five Lysander IIs after conversion for target-towing duties.

Lysander TT.Mk III. Designation of seven Lysander Is, 16 Lysander IIs, and 28 Lysander IIIs following conversion for target-towing duties.

Lysander TT.Mk IIIA. Designation of 100 new-production target-tugs with Mercury 30 engines.

EXPERIMENTAL VARIANTS: The original prototype was brought up to full Lysander I production standard after completing Air Ministry testing, and in early 1940 was used for a trial installation of two 20 mm cannon for attacks on German invasion barges. One was mounted above each wheel fairing, in such a position that the shells just cleared the propeller disc. Not ordered.

The above was the first of several anti-invasion experiments, intended to provide significant fire power for strafing shipping, or troops if a successful landing was made. K6127 was subsequently modified extensively, the fuselage length reduced to 7.85 m (25 ft 9 in), with the intention to install a four-gun power-operated turret at the tail. A de Lanne type secondary wing was mounted beneath the rear fuselage, just forward of the turret, and this incorporated full-span elevators, and twin endplate fins and rudders. Area of the de Lanne wing was 12.31 m² (132.5 sq ft). Aircraft tested by Harald Penrose, who considered that it handled well. None ordered.

Continuing the ground-strafing experiments, the first production Lysander I (L4673) was provided with an under-fuselage twin-gun installation. Known as the 'Pregnant Perch' at Yeovil, it was written off when engine failure caused a crash landing. In addition to the foregoing armament experiments, a mock up was made to show the possibility of mid-fuselage installation of a four-gun power-operated turret, but this did not progress beyond the mock up stage.

To investigate the problem of operating from unprepared landing strips, one aircraft was provided with caterpillar track main landing gear units. Another experiment to cater for cross-wind operations saw the installation of a Dowty castoring main landing gear system, which allowed the wheels to be offset to the aircraft's centreline.

Further experiments relating to aerodynamic research involved the installation of a Blackburn-Steiger parallel-chord high-lift wing on a Lysander II (P9105) in 1941. This wing, of only 11.58 m (38 ft) span, had 9° of forward sweep, and incorporated full-span leading-edge slats, and full-span trailing-edge flaps. Roll control was achieved by spoilers adjacent to the wingtips. One aircraft was known to have been provided with underwing bench-type airbrakes, although the purpose of this experiment is not known.

Westland Lysander with underwing airbrakes

WESTLAND-BUILT (Sub-contract)

HAWKER HECTOR

TYPE: Two-seat army co-operation aircraft.

NOTES: With a very large demand being made on Rolls-Royce for Kestrel engines, particularly to power Hawker Hinds ordered for the RAF's expansion programme, the Air Ministry considered it desirable to procure an Audax replacement with an alternative power plant. Hawker's proposal was a modified Hart, powered by a Napier Dagger III engine. It retained the fuselage, tail unit and landing gear of the Hart, but introduced a new straight (as opposed to slightly swept) upper wing to cater for the CG movement caused by installation of a heavier engine. In addition, refinements introduced on the Hind, and including an improved rear cockpit profile, and a tailwheel, were incorporated in the production Hector.

The prototype, K3719, was flown for the first time on 14 February 1936: before that date, however, Hawker Aircraft had received a production contract, which reflects the urgency of the requirement and the mood of that period in time. It had been intended to sub-contract these to A.V. Roe, but large contracts for the Anson, awarded to Avro in late 1935, meant that their production capacity was fully committed. The knowledge that Westland had gained a contract for the army co-operation Lysander, and that this association with the Hector might be helpful, led to selection of Westland as sub-contractor for the Hector. All 178 production Hectors, the first Westland-built aircraft being flown by Harald Penrose in February 1937, were built by the Yeovil company. Initial deliveries to No.50 Army Co-operation Wing, at Odiham, Hampshire, also began in February 1937. A total of 13 Hectors, 9 from the first production batch and 4 from the second, were supplied to the Irish Air Corps during 1941-42.

STRUCTURE: Single-bay biplane of unequal span. Basic structure of metal with fabric covering. Handley Page leading-edge slots, and ailerons on upper wings only. Fuselage and braced tail unit of metal with fabric covering. Non-retractable tailwheel landing gear.

ACCOMMODATION: Pilot and observer/gunner in open cockpits.

DATA:

POWER PLANT: One 600 kW (805 hp) Napier Dagger IIIMS 24-cylinder inline piston-engine.

Wing span	11.26 m (36 ft 11½ in)
Wing area, gross	32.14 m² (346 sq ft)
Length overall	9.09 m (29 ft 9¾ in)
Height overall	3.17 m (10 ft 5 in)
Weight empty	1,537 kg (3,389 lb)
Max T-O weight	2,227 kg (4,910 lb)
Max level speed at 2,000 m (6,560 ft)	
	162 nm (301 km/h; 187 mph)
Service ceiling	7,315 m (24,000 ft)
Endurance	2 h 25 min

License-built Hawker Hector

WESTLAND C.L.20 AUTOGIRO

First flight: 5 February 1935

TYPE: Two-seat lightweight autogyro.

NOTES: Although the C.29 Autogiro was gathering dust in the hangar, following the suspension of activities on that project, the company was still interested in the rotary-wing concept. As a result, a new arrangement was made with The Cierva Autogiro Company, possibly with the hope that a fresh look at the subject might also resolve the ground resonance problems of the five-seat C.29.

Work began in 1934 on the construction of a lightweight two-seat aircraft which had been designed in conjunction with Monsieur Lepere, chief engineer of the French licencees of the Cierva company. Although very much smaller, the airframe was similar to that of the earlier aircraft, but differed by having a different mounting for the main wheel units, and a much simpler tail unit. The rotor incorporated a direct control head, and had three untapered blades which had flapping and drag hinges. The rotor could be folded manually to simplify parking or storage problems.

Despite being basically a research project, Westland obviously hoped that a civil market could be found for the C.L.20, and had taken pains to produce an attractive cabin with side by side seats. Although first flown in 1935, the performance of the C.L.20 proved to be disappointing with an inexplicable deficiency of lift. Testing continued over an extended period, but further development was abandoned when the outbreak of World War II appeared to be imminent.

STRUCTURE: Fuselage and tail unit had a basic structure of light alloy, fabric-covered. Tail unit comprising tailplane, with one half having an inverted aerofoil section set at a negative angle of incidence to offset propeller torque, endplate fins, and central dorsal and ventral fins. Non-retractable tailwheel landing gear, with wheel fairings on all three units.

ACCOMMODATION: Two seats side by side in enclosed cabin.

DATA:

POWER PLANT: One 67 kW (90 hp) Pobjoy Niagra S radial piston-engine, driving a two-blade fixed-pitch wooden propeller.

Rotor diameter	9.75 m (32 ft 0 in)
Rotor disc area	74.71 m² (804.25 sq ft)
Length overall	6.17 m (20 ft 3 in)
Max T-O weight	635 kg (1,400 lb)
Max level speed	92 knots (171 km/h; 106 mph)

Westland C.L.20

WESTLAND WHIRLWIND

First flight:
Prototype (L6844): 11 October 1938

TYPE: Single-seat day or night fighter.

NOTES: Comments made on Westland's F.7/30 prototype mentioned the Air Ministry's growing concern to increase the fire power of fighter aircraft: that specification speeded the transition from two- to four-gun fighters. Negotiations that were initiated in 1934 were to lead to a licence agreement, in July 1935, which permitted the Birmingham Small Arms Company to manufacture a .303 calibre version of the American Colt Browning .300. The availability of this small, reliable and quick-firing machine-gun produced the Hurricane and Spitfire eight-gun fighters, which entered service with the RAF in 1937 and 1938 respectively. But in 1934 there was already growing concern that even eight .303 machine-guns would not prove adequate to stop new-generation fighters and bombers. Quick-firing cannon with large-calibre shells were beginning to arm aircraft produced on the European continent: Britain could not remain aloof to such developments. Air Ministry Specification F.37/35 was intended to start the ball rolling, calling for a single-seat day/night fighter to be armed with four 20 mm cannon.

Most of Britain's aircraft manufacturers were already committed heavily on production programmes to strengthen the RAF, which perhaps explains the small response to the F.37/35 specification. Proposals came from Bristol (Type 153), Hawker (a Hurricane variant), Supermarine (Type 313), and Westland (P8), and it was the latter that gained a contract to build two prototypes of what proved to be the first fighter of Westland design to serve with the RAF. The Whirlwind, as it became known, was designed by a team headed by 'Teddy' Petter. He had selected a low-wing monoplane layout with twin-engines, producing a beautifully streamlined structure that reduced drag to a minimum. So slender was the fuselage, that its cross-section was less than either of the engine nacelles which housed the Rolls-Royce Peregrine supercharged engines. Those installed in the first prototype (L6844) were geared to provide counter-rotating, or handed, propellers. Innovative features were the mounting of coolant radiators within wing centre-section ducts, providing a low-drag installation; the provision of a 'near' bubble canopy that gave an excellent all-round view; and the routing of engine exhausts through the wings. A wing fire during tests led to the installation of more conventional exhaust ejectors.

On 11 October 1938, Harald Penrose was able to fly the L6844 prototype for the first time, and realised very quickly that, at last, Westland had advanced to a new level of capability. The aircraft was highly manoeuvrable, with excellent low-level performance but, as might be expected, expansion of the flight envelope disclosed some shortcomings that needed remedy. Most important was a handling problem in a high-speed dive, traced to compressibility effects at the junction of fin and high-mounted tailplane. This was resolved within acceptable limits by the introduction of an acorn fairing at the point of intersection. Testing also showed that the stall characteristics were good enough to dispense with the wide-span Handley Page leading-edge slats installed in the outer wing panels. These were deleted from the majority of production aircraft, and locked in the closed position on the early aircraft which incorporated them. It did, however, raise the landing speed, which was one contributory factor to the low number of production aircraft (112), as the choice of airfields from which they could operate was very restricted.

The Whirlwind first entered service with the RAF's No.263 Squadron on 6 July 1940, but due to delays in engine deliveries from Rolls-Royce it was not until 7 December that the squadron became operational. These aircraft were found to be very fast at low level, and with their long-range capability proved to be excellent bomber escorts, and were to see also extensive service as fighter-bombers before being withdrawn from first-line service during 1943. Their demise was hastened by a fall off in performance at the higher altitudes at which combats were being fought as the war progressed. With Rolls-Royce committed to large-scale production and development of the Merlin engine, further development of the Peregrine was impossible. Production ended in December 1941, with the cancellation of outstanding orders for 288 aircraft.

STRUCTURE: Cantilever low-wing monoplane. Conventional all-metal stressed-skin structure. Handley Page leading-edge slats (not used) on outer wing panels of prototype and early production aircraft. Ailerons extending over trailing-edge of outer wing panels, trailing-edge flaps, in two sections, from inboard edge of aileron to fuselage on each wing. One section of these flaps doubled also to control airflow through the coolant radiators. Fuselage and tail unit of metal construction. Ailerons and tail unit control surfaces fabric-covered. Tailwheel landing gear with all units retractable.

ACCOMMODATION: Pilot only in enclosed cockpit with transparent canopy. Full blind-flying instrumentation. Radio. Oxygen. Accommodation heated and ventilated.

DATA:

POWER PLANT: Two 660 kW (885 hp) Rolls-Royce Peregrine I inline piston-engines, driving three-blade constant-speed propellers.

Westland Whirlwind prototype

Wing span	13.72 m (45 ft 0 in)
Wing area, gross	23.23 m² (250 sq ft)
Length overall	9.98 m (32 ft 9 in)
Height overall	3.53 m (11 ft 7 in)
Wheel track	3.89 m (12 ft 9 in)
Propeller diameter	3.05 m (10 ft 0 in)
Weight empty	3,769 kg (8,310 lb)
Max T-O weight (fighter)	4,697 kg (10,356 lb)
Max T-O weight (fighter/bomber)	5,166 kg (11,388 lb)
Max level speed, fighter at 4,570 m (15,000 ft)	
	313 knots (579 km/h; 360 mph)
Max level speed, bomber at 4,570 m (15,000 ft)	
	234 knots (435 km/h; 270 mph)
Service ceiling	9,145 m (30,000 ft)
Range (not recorded officially):	
	about 695 nm (1,287 km; 800 miles)

ARMAMENT: Four Hispano 20 mm cannon mounted in fuselage nose. Whirlwind IA fighter-bombers were converted in service by the installation of a Mk III Universal bomb-carrier beneath each wing, and making it possible to carry two 250 lb or two 500 lb bombs.

SPECIAL VARIANTS: As flown originally, the prototype (L6844) was without armament, but subsequently had the four cannon installation mentioned above. Armament variations proposed for the Whirlwind, some of which were fitted, flown, and fired on L6844, included:

1. Four 20 mm Hispano Mk 1 cannon with standard 60 round drum magazines, the guns in a two up and two down arrangement.

2. Four 20 mm Hispano Mk 2 cannon mounted in a horizontal line, with the outboard pair forward of the inboard guns. These were belt fed from large box magazines, containing some 100-120 rounds, with a Dessouter compressed air motor helping to drive the belt feeds.

3. Four 20 mm Hispano Mk 2 cannon mounted in a horizontal line, but with the outboard pair aft of the inboard guns. This made an external difference in the nose cowling by comparison with layout 2, the bulges to accommodate the corners of the box magazines being much smaller.

4. Four Hispano Mk 2s as in layout 3, plus three .303-in Browning machine-guns above and behind the centre 20 mm cannon.

5. A single large calibre cannon mounted slightly offset to port. The manufacturer of this weapon is uncertain, and whether it was of 37 mm or 40 mm calibre is also not clear.

6. Twelve .303-in Browning machine-guns mounted in a tubular steel unit, but there seems some doubt as to whether this was ever installed in the aircraft. It is believed that, chronologically, this installation, if made, would have come after the four Hispano Mk 1 cannon.

One aircraft which escaped the indignity of being scrapped after withdrawal from service (P7048), was refurbished at Yeovil and used as a company hack until 1947 under the civil registration G-AGOI.

WESTLAND-BUILT (Sub-contract)

SUPERMARINE SPITFIRE

TYPE: Single-seat fighter (Spitfire II) or fighter-bomber (Spitfire V).

NOTES: The significant role played by R.J. Mitchell's superb Supermarine Spitfire during six years of wartime service is so well-known that extended notes are entirely superfluous here. In addition to production in company factories at Castle Bromwich, Southampton, Swindon, and Winchester, the demand for this aircraft was such that it was sub-contracted on a wide basis. Westland was numbered among these sub-contractors, producing almost 700 examples which included IIAs, VBs, and VCs, with the first Westland-built Spitfire being flown by Harald Penrose on 8 July 1941.

STRUCTURE: Cantilever low-wing monoplane of all-metal construction. Split trailing-edge flaps between fuselage and ailerons. Fuselage and tail unit of metal construction, except for fabric-covered elevators and rudder. Retractable tailwheel landing gear, only main units retracting on earlier marks.

ACCOMMODATION: Pilot only in enclosed cockpit.

DATA (Spitfire VC):

POWER PLANT: One 1,074 kW (1,440 hp) Rolls-Royce Merlin 45 inline piston-engine.

Supermarine Spitfire VB/C

Wing span:	
Standard	11.23 m (36 ft 10 in)
Clipped	9.80 m (32 ft 2 in)
Wing area, gross:	
Standard	22.48 m² (242 sq ft)
Clipped	21.46 m² (231 sq ft)
Length overall	9.12 m (29 ft 11 in)
Max T-O weight	3,078 kg (6,785 lb)

Max level speed:
Standard wing at 3,960 m (13,000 ft)
325 knots (602 km/h; 374 mph)
Clipped wing at 1,830 m (6,000 ft)
310 knots (575 km/h; 357 mph)

Service ceiling:	
Standard wing	11,280 m (37,000 ft)
Clipped wing	11,125 m (36,500 ft)
Range, standard fuel	408 nm (756 km; 470 miles)

ARMAMENT: Spitfire VC had universal wing accommodating eight .303 machine-guns, or two 20 mm cannon and four .303 machine-guns, or four 20 mm cannon plus one 500 lb bomb or an extended range fuel tank beneath the fuselage, or two 250 lb bombs beneath the wings.

WESTLAND-BUILT (Sub-contract)

FAIREY BARRACUDA

TYPE: Three-seat carrier- or land-based torpedo-bomber/reconnaissance aircraft.

NOTES: Fairey's Barracuda, designed to meet the requirements of Specification S.24/37, was intended to replace the Fairey Albacore in service. A shoulder-wing monoplane of almost frail appearance, it hardly seemed possible that it was a weapon of war, and often appeared to possess the grace of a sailplane when in flight. Nothing could have been further from the truth than this apparent flimsy quality, as exemplified by the historic attack of 3 April 1944, launched by 42 of the Fleet Air Arm's Barracudas, against the German battleship *Tirpitz* lying in Norway's Kaafjord.

Barracuda production eventually exceeded 2,500, built not only by Fairey, but also by sub-contractors which included Blackburn, Boulton Paul, and Westland. The latter had anticipated fairly extensive involvement in this manufacturing programme, but had instead to switch priority to production of the Supermarine Seafire. As a result, Westland completed only 18 Barracudas (comprising both Mk Is and IIs) before having to withdraw from construction of these aircraft, in favour of both Merlin- and Griffon-engined versions of the Spitfire.

STRUCTURE: Cantilever shoulder-wing monoplane of metal construction. Fairey-Youngman flaps below and staggered aft of the wing trailing-edge. Fabric-covered ailerons. Wings folded for carrier stowage. Fuselage and braced tail unit of metal construction, with tailplane mounted high on the fin. Rudder and elevators fabric-covered. Retractable tailwheel landing gear, with only main units retracting.

ACCOMMODATION: Crew of three comprising pilot, observer/navigator, and gunner/radio operator in tandem cockpits beneath a continuous canopy.

DATA (Barracuda II):

POWER PLANT: One 1,223 kW (1,640 hp) Rolls-Royce Merlin 32 inline piston-engine.

Wing span	14.99 m (49 ft 2 in)
Wing area, gross	34.09 m^2 (367 sq ft)
Length overall	12.12 m (39 ft 9 in)
Height overall	4.60 m (15 ft 1 in)
Weight empty	4,241 kg (9,350 lb)
Max T-O weight	6,396 kg (14,100 lb)
Max level speed at 535 m (1,750 ft)	
	198 knots (367 km/h; 228 mph)
Max cruising speed at 1,525 m (5,000 ft)	
	168 knots (311 km/h; 193 mph)
Service ceiling	5,060 m (16,600 ft)
Range with 816 kg (1,800 lb) of bombs	
	455 nm (843 km; 524 miles)

ARMAMENT: Two Vickers machine-guns on flexible mounting in aft cockpit, one 18 in torpedo or four depth charges beneath the fuselage, or up to 816 kg (1,800 lb) bombs below the wings.

Fairey Barracuda

WESTLAND-BUILT (Sub-contract)

SUPERMARINE SEAFIRE

TYPE: Single-seat carrier-based fighter, fighter-bomber, or tactical reconnaissance aircraft.

NOTES: After the Sea Hurricane had proved that it was possible to operate a high-performance aircraft from an aircraft carrier, it seemed logical to use the Spitfire in a similar way. After testing of a VB, provided with an arrester hook, the development of a specialised Seafire went ahead with all speed. First production version, following the conversion of 48 Spitfire VBs to Seafire IBs, was the Seafire IIC. Westland built 110 of these under sub-contract, simultaneously working with Supermarine on the development of a folding wing, and then becoming prime contractor for the Seafire III. This was the first production version to incorporate a folding wing. The construction of all wartime production Seafires was carried out by Westland, in conjunction with Cunliffe-Owen Aircraft, this involving a total in excess of 2,400, of which Westland built almost two-thirds. These included Seafire IICs, IIICs, XVs, and XVIIs.

STRUCTURE: Cantilever low-wing monoplane of all-metal construction. Split trailing-edge flaps between fuselage and ailerons. Wings folded manually for carrier stowage, except on Seafire I/IIs. Fuselage and tail unit of metal construction, except for fabric-covered elevators and rudder. Fuselage incorporated an arrester hook and catapult spools. Retractable tailwheel landing gear, only main units retracting on earlier marks.

ACCOMMODATION: Pilot only in enclosed cockpit.

DATA (Seafire XV):

POWER PLANT: One 1,380 kW (1,850 hp) Rolls-Royce Griffon VI inline piston-engine.

Wing span	11.23 m (36 ft 10 in)
Wing area, gross	22.67 m² (244 sq ft)
Length overall	9.83 m (32 ft 3 in)
Height overall	3.25 m (10 ft 8 in)
Height empty	2,812 kg (6,200 lb)
Max T-O weight	3,629 kg (8,000 lb)
Max level speed at 4,115 m (13,500 ft)	333 knots (616 km/h; 383 mph)
Cruising speed at 6,100 m (20,000 ft)	290 knots (538 km/h; 334 mph)
Service ceiling	10,820 m (35,500 ft)
Range, standard fuel	373 nm (692 km; 430 miles)

Supermarine Seafire

114

WESTLAND WELKIN

First flight:
Prototype DG558/G 1 November 1942

TYPE: Single-seat high-altitude fighter.

NOTES: Use by the Luftwaffe of high-altitude fighter/reconnaissance aircraft was forseen by the Air Ministry soon after the outbreak of war, and Specification F.4/40 was drawn up to cover the design and development of a high altitude interceptor that could be deployed against aircraft of this category, in particular the Junkers Ju 86P, that might be used in attacks on Britain. Tenders were received from General Aircraft (GAL-46), Hawker (P.1004), and Westland (P14), and following study of these design proposals a new Specification F.7/41 was issued. This required an armament of six 20 mm cannon, and a pressurised cabin, and was required to be capable of adaptation for use by a crew of two, or to have provisions for AI radar. A minimum speed of 360 knots (668 km/h; 415 mph) was required at 10,060 m (33,000 ft), with a service ceiling of 12,800 m (42,000 ft). From a new round of proposals, prototypes were ordered from Vickers (Type 432) and Westland, but it was the latter company's Welkin which was awarded a production order, the first prototype flown by Harald Penrose on 1 November 1942. Its power plant comprised two 962 kW (1,290 hp) Rolls-Royce Merlin 61 two-stage supercharged engines.

As in the case of the Whirlwind, this had been designed under the leadership of 'Teddy' Petter, and retained a distinct likeness to the fighter that had preceded it. Very different was its high-aspect ratio wing, mounted in mid-wing configuration, but this incorporated coolant radiators within the leading-edge of the centre-section as introduced on the Whirlwind. Realisation of the pressurised cabin posed the major problem, and it was constructed as a separate bolt-on unit of bullet-resistant light alloy; this incorporated an armour steel bulkhead at the rear, and an openable bulkhead in its nose. Achievement of accurate control of the pressure differential led to the design and construction of a small compact valve that relieved the pilot of the task of continually monitoring and adjusting cabin pressure. Basically, this regulated the rate at which air that was pumped into the cabin was vented to atmosphere to maintain the desired cabin pressure: it proved to be effective and reliable. An inflatable

Westland Welkin prototype

rubber gasket sealed the sliding canopy after closure, this transparent canopy being of hollow sandwich construction to simplify de-icing and demisting.

Testing of the second prototype (DG562) at A & AEE Boscombe Down during 1943 was extensive, flown in mock combat against a Mosquito IX at 10,670 m (35,000 ft), and against another Welkin at heights of 11,580 to 12,190 m (38,000 to 40,000 ft). This left little doubt that the Welkin should be able to deal with any bomber or reconnaissance aircraft operating between the latter altitudes, but would almost certainly be out-manoeuvred by another single-seat fighter.

A contract for 100 aircraft was awarded, of which about 80 were built before production was cancelled because the threatened high altitude attacks never developed. None of these aircraft were issued to squadrons, but they were used instead for research into the problems of high altitude flying.

Westland Welkin I

STRUCTURE: Mid-wing cantilever monoplane. All-metal stressed skin structure with split trailing-edge flaps on centre-section, and ailerons in outer panels. Fuselage in two parts, comprising separate pressure cabin of duralumin, and the remainder of magnesium alloy monocoque construction. Cantilever tail unit of light alloy. Tailwheel landing gear, all three units retracting.

ACCOMMODATION: Pilot only in pressurised cabin, with automatic pressure and temperature regulation.

DATA (Welkin I):

POWER PLANT: Two 932 kW (1,250 hp) Rolls-Royce Merlin engines; Mk 72 or 76 starboard, Mk 73 or 77 port, driving four-blade constant-speed propellers, the port engine also driving the Rotol cabin supercharger.

Wing span	21.34 m (70 ft 0 in)
Wing area, gross	42.73 m² (460 sq ft)
Length overall	12.67 m (41 ft 7 in)
Height overall	4.09 m (13 ft 5 in)
Tailplane span	5.79 m (19 ft 0 in)
Wheel track	5.33 m (17 ft 6 in)
Propeller diameter	3.96 m (13 ft 0 in)
Weight empty	3,556 kg (7,840 lb)
Max T-O weight	4,658 kg (10,270 lb)
Max level speed at 7,925 m (26,000 ft)	
	336 knots (663 km/h; 387 mph)
Max rate of climb at S/L	1,173 m (3,850 ft)/min
Service ceiling	13,410 m (44,000 ft)
Range	approx 1,042 nm (1,931 km; 1,200 miles)

ARMAMENT: Four Hispano 20 mm cannon mounted in fuselage nose.

VARIANT: *Welkin NF.Mk II.* Night fighter version developed to Air Ministry Specification F.9/43. Generally similar to Welkin F.Mk I, except nose extended to accommodate AI radar installation, and provision in cabin for rearward-facing seat for the observer. Pilot's windscreen lowered, increased dihedral on outer wing panels, and power plant unchanged. One prototype, conversion of Welkin I, registration PF370 (later WE997). Max level speed 313 knots (579 km/h; 360 mph) at 7,925 m (26,000 ft).

SPECIAL VARIANTS: Two of the Welkin Is were used for special high altitude research. One of these was DG562, its Merlin engines modified so that they could be given injections of liquid oxygen to increase performance at high altitudes. Difficulties in handling the liquid oxygen brought these experiments to a premature close. The other Welkin I (DX340), was provided with two Rolls-Royce Merlin RM16SM engines, and with beard-type coolant radiators augmenting the standard wing centre-section installation. This one-off conversion demonstrated a max speed of 346 knots (641 km/h; 398 mph) at 9,145 m (30,000 ft) during tests.

Westland Welkin II with radar nose

WESTLAND WYVERN

First flights:
1st prototype (TS371): 12 December 1946
TF.Mk 2 prototype (Clyde engine) (VP120):
18 January 1949
TF.Mk 2 prototype (Python engine) (VP109):
22 March 1949
TF.Mk 4 (later S.4): May 1951

TYPE: Single-seat ship-based strike aircraft.

NOTES: During 1944, the Naval Air Staff of the Admiralty drew up Specification N.11/44 covering the design and development of a new long-range day fighter. It was a complicated and demanding requirement, calling for use of the Rolls-Royce Eagle 24-cylinder sleeve valve engine, but requiring also that it should be suitable for the use of turboprop power plant as soon as this became available. Structural requirements included powered wing folding, and landing gear able to withstand a maximum impact velocity of 4.27 m (14 ft)/sec. Provisions were to be made for the use, when necessary, of RATO units. Weapons were to include two or four 20 mm cannon, eight rocket projectiles, three 1,000 lb bombs, and an 18 in torpedo or a 1,820 lb mine.

Only two manufacturers submitted proposals: General Aircraft (GAL-56) and Westland, and prototypes of the latter company's W34 design were ordered. During their construction Air Ministry Specification F.13/44 was issued for a structurally similar aircraft for the Royal Air Force, but with considerable complication in detail requirements: beyond allocation of the Westland identification W34/1, no further action appears to have been taken to meet this specification, and the requirement itself disappeared with the advent of turbojet engines. Meanwhile, work on the six prototypes was progressing and the first of these (TS371) was flown for the first time by Harald Penrose on 12 December 1946. It was an attractive aircraft, a clean low-wing monoplane, but with a distinct hump-backed line to the upper fuselage as a result of the need to provide the pilot with a high viewpoint for deck landings. The development work on the Wyvern was most extensive, primarily because of the power plant involved. For example, it was the only aircraft to be flown with the 2,006 kW (2,690 hp) Rolls-Royce Eagle 22, a new high-powered engine that itself needed a long development programme. Further difficulties were encountered with the large-diameter contra-rotating propellers that were needed, and the combination of engine, propeller, and resulting aerodynamic problems, must have convinced Westland's engineers that they had created a giant Pandora's Box which threatened their continued existence.

To help speed the development programme ten pre-production TF.Mk 1 Wyverns were built, also with the Rolls-Royce Eagle engine. These, plus the prototypes, were the only Wyverns to use this power plant, for British engine manufacturers had by then made such progress with turboprop engines that it was possible to begin flight evaluation of the most suitable. It did not prove possible, and perhaps was not really desirable, to limit the exercise to a single power plant. After consideration of the alternatives, the 3,065 kW (4,110 shp) Armstrong Siddeley Python 3 and 3,005 kW (4,030 shp) Rolls-Royce Clyde were chosen, and three TF.Mk 2 prototypes (two Python-engined) were completed to the new Specification N.12/45, identified by Westland as W35s.

Following the first flights of these aircraft, the difficulties facing Westland engineers were compounded to involve the development programmes of two more untried engines. This was bad enough, but a completely new problem was encountered in the turbine engine/propeller combination as it related to carrier deck operations, and the requirements of high speed operational performance. In the latter case, testing showed that rapid changes of altitude and power setting, as would be expected in service use, caused unexpected and violent power surges. It resulted in temporary grounding of the turbine-powered aircraft until the cause was identified and cured, involving the development of an inertia controller by Armstrong Siddeley and Rotol.

Armstrong Siddeley's Python, the most powerful of the two turboprops under evaluation, was selected for installation in the 20 pre-production TF.Mk 2s. Of these 13 were delivered as TF.Mk 2s, the remainder being completed to TF.Mk 4 (later S.4) standard before delivery. Four of the 13 TF.Mk 2s were subsequently converted to TF.Mk 4s. The Python was also used to power the 90 production Wyvern S.4s, these having a cut-back engine cowling to permit cartridge starting, and several airframe refinements. Retrospective modifications, after the Wyvern entered service, introduced a bullet-proof windscreen, provisions for the installation of wingtip fuel tanks, and perforated airbrakes beneath the wing centre-section.

In May 1953, just five months short of seven years from the first flight of the prototype, Wyverns entered operational service with No.813 Squadron. Remaining shore-based until 1954, this squadron's aircraft served subsequently with HMS *Eagle* and *Albion*, and the other Wyvern operational squadrons (Nos. 827, 830 and 831) also saw service aboard *Eagle*.

STRUCTURE: Cantilever low-wing monoplane of light alloy stressed skin construction. Youngman type trailing-edge flaps on inner wing; ailerons and airbrakes in outer wing panels. Supplementary airbrakes beneath wing centre-section added retrospectively. Outer wing panels folded hydraulically for carrier stowage. Fuselage and tail unit of conventional light alloy construction. Sting type arrester hook in rear fuselage. Auxiliary fins incorporated in tailplane structure retrospectively. Hydraulically-retractable tailwheel landing gear, all units retracting.

ACCOMMODATION: Pilot only on Martin Baker ejection seat in enclosed cockpit.

DATA (Wyvern S.4):

POWER PLANT: One 3,065 kW (4,110 shp) Armstrong Siddeley Python ASp.3 turboprop engine, driving Rotol four-blade constant-speed contra-rotating propellers.

Wing span	13.41 m (44 ft 0 in)
Wing area, gross	32.98 m² (355 sq ft)
Length overall	12.88 m (42 ft 3 in)
Length overall (Eagle engine)	11.96 m (39 ft 3 in)
Length overall (Clyde engine)	12.50 m (41 ft 0 in)
Height overall	4.80 m (15 ft 9 in)
Width (wings folded)	6.10 m (20 ft 0 in)
Weight empty	7,080 kg (15,608 lb)
Max T-O weight	11,113 kg (24,500 lb)
Max level speed at S/L	333 knots (616 km/h; 383 mph)
Max cruising speed at 6,100 m (20,000 ft)	298 knots (552 km/h; 343 mph)
Max rate of climb at S/L	716 m (2,350 ft)/min
Service ceiling	8,535 m (28,000 ft)
Combat range	781 nm (1,448 km; 900 miles)

ARMAMENT: Four Hispano Mk V 20 mm cannon, two in each wing; one 20 in air torpedo, bombs, mines, or depth charges; and 16 × 60 lb rockets.

AVIONICS: Extensive avionics included VHF/HF transceiver, and IFF.

VARIANT: *Wyvern T.Mk 3*. Designation of two-seat trainer prototype, of which only a single example was built (VZ 739). Generally similar to Wyvern S.4, except for modification of rear fuselage to provide a second cockpit (aft). Both had ejection seats, and a periscopic mirror was introduced to provide an optimum view for the instructor, accommodated in the rear seat.

Westland Wyvern S.4

WESTLAND-FAIREY GANNET

First flight:
Fairey prototype (VR546) 19 September 1949
Fairey Gannet AEW. Mk 3 prototype 20 August 1958

TYPE: Carrier-based ASW search and strike aircraft.
NOTES: Westland's acquisition of the UK aviation interests of Fairey Aviation Ltd, on 2 May 1960, brought responsibility for continued production of the Fairey Gannet AEW. Mk 3 three-seat airborne early warning aircraft. This had been developed by Fairey from the ASW versions of the Gannet, to provide the Royal Navy with a replacement for its Douglas AEW.Mk 1 Skyraider early warning air-

Westland-Fairey Gannet of the Royal Australian Navy
(*RAF Museum/Charles Brown*)

craft, which had been in service since late 1951. Fairey received a contract for 44 Gannet AEW.Mk 3s, and the majority of these were completed after Westland had taken control of the company. Production was completed in December 1962.

Two other variants were to appear under the Westland-Fairey name, these being the Gannet AS.Mk 6 and AS.Mk 7 ASW aircraft updated from the earlier AS.Mk 4 by the installation of more advanced avionics and equipment.
DATA (AEW.Mk 3):
POWER PLANT: One 2,890 ekw (3,875 ehp) Bristol Siddeley Double Mamba 102 turboprop engine.

Wing span	16.56 m (54 ft 4 in)
Length overall	13.41 m (44 ft 0 in)
Height overall	5.13 m (16 ft 10 in)
Max T-O weight	approx 11,340 kg (25,000 lb)
Max level speed	217 knots (402 km/h; 250 mph)
Econ cruising speed	113 knots (209 km/h; 130 mph)
Service ceiling	7,620 m (25,000 ft)
Range	608 nm (1,127 km; 700 miles)

WESTLAND DRAGONFLY

First flight: Dragonfly Mk 1A 5 October 1948

TYPE: Four-seat general-purpose helicopter.

NOTES: The Dragonfly has a particular niche in the history of Westland Aircraft, representing the first helicopter to be built by the company. It derived from the Sikorsky S-51, for which licence construction rights were acquired as the result of an agreement signed in December 1946. This agreement was very favourable from the Westland point of view, allowing them to build the S-51 for marketing throughout the world except in the USA and Canada. In addition, Westland was permitted great freedom to develop and improve the Sikorsky design.

Monetary control of the period meant that no components could be acquired from the US company, with the result that all of the detail drawings of the Sikorsky S-51 had to be anglicised before manufacture could begin. Few people realised just how much work this involved, but it is put into sharp perspective by a comment of the Chief Engineer of that period, O. Fitzwilliams: 'the . . . (work) . . . was very extensive, every part of the helicopter being in some respects (and many parts in very major respects) different from the American original.' This work began in late May 1947, when all the drawings were received from Sikorsky, so the company did extremely well to record the first flight of the first Westland-built S-51 (G-AKTW) on 5 October 1948. An initial batch of 30 were built on a speculative basis, and without the use of production tooling. The result was that when the Ministry of Supply completed an evaluation of three of these early production aircraft, and placed contracts

Royal Navy Westland Dragonfly

covering initial supplies for both the Royal Navy and Royal Air Force, there was a delay of almost 18 months before the first delivery was made, due to the time involved in equipping with production tooling.

The civil Westland/Sikorsky S-51 was the first British-built helicopter to gain a Certificate of Airworthiness, on 24 July 1951, and civil S-51s were to see exploratory service with several airlines. They were adopted by industrial operators at a fairly early date, able to appreciate their value for agricultural spraying and dusting operations. The initial military version was the Navy's HR.Mk 1, to which this service gave the name Dragonfly, one that was to become general for all of the military variants. It was equipped primarily for the role then known as Air/Sea Rescue, with a secondary use for photographic sorties. The HR.Mk 1s equipped the Navy's first helicopter squadron, No.705, formed at RNAS Gosport in 1950, which had the distinction of being the world's first helicopter squadron formed outside of the USA.

Production of HR.Mk 1s totalled 13, and their initial use was mainly for 'plane guard' duties, hovering just off a carrier during deck operations and providing an instant rescue service for fixed-wing aircraft crews if needed. They also demonstrated their value for rapid ship-to-ship or ship-to-shore communications. It was in the first role that they proved to be of great practical and economic value, able to carry out more quickly and more economically a role that had traditionally become a task of escorting destroyers. It was not long before the Navy found that it needed far more than its initial 13 aircraft, one of which was flown with an experimental four-blade main rotor. The RAF had also received a batch of 12 of these helicopters, equipped primarily for casualty evacuation, and in April 1950 they were deployed in Malaya to form a Casualty Evacuation Flight. There they quickly made their presence felt and, like the Navy, the Air Force realised that it had gained a valuable new tool. On 1 February 1953 the RAF expanded this flight to form No.194 Squadron, the first helicopter squadron of the Royal Air Force.

STRUCTURE: Three-blade main rotor of composite construction, three-blade tail rotor. Basic centre fuselage structure of steel tube with light alloy skins; forward fuselage and tail cone of semi-monocoque light alloy structures. Non-retractable tricycle landing gear with fully-castoring nosewheel.

ACCOMMODATION: Pilot on individual seat forward, and up to three passengers side by side on aft bench seat. A dual control arrangement, with pilot and co-pilot in tandem, was possible.

DATA (HR.Mk 1):

POWER PLANT: One 403 kW (540 hp) Alvis Leonides 50 radial piston-engine mounted horizontally in fuselage. 377 litres (83 Imp gallons) fuel in two fuselage tanks.

Main rotor diameter	14.63 m (48 ft 0 in)
Tail rotor diameter	2.57 m (8 ft 5 in)
Length overall, rotors turning	17.54 m (57 ft 6½ in)
Height overall	3.95 m (12 ft 11½ in)
Weight empty	1,987 kg (4,380 lb)
Max T-O weight	2,663 kg (5,870 lb)
Max level speed at S/L	82.5 knots (153 km/h; 95 mph)
Max rate of climb at S/L	244 m (800 ft)/min
Hovering ceiling IGE	1,705 m (5,600 ft)
Hovering ceiling OGE	1,400 m (4,600 ft)
Service ceiling	3,780 m (12,400 ft)
Range	260 nm (483 km; 300 miles)

VARIANTS: *Dragonfly HC.Mk 2.* Initial version for the RAF with Alvis Leonides 50 engine, and intended primarily for casualty evacuation. Two stretcher cases could be carried in enclosed panniers, one mounted on each side of the fuselage, with alternative cabin accommodation for sitting casualties. Three built.

Dragonfly HR.Mk 3. Rescue version for the Royal Navy with Alvis Leonides 50 engine, and introducing an all-metal three-blade rotor and hydraulic servo-control mechanism. Otherwise generally similar to HR.Mk 1. Fifty-eight built.

Dragonfly HC.Mk 4. Casualty evacuation version for the RAF with Alvis Leonides 50 engine, but introducing the three-blade rotor and servo-control mechanism of the HR.Mk 3, and retaining the pannier stretcher containers. Twelve built.

Dragonfly HR.Mk 5. Final rescue version for the Royal Navy, with Alvis Leonides 50, and generally similar to HR. Mk 3. Nine built.

Dragonfly Mk 1A. Civil version with 388 kW (520 hp) Alvis Leonides 521/1 engine. Most were equipped as passenger transports, but small numbers served also with the Italian and Thai air forces, and were used in Japan for military rescue work.

Dragonfly Mk 1B. Civil version, generally similar to Mk 1A, powered by a 336 kW (450 hp) Pratt & Whitney R-985-B4 Wasp Junior radial engine.

WESTLAND WIDGEON

First flight: (G-ALIK) 23 August 1955

TYPE: Five-seat general-purpose helicopter.

NOTES: Sikorsky's S-51 had been designed around the 336 kW (450 hp) Pratt & Whitney R-985 engine, but the installation by Westland of the Alvis Leonides 50 in the Dragonfly, producing 20 per cent more power, meant that it would be possible to carry an increased payload. Accordingly, the company began development of a five-seat version of the Dragonfly as a private venture, this requiring the design and construction of a new front fuselage to provide the increased accommodation. At the same time, it was decided to install the improved main rotor of the Whirlwind, which was of increased diameter and incorporated blades that were attached to the hub through offset flapping hinges. This rotor, by comparison with that of the Dragonfly which had free-flapping blades with hinges on the centreline, not only offered improved efficiency, but provided a much greater CG range.

The prototype Widgeon (G-ALIK) was a conversion of a Dragonfly Mk 1A, and flew for the first time on 23 August 1955. Its larger cabin offered greater versatility, and Westland went to considerable trouble to ensure that not only would the Widgeon be capable of operation in several roles, but that it should be possible for an operator to convert it fairly easily for use in any of them. These included the basic five-seat passenger transport; and they were suitable also as an air ambulance, with two stretchers and an attendant carried within the cabin; as a rescue aircraft when equipped with a hydraulically-powered winch; or as a freight transport that could airlift an external load of up to 454 kg (1,000 lb). And to make it possible to operate the Widgeon from land and water, inflatable neoprene pontoon landing gear was available as an option.

Despite the efforts made by Westland, only 14 Widgeons were built, of which a number were conversions from Dragonflies. This was mainly due to introduction of the larger capacity Whirlwind with improved performance.

STRUCTURE: Three-blade main rotor of all-metal construction, and three-blade tail rotor. Basic centre fuselage structure of steel tube with light alloy skins; forward fuselage and tail-cone semi-mono-coque light alloy structures. Non-retractable tricycle landing gear with fully-castoring nosewheel or, optionally, inflatable pontoons of neoprene.

ACCOMMODATION: Pilot and passenger side by side in front, and three passengers on aft bench seat. Sliding door on each side of cabin, and clamshell door on port side of nose for stretcher loading.

DATA:

POWER PLANT: One 388 kW (520 hp) Alvis Leonides 521/1 radial piston-engine mounted within the fuselage.

Main rotor diameter	14.99 m (49 ft 2 in)
Tail rotor diameter	2.57 m (8 ft 5 in)
Length overall, rotors turning	17.72 m (58 ft 1½ in)
Height overall	4.03 m (13 ft 2¾ in)
Wheel track	3.66 m (12 ft 0 in)
Weight empty	2,007 kg (4,424 lb)
Max T-O weight	2,676 kg (5,900 lb)
Max level speed at S/L	90 knots (167 km/h; 104 mph)
Cruising speed	70 knots (130 km/h; 81mph)
Max rate of climb at S/L	213 m (700 ft)/min
Service ceiling	3,200 m (10,500 ft)
Hovering ceiling IGE	1,525 m (5,000 ft)
Range	269 nm (499 km; 310 miles)

Westland Widgeon prototype G-ALIK

WESTLAND WHIRLWIND

First flights:
Whirlwind Srs 1: 12 November 1952
Whirlwind Srs 3: 28 February 1959
Whirlwind HAR.Mk 1: 15 August 1953
Whirlwind HAR.Mk 5: 28 August 1955
Whirlwind HAS.Mk 7: 17 October 1956

TYPE: General-purpose helicopter.
NOTES: Early experience with the S-51 developments built by Westland, left the company in little doubt that a larger and more powerful helicopter would prove attractive to both civil and military users. Not long after the first Dragonflies had entered service, Westland announced that licence agreements had been finalised with Sikorsky for construction of the Sikorsky S-55 for the British forces, and for export to certain approved countries. The negotiations that had been initiated with Sikorsky, in June 1950, were finalised in November of that year, but it was not until two years later that the first Westland-built aircraft was flown. Almost simultaneously, the first of 25 S-55s obtained from Sikorsky under the Mutual Defense Assistance Program began to enter service with the Royal Navy for evaluation and familiarisation purposes. Given the name Whirlwind, ten, each with 447 kW (600 hp) Pratt & Whitney Wasp R-1340-40 radial engines, were designated HAR.Mk 21; the remaining 15 were designated HAS.Mk 22, and were powered by 522 kW (700 hp) Wright R-1300-3 engines. In Navy service the Westland Dragonfly had been used to establish its first helicopter squadron (No.705); now the HAR.Mk 21 Whirlwind was to equip the Royal Navy's first operational helicopter squadron in November 1952 (No.848), and this unit used its aircraft in action for the first time, in Malaya, on 20 March 1953. The Whirlwind HAS.Mk 22s were equipped with dipping sonar gear, and these were used to form the Navy's first helicopter anti-submarine squadron (No.845), which became operational on 15 March 1954.

Westland's initial versions of the Whirlwind followed the same general engineering pattern as the American-built S-55s, but with performance improvements that came from the installation of different power plants several modifications were introduced. In addition, the larger cabin of the

Westland S-55 demonstrator

Whirlwind, and its increased payload capability, added a variety of equipment, so that in addition to the basic civil and military roles Whirlwinds were operated for agricultural, cargo, crowd control, flying crane, oil prospecting, and whale spotting duties. Naval versions could also be equipped with a hook, attached to the fuselage structure aft of the cabin, which enabled them to tow mine-sweeping gear.

First of the Westland production versions was the civil Whirlwind Srs 1, first flown on 12 November 1952. This version is remembered for inaugurating BEA's experimental passenger service between London's South Bank and Heathrow on 25 July 1955. Before Whirlwind production ended, eleven other versions had been developed and manufactured.

STRUCTURE: Three-blade all-metal main rotor, and two-blade tail rotor. Pod and boom semi-monocoque fuselage structure of light alloy. Small tail stabiliser with pronounced anhedral. Quadricycle landing gear, forward wheels fully-castoring; complementary floats available optionally for amphibious operations.

ACCOMMODATION: Pilot and co-pilot on flight deck in nose, above engine. Dual controls standard.

Westland S-55 Series 1 of BEA

Maximum accommodation in main cabin for ten troops; civil versions usually seated seven passengers.

DATA (Srs 1):

POWER PLANT: One 447 kW (600 hp) Pratt & Whitney Wasp R-1340-40, or one 522 kW (700 hp) Wright Cyclone R-1300-3 radial piston-engine. Fuel capacity 659 litres (145 Imp gallons).

Main rotor diameter	16.15 m (53 ft 0 in)
Tail rotor diameter	2.72 m (8 ft 11 in)
Length overall, rotors turning	18.94 m (62 ft 1½ in)
Height overall	4.04 m (13 ft 3 in)
Wheel track (fwd wheels)	1.37 m (4 ft 6 in)
Wheel track (aft wheels)	3.35 m (11 ft 0 in)
Wheelbase	3.15 m (10 ft 4 in)
Weight, empty	2,272 kg (5,010 lb)
Max T-O weight	3,402 kg (7,500 lb)
Max level speed at S/L	95 knots (175 km/h; 109 mph)
Cruising speed	75 knots (138 km/h; 86 mph)
Max rate of climb at S/L	244 m (800 ft)/min
Service ceiling	2,135 m (7,000 ft)
Range	260 nm (483 km; 300 miles)

Westland Whirlwinds of the Queens Flight

ARMAMENT: Royal Navy HAS.Mk 7s could carry a lightweight homing torpedo, bombs, or depth charges. Some RAF HAR.Mk 10s were provided with mountings for four Nord A.S.11 anti-tank missiles.

VARIANTS: *Whirlwind Srs 2*. Civil version, generally similar to Srs 1, but powered by one 582 kW (780 hp) Alvis Leonides Major Mk 155 or Mk 755 radial piston-engine derated to 559 kW (750 hp). Fuel capacity increased by 114 litres (25 Imp gallons), to a maximum of 773 litres (170 Imp gallons).

Whirlwind Srs 3. Civil version, generally similar to Srs 1 and 2, but with turboshaft power plant. The prototype Srs 3 was powered originally by a General Electric T58 turboshaft of 783 kW (1,050 shp), and flew for the first time with this engine on 28 February 1959. The T58 was built under licence as the Gnome H.1000 by Bristol Siddeley, and this installation was first flown in the Whirlwind in September 1959. The turboshaft-engined Whirlwinds could be distinguished from those with a piston-engine by having an extended fuselage nose. The gearbox and transmission system of the piston-engine power plant was retained to facilitate conversion to turbine power. Standard fuel capacity 814 litres (179 Imp gallons). Optional auxiliary fuel to provide maximum capacity of 1,314 litres (289 Imp gallons).

Whirlwind HAR.Mk 1. Military version for the Royal Navy with Pratt & Whitney R-1340-40 engine. Only ten produced, and used to equip the Navy's No. 705 Squadron.

Whirlwind HAR.Mk 2. Version for the RAF, generally similar to the Navy's HAR.Mk 1. About 60 produced and used for communications and SAR duties with Coastal and Transport Commands.

Whirlwind HAR.Mk 3. Version for the Royal Navy, generally similar to HAR.Mk 1 and 2, but powered by an R-1300-3 Wright Cyclone engine. Twenty built.

Whirlwind HAR.Mk 4. Version for the RAF with 447 kW (600 hp) Pratt & Whitney R-1340-57 engine suitable for operation in high temperatures and at high altitudes. Served in Malaya for troop transport and jungle rescue operations. About 30 built.

Whirlwind HAR.Mk 5. Version intended for the Royal Navy with a 582 kW (780 hp) Alvis Leonides Major Mk 155 or Mk 755 radial piston-engine derated to 559 kW (750 hp). The HAR.Mk 5 introduced a modified tail cone and rear pylon to give 3° of droop on the tail boom, allowing greater clearance for the main rotor blades, and a new horizontal tail stabiliser. These features became standard on subsequent versions. Total of seven built, three being supplied to the Royal Navy, the remainder to Austria.

Whirlwind Mk 6. Projected version only, which was to have been powered by a 559 kW (750 hp) Blackburn-Turboméca A.129 Twin Turmo turboshaft. None built.

Whirlwind HAS.Mk 7. Final production version for the Royal Navy with the same power plant as the HAR.Mk 5, but equipped for ASW. First British helicopter for use in this role, the HAS.Mk 7 carried radar and dipping Asdic for submarine detection: for attack a lightweight homing torpedo, bombs, or depth charges, could be carried in an open bay, beneath the cabin floor. A two-helicopter team could combine the detection equipment and attack weapons, making an effective hunter/killer group. It had the distinction of being the first helicopter in the world to become operational that was suitable for ASW search or strike missions. The first squadron to become operational was No. 845 in August 1957. About 120 built.

Whirlwind HCC.Mk 8. Designation of two aircraft for The Queen's Flight, powered by a 552 kW (740 hp) Alvis Leonides Major Mk 160, and with dual controls, and special interior furnishings for four to seven passengers.

Whirlwind HAR.Mk 9. Designation of turbine-engined conversions of piston-engined HAS.Mk 7s for use in SAR and ice patrol duties. Powered by the 783 kW (1,050 shp) Bristol Siddeley Gnome H.1000 turboshaft, and introduced into service in mid-1966.

Whirlwind HAR.Mk 10. Version for the RAF, powered by the Bristol Siddeley Gnome H.1000, of which the prototype flew for the first time in Spring 1961. Entered service with No. 225 Squadron, Transport Command, on 4 November 1961. In addition to new-production HAR.Mk 10s, the designation applied also to piston-engined aircraft in RAF service that were converted subsequently to Gnome H.1000 power plant. Some HAR.Mk 10s were equipped to carry four Nord A.S.11 air-to-ground anti-tank missiles.

Whirlwind HCC.Mk 12. Designation of two aircraft for The Queen's Flight, powered by Gnome H.1000 engines, and with special interior furnishings.

Westland Whirlwind HAR Mk 10

Westland Westminster, naked

The same aircraft G-APLE, skinned conventionally

WESTLAND WESTMINSTER

First flights:
First prototype (G-APLE) 15 June 1958
Second prototype (G-APTX) 4 September 1959

TYPE: Single-rotor transport helicopter research vehicle.
NOTES: In late 1953 Sikorsky flew the prototype of its S-56 design in the form of the XHR2S-1 assault helicopter for the US Marine Corps. At that time it was the largest helicopter that had been flown outside of the Soviet Union. In the following year Westland considered licence-construction of the S-56, but decided instead to proceed with the private-venture development of a large transport helicopter seating a maximum of 45 passengers. To reduce design and development costs, Westland concluded an agreement with Sikorsky to use the five-blade main rotor, reduction gear, and four-blade tail rotor of the S-56; and with the need to restrain labour and financial commitment as much as possible, because of the company's heavy involvement in the Wessex programme, only an absolute minimum of staff and resources could be allocated to this new project.

The first prototype (G-APLE) of the Westminster, as this helicopter was named, was a functional flying test rig. As flown originally it had an uncovered fuselage structure of heavy gauge steel tube; this construction was used intentionally so that lead weights could be added to the airframe to simulate full AUW. Only the tail rotor pylon was skinned, but of course the flight deck was totally enclosed, accommodating a pilot and co-pilot, and equipment included full blind-flying instrumentation. The power plant installation represented the most innovative feature of the design, two 2,349 kW (3,150 shp) Napier Eland E229A turboshafts mounted above the cabin roof, forward of the main rotor. Westland was one of the first helicopter manufacturers to appreciate that the comparatively light weight of these high-power turbine engines made such an installation possible, not only freeing the interior of the fuselage of power plant, to provide maximum passenger/cargo capacity, but also making possible the design of an improved rotor drive system.

The Westminster's rotor drive incorporated automatic rotor speed governing which, in conjunction with improved rotor control design by Westland, produced a helicopter that was, reportedly, very pleasant to fly. Admiralty belief that the company's work on the Westminster was causing delay to the Wessex programme was so strong, although unfounded, that it led to the large transport project being abandoned. Just before this happened, however, Westland decided to build a second prototype in airline configuration. This incorporated a lighter-weight monocoque airframe structure (its design carried out by Saunders-Roe at Cowes), many other refinements, the same power plant, and of course the entire structure was enclosed by skins or cowlings.

While this work was in progress, the first prototype was faired in so that it could be flown to supplement wind tunnel estimates of performance for the airliner. This 'fairing' consisted of Terylene fabric, treated with special dope that was impervious to the lubricant of the main transmission. When flown in this form, with a six-blade main rotor manufactured by Sikorsky, G-APLE demonstrated a maximum speed of 135 knots (249 km/h; 155 mph) 'with a very low vibration level'. The second prototype was flown for the first time on 4 September 1959, but although early testing progressed satisfactorily, the Westminster project was finally abandoned. This came in early 1960 after Westland's acquisition of the Helicopter Division of Bristol Aircraft, and the UK aviation interests of Fairey Aviation Ltd, when early evaluation of Bristol's Type 194 project, and Fairey's Rotodyne programme, showed that both were more advanced concepts.
STRUCTURE (1st prototype): Five-blade main rotor and four-blade tail rotor of all-metal construction. This aircraft flown finally with a six-blade main rotor. Basic airframe structure of heavy gauge steel tube. Non-retractable tailwheel landing gear.
ACCOMMODATION (1st prototype): Pilot and co-pilot only, side by side on enclosed flight deck.
DATA (1st prototype):
POWER PLANT: Two 2,349 kW (3,150 shp) Napier Eland E229A turboshaft engines, mounted side by side on the cabin roof, forward of the main rotor. Both engines were coupled to a common gearbox so that either engine could maintain the helicopter in flight. Fuel tanks were mounted within the open fuselage structure.

Main rotor diameter	21.95 m (72 ft 0 in)
Tail rotor diameter	4.57 m (15 ft 0 in)
Length of fuselage	26.44 m (86 ft 9 in)
Height overall	6.43 m (21 ft 1 in)
Weight empty equipped	9,072 kg (20,000 lb)
Normal T-O weight	14,969 kg (33,000 lb)
Max overload T-O weight	16,329 kg (36,000 lb)

Performance (estimated for production version):
Cruising speed at S/L 130 knots (241 km/h; 150 mph)
Max rate of climb at S/L more than 610 m (2,000 ft)/min
Rate of climb at S/L, one engine out 183 m (600 ft)/min
Range with max payload 130 nm (241 km; 150 miles)

WESTLAND WESSEX

First flights:
American-built S-58 (HSS-1) re-engined by Westland as Wessex prototype/demonstrator (XL722)
17 May 1957
Westland-built Wessex prototype (XL727)
20 June 1958
Wessex HC.Mk 2 prototype (XM299)
18 January 1962
Wessex HC.Mk 2, first production (XR588)
5 October 1962
Wessex HC.Mk 4 17 March 1969
Wessex HU.Mk 5, first prototype (XS241)
31 May 1963
Wessex HU.Mk 5, first production (XS479)
17 November 1963

TYPE: Turbine-engined general-purpose medium
helicopter.
NOTES: The undoubted success of the Whirlwind
with turboshaft power plant led Westland to believe
that a larger airframe, with more powerful turbine or
twin-turbine engines, would prove even more versa-
tile. More importantly for naval use, greater payload
capacity should make it possible to combine the
hunter/killer ASW roles in one aircraft, adding
greater efficiency and capability. Such a concept
was not realised in this new helicopter, named
Wessex, and which derived very directly from the
Sikorsky S-58. Following the conclusion of licence
arrangements with Sikorsky for construction of the
S-58, one example was imported (an HSS-1 airframe) and instead of the standard Wright R-1820
piston-engine, a 820 kW (1,100 shp) Napier Gazelle
NGa.11 turboshaft engine was installed. This was
less powerful than the piston-engine, but was also
much lighter, and the performance of the resulting
prototype/demonstrator (XL722) was sufficiently
promising for development of the Wessex to continue. The first Westland-built prototype, and the
pre-production aircraft, had a 1,081 kW (1,450 shp)
Napier Gazelle Mk 161, and this was to be the power
plant of the first production version, the Royal
Navy's HAS.Mk 1 anti-submarine helicopter. Like
the Whirlwind which it at first complemented, and
subsequently superseded, the HAS.Mk 1s were used
in hunter/killer pairs in the ASW role; later they
served also as Marine Commando transports, able
to accommodate up to 16 fully-equipped Marines.

Wessex HAS.Mk 1s, of which about 130 were
built, began to enter service with No.815 Squadron
on 4 July 1961, and this unit embarked on HMS *Ark
Royal* in September of that year. It is interesting to
record that the last 25 Mk 1s were built quite late in
the programme, these being needed to fill the gap
made by those required for conversion to Mk 3. This
new helicopter represented a tremendous advance
in airborne ASW capability, for being large enough
to accommodate Doppler navigation radar and
autostabilisation equipment, the HAS.Mk 1 could

**Westland Wessex HAS Mk 3 equipped with flotation
bags**

operate by day or night. It was also suitable for deployment from small platforms on fleet escort destroyers. In addition to service in the ASW role, the Wessex was equally at home when used for cargo carrying, casualty evacuation, communications, SAR, and training duties. A load of up to 1,814 kg (4,000 lb) could be carried on an external cargo sling. Such versatility meant that this helicopter appealed to services other than the Royal Navy, and in addition to the HAS.Mk 1, nine other versions were developed and built.

STRUCTURE: Main rotor and tail rotor each with four metal blades. Main rotor blades fold manually. Light alloy semi-monocoque fuselage structure, with steel tube support structure for main rotor gearbox. Fuselage tail folds 180° to port for stowage. Non-retractable tailwheel landing gear.

ACCOMMODATION: Crew of one to three, according to role, and up to 16 passengers in main cabin, or eight stretchers.

DATA (HAS.Mk 1):

POWER PLANT: One 1,081 kW (1,450 shp) Napier Gazelle Mk 161 (NGa.13) turboshaft engine mounted in nose. Standard fuel capacity 1,364 litres (300 Imp gallons); optional auxiliary tankage to provide a maximum capacity of 2,273 litres (500 Imp gallons).

Main rotor diameter	17.07 m (56 ft 0 in)
Tail rotor diameter	2.90 m (9 ft 6 in)
Main rotor disc area	228.8 m² (2,463 sq ft)
Length overall, rotor turning	20.04 m (65 ft 9 in)
Length overall, blades and tail folded	
	11.73 m (38 ft 6 in)
Height overall	4.93 m (16 ft 2 in)
Wheel track	3.66 m (12 ft 0 in)
Weight empty, equipped	3,447 kg (7,600 lb)
Max T-O weight	5,715 kg (12,600 lb)
Max level speed at S/L	115 knots (212 km/h; 132 mph)
Max cruising speed	105 knots (195 km/h; 121 mph)
Max rate of climb at S/L	475 m (1,560 ft)/min
Service ceiling	4,300 m (14,100 ft)
Hovering ceiling IGE	1,800 m (5,900 ft)
Hovering ceiling OGE	1,100 m (3,600 ft)
Range with standard fuel	339 nm (628 km; 390 miles)
Range with standard plus optional fuel,	
10 per cent reserves	560 nm (1,038 km; 645 miles)

AVIONICS: Differs according to service and role: Royal Navy ASW aircraft included UHF transceiver and homer, standby UHF, HF transceiver, Telebriefing system, Ryan AN/APN-97A Doppler radar, and Louis Newmark Mk 19 autostabilisation system.

ARMAMENT: Royal Navy aircraft were equipped to carry, according to role, homing torpedoes, machine-guns, 2 in air-to-surface rockets, and Nord SS.11 wire-guided air-to-surface missiles.

VARIANTS: *Wessex HC.Mk 2.* High-performance development of the HAS.Mk 1 for service with the RAF, powered by two coupled Bristol Siddeley Gnome turboshafts (one Mk 110 and one Mk 111),

each rated at 1,007 kW (1,350 shp). These turbine engines were intercoupled so that either engine was capable of driving the rotor system in the event of one engine failing. Ordered for service with the RAF in August 1961, began to equip No.18 Squadron on 9 February 1964. Primary roles ambulance and transport, but used also for general purpose duties, including ground attack. Max T-O weight increased to 6,123 kg (13,500 lb).

Wessex HAS.Mk 3. More powerful version of the HAS.Mk 1 for service with the Royal Navy, with power plant comprising one 1,193 kW (1,600 shp) Napier Gazelle Mk 165 (NGa.22) turboshaft engine. Comprehensive AFCS of Westland design, which allowed all phases of the aircraft's anti-submarine search and strike capability to be met automatically, from initial lift-off to positioning for landing. Features included automatic transition to and from the hover, coupled hover, and turns to pre-selected headings, all in a fully duplicated system. More sophisticated weapons system. Although used in hunter/killer pairs, this version was capable of combining the hunter/killer role. The HAS.Mk 3 was distinguished readily by large dorsal radome associated with new search radar. Approximately 50 entered service, all but three being conversions from HAS.Mk 1s.

Wessex HC.Mk 4. Designation of two aircraft for The Queen's Flight with special furnishings and equipment, otherwise as for HC.Mk 2. Delivered to RAF Benson in April 1969.

Wessex HU Mk 5 equipped for ground attack operations

Iraqi Wessex Mk 52

Wessex civil Srs 60 of Bristow Helicopters

Wessex HU.Mk 5. Ship- or shore-based troop-carrying assault helicopter, similar to the HC.Mk 2, for service with the Marine Commandos. Accommodation for crew of 1-3, according to role, with three fixed, and 13 removable troop seats, or seven stretchers, or 1,814 kg (4,000 lb) freight. The HU.Mk 5 could be equipped alternatively with weapons for action against ground targets. About 100 built, equipping first No.707 Training Squadron at RNAS Culdrose in December 1964. The first operational unit was No. 845 Squadron.

Wessex HAS.Mk 31. Version for the Royal Australian Navy, generally similar to HAS.Mk 1, but powered by one 1,174 kW (1,575 shp) Napier Gazelle Mk 162 (NGa.13/2), flat rated to 1,148 kW (1,540 shp). Delivery of 27 began in August 1962. At a later date many of these were given improved ASW systems and components, and becoming redesignated HAS.Mk 31B following conversion.

Wessex Mk 52. Version of the HC.Mk 2 for service with the Iraqi Air Force, of which twelve were delivered between April 1964 and February 1965.

Wessex Mk 53. Version of the HC.Mk 2 for service with the Ghana Air Force. Three delivered.

Wessex Mk 54. One example for service in Brunei, generally similar to HC.Mk 2, and delivered in January 1967.

Wessex Mk 60. Civil version of the HC.Mk 2, designed to carry 10 passengers to airline standards, or a maximum of 16 for aerial work duties; or eight stretchers, two sitting casualties, and a medical attendant; or 15 survivors in a rescue operation. About 15 built, the majority of which were in service with Bristow Helicopters Ltd in early 1981.

WESTLAND BELVEDERE

First flights:
Bristol Type 173 3 January 1952
Bristol Type 192 5 July 1958
Bristol Type 192 with powered controls (XG450)
12 December 1960

TYPE: Short-range twin-rotor tactical transport.
NOTES: Following acquisition of the Helicopter Division of Bristol Aircraft Ltd, on 23 March 1960, this became known as Westland's Bristol Helicopter Division. Bristol had developed a tandem-rotor helicopter identified as the Type 173: when the first example was flown in 1952, it was the first helicopter of this configuration to be flown in Britain. Engine development problems led to the demise of the Type 173, and leading to design submissions for Types 191, 192 and 193 to meet respectively the requirements of the Royal Navy, the Royal Air Force, and the Royal Canadian Navy. Still-unresolved engine and transmission problems led to cancellation of the Type 191s in 1957: economic problems in Canada meant that the 193s were also stillborn. Only the RAF Type 192s survived, the prototype (XG447) flying in 1958. Development was continuing at the time of Westland's acquisition, and it was not until six months later that the first three pre-production aircraft were delivered to the RAF's Trials Unit, at Odiham, Hampshire. Thus, production of these helicopters, which were designated as the HC.Mk 1 Belvedere, was completed under the Westland banner although construction continued at Bristol's former works at Weston-Super-Mare, Somerset.

The Type 192 had manual controls in its initial configuration and, in fact, the pre-production aircraft delivered to RAF Odiham also had manual controls. However, one aircraft (XG450) had been taken out of the development flying programme so that it could be modified to incorporate fully-duplicated power-operated flying controls, and this aircraft, with other improvements and refinements, established the standard for production aircraft. A total of 24 Belvederes was built for the RAF, No.66 Squadron being the first to receive them on 15 September 1961, and the type remained in service until March 1969. It had gained the distinction of being the first twin-engined tandem-rotor helicopter in RAF service.
STRUCTURE: Tandem four-blade rotors of all-metal construction. Conventional semi-monocoque fuselage structure of light alloy. Braced inverted V stabiliser mounted at aft end of fuselage. Non-retractable quadricycle landing gear with fully-castoring forward wheels.
ACCOMMODATION: Crew of two side by side on flight deck. Cabin with standard seating for 19 troopers, but a maximum of 30 survivors could be carried in an emergency SAR role. Alternative arrangements for 12 stretchers, two sitting casual-

Westland/Bristol 192 prototype

Westland Belvedere

Diameter of main rotors (each)	14.91 m (48 ft 11 in)
Main rotor disc area (each)	174.59 m² (1,879 33 sq ft)
Length overall, rotors turning	27.36 m (89 ft 9 in)
Height overall	5.26 m (17 ft 3 in)
Weight empty	5,277 kg (11,634 lb)
Normal T-O weight	8,618 kg (19,000 lb)
Max overload T-O weight	9,072 kg (20,000 lb)
Max level speed	120 knots (222 km/h; 138 mph)
Econ cruising speed, for max range	100 knots (185 km/h; 115 mph)
Econ cruising speed, for max endurance	65 knots (121 km/h; 75 mph)
Max rate of climb at S/L	305 m (1,000 ft)/min
Rate of climb at S/L, one engine at emergency power	146 m (480 ft)/min
Service ceiling	3,050 m (10,000 ft)
Hovering ceiling OGE	1,830 m (6,000 ft)
Max range with standard fuel, no allowances	386 nm (716 km; 445 miles)
Max range with standard plus max optional fuel, no allowances	608 nm (1,127 km; 700 miles)

ties, and a medical attendant; or up to 2,722 kg (6,000 lb) of internal freight. A similar load could be carried alternatively suspended beneath the fuselage, with mechanical or electrical quick-release gear.

DATA:

POWER PLANT: Two 1,230 kW (1,650 shp) Napier Gazelle NGa.2 Mk 101 turboshaft engines, mounted in compartments at the forward and rear ends of the cabin. Fuselage fuel tanks with standard combined capacity of 2,609 litres (574 Imp gallons). One or two overload tanks, each of 1,209 litres (266 Imp gallons) optional.

WESTLAND WASP

First flights:
P.531 prototype (G-APNU) 20 July 1958
Pre-production HAS.Mk 1 (XS463) 28 October 1962
Production HAS.Mk 1 (XS527) January 1963

TYPE: Five-seat general-purpose helicopter.
NOTES: The Westland Wasp shares its origin with the Scout (which see), derived from the Saunders-Roe P.531 prototypes flown in 1958. Following the initial evaluation by pilots at A & AEE Boscombe Down, exhaustive naval trials were carried out from November 1959, using at first the second prototype (G-APNV). This was followed by three P.531-O/N prototypes, also powered by the 298 kW (400 shp) Blackburn-Turboméca Turmo 603 turboshaft engine, derated to 242 kW (325 shp). During these trials, conducted by the Navy in conjunction with RAE Bedford, the P.531-O/Ns made a vital contribution to the appreciation, investigation, and solution of the problems associated with helicopter operations from small ships. Hundreds of take-offs and land-ings were made aboard frigates, by day and night, and no fewer than 19 different landing gear/deck securing systems were investigated. Among these latter tests one P.531-O/N, with specially-designed suction pads beneath skid landing gear, carried out a programme of take-offs and landings aboard a frigate. The development of an autopilot/autostabi-lisation system was taking place simultaneously in a Saro Skeeter, this having been re-engined with a Turmo turboshaft engine to provide a constant-speed rotor system.

Following the satisfactory conclusion of these trials, the P.531 was ordered into production with the designation Sea Scout HAS.Mk 1, this name being changed subsequently to Wasp. Although generally similar to the Scout, this version differs externally by the use of quadricycle wheeled land-ing gear instead of skids, and by having a stabiliser which is mounted on the starboard side only of the tail rotor pylon. The other major change involved the provision of folding rotor blades and tail section, to facilitate shipboard stowage.

Production Wasps first entered service with No. 700W Squadron, the Initial Flying Trials Unit, formed

Brazilian Navy Westland Wasp

Royal Navy Westland Wasp

at RNAS Culdrose in the Summer of 1963, and going later to No.829 Squadron which became commissioned as the Headquarters Squadron for Small Ships Flights. A total of 98 Wasps were built for service with the Royal Navy, of which more than 60 remained in service in early 1981. In addition to these aircraft, generally similar helicopters have been exported for service with the navies of Brazil (3), the Netherlands, which designates them AH-12A (12), New Zealand (3), and South Africa (17). Some of the Netherlands aircraft (about 8) have been refurbished recently for service with the Indonesian Navy.

STRUCTURE: Four-blade main and two-blade tail rotors of metal construction. Main rotor blades and tail rotor pylon folds for stowage. Pod and boom type fuselage of conventional light alloy stressed skin construction. Horizontal stabiliser on starboard side of tail rotor pylon. Non-retractable quadricycle type landing gear; all wheels fully castoring and provided with sprag type brakes.

ACCOMMODATION: Two seats side by side at front of cabin, bench seat for three at rear. Bench seat can be removed for freight carrying. Full blind-flying instrumentation, autopilot/autostabilisation, and radio altimeter standard.

DATA:

POWER PLANT: One 783 kW (1,050 shp) Rolls-Royce Bristol Nimbus 103 or 104 turboshaft engine, derated to 529 kW (710 shp). Standard fuel capacity 705 litres (155 Imp gallons), contained in three interconnected flexible fuselage tanks.

Main rotor diameter	9.83 m (32 ft 3 in)
Main rotor disc area	75.89 m² (816.86 sq ft)
Tail rotor diameter	2.29 m (7 ft 6 in)
Length overall, rotors turning	12.29 m (40 ft 4 in)
Height overall	2.72 m (8 ft 11 in)
Wheel track	2.44 m (8 ft 0 in)
Wheelbase	2.44 m (8 ft 0 in)
Manufacturer's empty weight	1,566 kg (3,452 lb)
Max T-O weight	2,495 kg (5,500 lb)
Max level speed at S/L	104 knots (193 km/h; 120 mph)
Max cruising speed	96 knots (179 km/h; 111 mph)
Max rate of climb at S/L	439 m (1,440 ft)/min
Practical ceiling	3,720 m (12,200 ft)
Hovering ceiling IGE	3,810 m (12,500 ft)
Hovering ceiling OGE	2,680 m (8,800 ft)
Max range with standard fuel	
	263 nm (488 km; 303 miles)

ARMAMENT: A weapons load of approximately 245 kg (540 lb) can be carried beneath the fuselage, comprising usually two Mk 44 or 46 homing torpedoes, or an equivalent weight of bombs or depth charges. Some aircraft have been equipped to carry Nord AS.11 or AS.12 missiles, with an APX Bézu M.260 gyrostabilised sight.

AVIONICS: PTR.170 and PV.141 UHF transceivers, standby UHF, UHF homer, and intercom.

WESTLAND SCOUT

First flights:
P.531 prototype (G-APNU) 20 July 1958
P.531-2 prototype (G-APVL) 9 August 1959
P.531-2 Mk 1 pre-production (XP165) 4 August 1960
Scout AH.Mk 1 (XP847) 6 March 1961

TYPE: Five-seat general-purpose helicopter.
NOTES: In a manner similar to its acquisition of the Helicopter Division of Bristol Aircraft, Westland added Saunders-Roe Ltd to its strength in August 1959. This latter company became Westland's Saunders-Roe Division, its experience in rotary-wing aircraft dating from January 1951 when it had itself taken over The Cierva Autogiro Company. At that time Cierva was developing the Skeeter light helicopter, a task that Saunders-Roe continued, followed by production of this aircraft for the British Army Air Corps, and in much smaller numbers for the Federal German Army and Navy.

Successful development and production of the Skeeter led Saunders-Roe to initiate design studies for a new light helicopter. This, it was hoped, would be considered a valuable tool for service with the Army Air Corps which, clearly, represented an expanding market for light multi-role helicopters. Preliminary design studies began in 1956, with the construction of two prototype Saunders-Roe P.531s beginning in early 1958. Both incorporated a number of Skeeter components in their construction, and

Westland Scout with rigid rotor

they were flown for the first time on 20 July (G-APNU) and 30 September 1958 (G-APNV). Both of the aircraft were powered by 298 kW (400 shp) Blackburn-Turboméca Turmo 603 turboshaft engines derated to 242 kW (325 shp). Early evaluation of these prototypes by Navy and Army pilots at A & AEE, Boscombe Down, led to continuing development, pursued actively by Westland following acquisition of Saunders-Roe in the Summer of 1959. By that time an additional P.531-2 prototype had been flown (G-APVL), on 9 August 1959, this being powered by a Blackburn-Turboméca A.129 turboshaft of 529 kW (710 shp), derated to 474 kW (635 shp). This engine was developed subsequently by Bristol Siddeley, becoming named Nimbus. A second P.531-2 prototype (G-APVM) was flown on 3 May 1960. This was used to evaluate a 783 kW (1,050 shp) Bristol-Siddeley Gnome H.100 turboshaft engine, derated to 511 kW (685 shp). It was the only example of the P.531s to use this power plant. One other development Scout (XR493) was fitted with a semi-rigid rotor as a technology prover for the Lynx.

Shortly after this first flight, the Army Air Corps placed an order for a pre-production batch of P.531-2 Mk 1s, for familiarisation and more extensive evaluation, the first of them flying in August 1960. In the following month the first production batch was ordered under the designation Scout AH.Mk 1, these differing from the earlier helicopters by incorporating powered controls. The first of these was flown in March 1961, and they began to enter service in early 1963, gradually replacing the Skeeter. Production of the Scout has ended, but more than 100 remained in service with British Army Aviation in early 1981. The Scout is used extensively for a variety of purposes, both at home and abroad, including air-to-ground attack, casualty evacuation, freight transport, liaison, passenger transport, reconnaissance, SAR, and training. In addition to AH.Mk 1 Scouts supplied to the British Army, exports have included examples for the Royal Australian Navy (2), Royal Jordanian Air Force (3), and the police departments of Bahrain (2) and Uganda (2).

STRUCTURE: Four-blade all-metal main rotor, two-blade wooden tail rotor. Conventional light alloy stressed skin fuselage structure of pod and boom type. Horizontal stabiliser mounted beneath tail boom at rear. Tubular skid type landing gear with ground handling wheels.

ACCOMMODATION: Two seats side by side at front of cabin, bench seat for three at rear. Rear seat removable to accommodate cargo, or two stretchers in a casualty evacuation role. Two additional stretcher cases can be carried in externally-mounted panniers. Full blind-flying instrumentation standard; dual controls and basic instrument panel for trainee pilot optional. Autopilot/autostabiliser, cabin heating and demisting optional.

DATA:

POWER PLANT: One 783 kW (1,050 shp) Rolls-Royce Bristol Nimbus 101 or 102 turboshaft engine, derated to 511 kW (685 shp). Standard fuel capacity 705 litres (155 Imp gallons), contained in three interconnected flexible fuselage tanks.

Main rotor diameter	9.83 m (32 ft 3 in)
Main rotor disc area	75.89 m² (816.86 sq ft)
Tail rotor diameter	2.29 m (7 ft 6 in)
Length overall, rotors turning	12.29 m (40 ft 4 in)
Height overall	2.72 m (8 ft 11 in)
Skid track	2.59 m (8 ft 6 in)
Basic operating weight	1,466 kg (3,232 lb)
Max T-O weight	2,404 kg (5,300 lb)
Max level speed at S/L	114 knots (211 km/h; 131 mph)
Max cruising speed	106 knots (196 km/h; 122 mph)
Max rate of climb at S/L	509 m (1,670 ft)/min
Practical ceiling	4,085 m (13,400 ft)
Range with max fuel, pilot and four passengers, allowances for T-O and landing and 15 min reserves at best cruising height	273 nm (505 km; 314 miles)

ARMAMENT: Can include various gun installations, air-to-ground rockets, and Nord AS.11 air-to-surface missiles.

AVIONICS: PTR.161F and TR.1998A VHF transceivers, Army B.47/48 radio, and Ultra U.A.60 intercom.

Westland Sioux

WESTLAND/AGUSTA-BELL SIOUX

First flight:
Westland-built 47G-3B-4 9 March 1965

TYPE: Three-seat general-purpose helicopter.

NOTES: The Bell Model 47 helicopter, that had been in production from early 1947 and which was supplied extensively to the US armed services, was selected as standard equipment for the British Army under the designation Sioux AH.Mk 1. An initial batch of 50 was supplied to the Army by the Italian company of Agusta, which manufactured them under licence from Bell for the European market, and it was arranged that additional production for UK requirements would be carried out by Westland under licence from Agusta. This was to result in the construction of 250 47G-3B-4s, using many components of Italian manufacture. Most of these were supplied to the Army, but some saw service as HT.Mk 2 trainers with the RAF's Central Flying School, and at RAF Tern Hill.

STRUCTURE: Two-blade main and tail rotors of metal construction. Fuselage of welded steel tube, with tail boom of triangular cross-section left uncovered. Tubular skid type landing gear with small ground handling wheels.

ACCOMMODATION: Individual bucket seats side by side for pilot and two passengers, enclosed by a free-blown Plexiglas canopy. Door on each side, easily removable if required for special operations. Passenger seats removable to accommodate 454 kg (1,000 lb) internal cargo.

DATA:

POWER PLANT: One 194 kW (260 hp) Avco Lycoming TVO-435-A1A turbocharged piston-engine.

Main rotor diameter	11.32 m (37 ft 1½ in)
Main rotor disc area	100.56 m² (1,082.49 sq ft)
Tail rotor diameter	1.78 m (5 ft 10 in)
Length overall, rotors turning	13.17 m (43 ft 2½ in)
Height overall	2.84 m (9 ft 3¾ in)
Landing skid track	2.29 m (7 ft 6 in)
Weight empty	806 kg (1,778 lb)
Max T-O weight	1,338 kg (2,950 lb)
Max level speed at S/L	91 knots (169 km/h; 105 mph)
Cruising speed at 1,525 m (5,000 ft)	73 knots (135 km/h; 84 mph)
Max rate of climb at S/L	268 m (880 ft)/min
Service ceiling	6,100 m (20,000 ft)
Hovering ceiling IGE	6,100 m (20,000 ft)
Hovering ceiling OGE	3,230 m (10,600 ft)
Range with max fuel	274 nm (507 km; 315 miles)

VARIANT: *Westland/Agusta-Bell 47G-4A.* Westland-built under licence from Agusta 16 aircraft of this designation during 1969. These were required by Bristow Helicopters for the training of Army pilots at the Company's Middle Wallop, Hampshire, civil flying school. Generally similar to the Sioux AH.Mk 1 and HT.Mk 2 aircraft in Army and RAF service respectively, they differed by having a 227 kW (305 hp) Avco Lycoming VO-540 piston-engine derated to 201 kW (270 hp).

Westland/Aérospatiale Puma

WESTLAND/AÉROSPATIALE PUMA

First flights:
SA.330 prototype (F-ZWWN) 15 April 1965
SA.330-08 RAF trials aircraft (XW241) 30 July 1968
Puma HC.Mk 1 (XW198) 25 November 1970

TYPE: Medium-sized transport helicopter.

NOTES: Similar requirements for new helicopters to serve with the armed forces of Britain and France resulted in discussions, originating in 1967, that led to Westland and Aérospatiale collaborating closely in the production of three helicopters. Under this agreement, finalised on 2 April 1968, the two companies shared in varying proportions responsibility for design, manufacture and assembly of the Gazelle, Lynx and Puma. Like Westland, Sud-Aviation (one of the three companies that were merged to form Aérospatiale on 1 January 1970) had held licence-construction agreements with Sikorsky in the USA, covering manufacture of the S-58. A development of the S-58, with a 1,417 kW (1,900 shp) Turboméca Bi-Bastan turboshaft engine, was flown on 5 October 1962, but this line was not followed. Instead, design of the SA. (Sud-Aviation) 330 was started, planned initially to have a power plant of two 969 kW (1,300 shp) Turboméca Bastan VII turboshafts. However, by the time that approval for development of the SA.330 had been given, the Turboméca Turmo III turboshaft was considered to be more suitable for this new helicopter, having an improved power/weight ratio and a lower fully-equipped dry weight. Construction of two prototypes and six-pre-production aircraft began, the first of them flying in April 1965. Last of these to fly, SA.330-08, on 30 July 1968, was the RAF's trials aircraft (XW241).

By that time the Aérospatiale/Westland production agreement had been concluded, with both companies manufacturing components. Westland was responsible also for the assembly and completion of the 40 examples ordered for service with the Royal Air Force under the designation Puma HC.Mk 1, the first Westland-built aircraft (XW198) making its first flight on 25 November 1970. HC.Mk 1s entered service with the RAF's No.33 Squadron in late 1971, and with No.230 Squadron in 1972, all 40 being delivered before the end of 1973. An additional eight HC.Mk 1s were ordered subsequently, the first of them being delivered on 23 May 1980. This later batch of RAF Pumas differ by having composite main rotor blades, which will be introduced retrospectively on the other aircraft, more powerful Turmo IVC engines with new air intakes that can prevent both ice and sand ingestion; and operate at the higher gross weight of 7,000 kg (15,432 lb). Westland manufacture of SA.330 components for Aérospatiale's production line was continuing in 1981.

STRUCTURE: Four-blade main and five-blade tail rotors of metal construction. Main rotor blades can be folded manually. Conventional semi-monocoque fuselage structure of light alloy, with monocoque tail boom. Horizontal stabiliser on port side of rotor pylon. Semi-retractable tricycle landing gear with twin wheels on each unit; pop-out flotation units optional.

ACCOMMODATION: Crew of two side by side on flight deck with dual controls as standard. Main cabin seats 16 fully-equipped troops; six stretchers and four seated patients; or an equivalent weight of cargo. RAF Pumas have as standard a rescue hoist of 275 kg (606 lb) capacity, and an internally mounted cargo sling of 2,500 kg (5,512 lb) capacity.

DATA (HC.Mk 1):

POWER PLANT: Two 984 kW (1,320 shp) Turboméca Turmo IIIC turboshaft engines. Standard fuel capacity 1,550 litres (341 Imp gallons). Provision for an additional 1,900 litres (418 Imp gallons) in auxiliary ferry tanks.

Main rotor diameter	15.00 m (49 ft 2½ in)
Main rotor disc area	177.00 m² (1,905.3 sq ft)
Tail rotor diameter	3.12 m (10 ft 2¾ in)
Length overall, rotors turning	18.18 m (59 ft 7¾ in)
Height overall	5.12 m (16 ft 9½ in)
Width over wheel fairings	3.00 m (9 ft 10 in)
Wheelbase	4.04 m (13 ft 3 in)
Basic empty weight	3,430 kg (7,562 lb)
Max T-O weight	6,400 kg (14,110 lb)
Max level speed at S/L	151 knots (280 km/h; 174 mph)
Max cruising speed at S/L	143 knots (265 km/h; 165 mph)
Max rate of climb at S/L	426 m (1,398 ft)/min
Rate of climb at S/L, one engine out	180 m (591 ft)/min
Service ceiling	4,800 m (15,750 ft)
Hovering ceiling IGE	2,800 m (9,185 ft)
Hovering ceiling OGE	1,900 m (6,235 ft)
Max range at S/L with standard fuel	340 nm (630 km; 391 miles)
Max range at S/L with standard and auxiliary fuel	756 nm (1,400 km; 870 miles)

ARMAMENT: Optional, and can include side-firing 20 mm cannon, axial-firing 7.62 mm machine-guns, and missiles.

AVIONICS: VHF/UHF transceivers, standby UHF, UHF homer, Decca navigation with flight log, radio altimeter, IFF/SSR, ICS, and intercom.

WESTLAND/AÉROSPATIALE GAZELLE

First flights:
SA.340 prototype (F-WOFH) 7 April 1967
SA.340 2nd prototype (F-ZWRA) 17 April 1968
SA.341 Gazelle, pre-production 2 August 1968
SA.341 Gazelle, first production 6 August 1971
Gazelle AH.Mk 1 prototype, Westland-built 28 April 1970
Gazelle AH.Mk 1 production 31 January 1972
Gazelle HT.Mk 2 production 6 July 1972

TYPE: Five-seat light utility helicopter.
NOTES: The second of the helicopters to be covered by the Aérospatiale/Westland co-production agreement, the SA.341 Gazelle was designed as a replacement for the Alouette II series, which dated from 1961, to meet a French army requirement for a light observation helicopter. Then designated SA.340, the prototype had the power plant and transmission of the Alouette II Astazou combined with the tail rotor and skid of the Alouette II, and differed conspicuously by having a semi-monocoque stressed skin fuselage structure, instead of the uncovered triangulated steel tube tail boom of the earlier helicopter. Soon after this had flown, the Aérospatiale/Westland co-production discussions began and the Gazelle, which would meet also the requirements of the British armed forces, represented a significant proportion of the initial programme. The second prototype (F-ZWRA) was more like the production aircraft, and introduced a vertical fin which incorporated a fenestron or shrouded-fan tail rotor, and a main rotor of composite construction that had been developed in collaboration with Bölköw in Germany. These factors, and power plant changes, meant that the design had strayed some distance from the

Westland/Aérospatiale Gazelle

original concept, and resulting in the designation of SA.341 for the four pre-production Gazelles. The third of these (XW276) was equipped to British Army requirements and used for service trials. The first production SA.341 Gazelle, flown in the Summer of 1971, introduced a number of improvements, including a lengthened cabin and a more powerful Turboméca Astazou III turboshaft engine.

Most important of the four versions that have been built by Westland for the British armed services is the Gazelle AH.Mk 1 (SA.341B), the first of which was flown for the first time on 31 January 1972. All four versions are generally similar in construction and power plant, but differ in equipment according to the role for which they are intended. A total of 187 AH.Mk 1s have been delivered for service with Army Aviation, entering operational service with No.660 Squadron at Soest, Germany, on 6 July 1974. With total requirements for the British forces close on 300 aircraft, and combined Aérospatiale/Westland production approaching 900 examples in 1981, the Gazelle has proved to be an important project for the British company.

STRUCTURE: Three-blade main rotor of composite construction, and shrouded-fan tail rotor of light alloy. Main rotor blades can be folded manually. The fuselage is basically a light alloy semi-monocoque structure. Ventral fin beneath shrouded rotor; horizontal stabiliser and small endplate fins just forward of this fin. Skid landing gear of tubular steel. Ground handling wheel, and float or ski landing gear optional.

ACCOMMODATION: Crew of two side by side at front of cabin, bench seat for three at rear. Dual controls optional. Bench seat folds into floor wells to provide cargo space.

DATA:

POWER PLANT: One 440 kW (590 shp) Turboméca Astazou IIIA turboshaft engine, with max continuous rating of 390 kW (523 shp), mounted above fuselage aft of cabin. Standard fuel capacity 464 litres (102 Imp gallons). Provision for 90 litre (19.8 Imp gallon) and/or 200 litre (44 Imp gallon) auxiliary and ferry tanks respectively.

Main rotor diameter	10.50 m (34 ft 5½ in)
Main rotor disc area	85.59 m² (932.08 sq ft)
Tail rotor diameter	0.695 m (2 ft 3¼ in)
Length overall, rotors turning	11.97 m (39 ft 3¼ in)
Height overall	3.15 m (10 ft 4 in)
Skid track	2.02 m (6 ft 7½ in)
Weight empty	850 kg (1,874 lb)
Max T-O weight	1,800 kg (3,968 lb)
Max cruising speed at S/L	142 knots (264 km/h; 164 mph)
Econ cruising speed at S/L	126 knots (233 km/h; 145 mph)
Max rate of climb at S/L	540 m (1,772 ft)/min
Service ceiling	5,000 m (16,405 ft)
Hovering ceiling IGE	2,850 m (9,350 ft)
Hovering ceiling OGE	2,000 m (6,560 ft)
Range at S/L with max fuel	361 nm (670 km; 416 miles)
Range with pilot only, max fuel, and 500 kg (1,102 lb) payload	195 nm (360 km; 224 miles)

VARIANTS: *Gazelle HT.Mk 2 (SA.341C)*. Training version for service with the Royal Navy, generally similar to AH.Mk 1. Incorporates a stability augmentation system, and a rescue hoist of 120 kg (265 lb) capacity. The first of 36 (XW845) was flown on 6 July 1972, entering operational service with No. 706 Squadron at RNAS Culdrose on 10 December 1974.

Gazelle HT.Mk 3 (SA.341D). Training version for service with the Royal Air Force, generally similar to AH.Mk 1. Incorporates a stability augmentation system, and a Schermuly flares installation. The first example was delivered to the RAF's Central Flying School on 16 July 1973.

Gazelle HCC.Mk 4 (SA.341E). Communications version for service with the Royal Air Force. Due to funding problems has been procured in only very small numbers.

AVIONICS: Nav/com systems according to individual service requirements, plus intercom. Army AH.Mk 1s have Decca Doppler 80 radar and automatic chart display.

WESTLAND SEA KING

First flights:
Sea King prototype (XV370) 8 September 1967
HAS.Mk 1 Sea King (XV642) 7 May 1969
HAS.Mk 2 Sea King (XZ570) 18 June 1976
HAR.Mk 3 Sea King (XZ583) 6 September 1977
HC.Mk 4 Sea King (ZA290) 26 September 1979
Commando Mk 1 12 September 1973
Commando Mk 2 (G-17-12) 16 January 1975

TYPE: Twin-turbine ASW and general-purpose helicopter.

NOTES: In 1959, Westland concluded licence agreements with Sikorsky that related to that company's S-61 design of a twin-turbine helicopter with amphibious capability. The first of Sikorsky's production versions of this aircraft was the SH-3D (formerly HSS-2) Sea King, and of which the prototype made its first flight on 11 March 1959. Westland was interested in the development of a new ASW helicopter for service with the Royal Navy, and the licence agreements concluded in 1959 allowed the British company to use the basic airframe and rotor system of the SH-3 for this purpose.

Despite the conclusion of this early agreement, it was not until the Autumn of 1967 that the first of four aircraft which were assembled from Sikorsky-supplied components reached completion (XV370), and serving as the Sea King prototype. This aircraft was reassembled on the dockside at Avonmouth after the assemblies were received in Britain, and was flown out from there by Westland's Chief Test Pilot, 'Slim' Sear. It was followed by the other three pre-production aircraft that were built up from the US components (XV371-XV373), and then by the first of the Sea Kings manufactured completely by Westland (XV641). The first production HAS.Mk 1 Sea King for the Royal Navy (XV642) made its first

RAF Westland Sea King Mk 3

flight on 7 May 1969, and leading to No.700S Squadron, the Navy's Sea King Intensive Flying Trials Unit, being commissioned at RNAS Culdrose on 19 August 1969. XV642 was joined later by XV643, and the former continues to serve as a trials aircraft in 1981. The first operational unit to be equipped with Sea Kings was No.824 Squadron, which was formed at Culdrose in February 1970, and served subsequently aboard HMS *Ark Royal*.

With the entry into service of the Sea King, the Royal Navy had acquired rather more than a version of the Sikorsky S-61/SH-3 which had been supplied to the US Navy. Both were intended primarily as submarine hunter/killers, and this, plus retention of the Sea King name, led many journalists to believe that Westland's new helicopter was a pure and simple licence-built aircraft of Sikorsky design. Only the basic airframe and rotor system were virtually identical in the original HAS.Mk 1, and since then modifications introduced by Westland have made it a better aircraft for the specific RN requirement. One of the original major differences was the idea of using the large cabin to provide a tactical compartment for ASW operations, and thereby enabling the British Sea King to be equipped to operate completely independently in the ASW role. Advanced equipment included Ekco search radar, Marconi Doppler, a Newmark automatic flight control system that was an improvement upon that developed for the Wessex, and Plessey sonar: British-built power plant was installed in the form of two Rolls-Royce Gnome H.1400 turboshaft engines. When the Sea King entered service with the Royal Navy, not only was it technically advanced, but it was also its first helicopter with a power-folding five-blade rotor, retractable landing gear, and a hull that made possible emergency operations on water. A total of 56 HAS.Mk 1 Sea Kings were built.

In addition to the naval ASW/SAR versions, Sea Kings have been developed also for tactical and logistics operations, and a specialised version for operation in the foregoing roles, plus cargo transport, casualty evacuation, and secondary capability for air-to-surface strike and SAR has the name Commando. The first Mk 1 version of the Commando was flown for the first time on 12 September 1973. In Mk 2 form it dispensed with the retractable landing gear of the Sea King, and has small stub-wings instead of sponsons. Most importantly, because of the intended roles, every effort has been made to optimise payload/range performance and endurance.

STRUCTURE: Five-blade all-metal main rotor with an automatic powered folding system; five-blade (Mk 1), six-blade (Mk 2) tail rotor mounted on tail section that folds for stowage. Commando main rotor does not fold. The rotor gearbox incorporates freewheel units that permits both or either engine to drive both rotors, and also to allow for autorotation

Royal Navy Westland Sea King Mk 4 demonstrates its vehicle lift capacity

in the case of complete power plant failure. Single-step boat hull to allow emergency operation from water. Tailwheel landing gear with retractable main units, except for Commando which has non-retractable main gear.

ACCOMMODATION (Sea King): Crew of four in ASW role, with space for up to 22 survivors in SAR role; (Commando): crew of two on flight deck, and seats for up to 28 troops.

DATA (A: HAS.Mk 1; B: Commando):

POWER PLANT: HAS.Mk 1: Two 1,119 kW (1,500 shp) Rolls-Royce Gnome H.1400 turboshaft engines, each with a maximum continuous rating of 932 kW (1,250 shp). Optional fuel systems of 3,200 litres (704 Imp gallons) or 3,714 litres (817 Imp gallons) for SAR and Commando versions only; plus optional external

fuel of 909 litres (200 Imp gallons) for Commando only; and for ferry purposes one or two fuselage tanks with capacity of 680 kg (1,500 lb) fuel each.

Main rotor diameter	18.90 m (62 ft 0 in)
Tail rotor diameter	3.15 m (10 ft 4 in)
Main rotor disc area	280.5 m² (3,019 sq ft)
Length overall, rotors turning:	22.15 m (72 ft 8 in)
Length overall, rotors and tail folded:	
A only	14.40 m (47 ft 3 in)
Height overall, rotors turning:	5.13 m (16 ft 10 in)
Wheel track	3.96 m (13 ft 0 in)
Wheelbase:	
B	7.21 m (23 ft 8 in)
Weight empty equipped:	
A (ASW role)	7,019 kg (15,474 lb)
B (troop transport role)	5,700 kg (12,566 lb)
Max T-O weight:	
A	9,707 kg (21,400 lb)
B	9,525 kg (21,000 lb)
Normal cruising speed:	
A	113 knots (209 km/h; 130 mph)
B	112 knots (208 km/h; 129 mph)
Max endurance speed:	
A	75 knots (138 km/h; 86 mph)
Range with max standard fuel:	
A	600 nm (1,112 km; 691 miles)
B	664 nm (1,231 km; 765 miles)

AVIONICS (HAS.Mk 1, ASW role): Ekco AW.391 search radar and transponder, Marconi AW.96 Doppler navigation system, Newmark Mk 31 AFCS, Plessey Type 195 dipping sonar, Sperry Mk.7B compass system, STR.70 radio altimeter, AN/ARC-52 UHF and homer, Ultra D.403 standby UHF, HF transceiver, Ultra UA.60M intercom, Telebrief system, and IFF provisions. (Commando): a wide range of radar, radio, and navigation avionics to customer's requirements.
ARMAMENT: (HAS.Mk 1, ASW role): Four No. 2 Mk 2 smoke floats, two No.4 marine markers, up to four Mk 44 homing torpedoes, or four Mk 11 depth charges, or one Clevite simulator. (Commando):

Westland Sea Kings of the Royal Australian Navy on patrol

Able to carry a variety of guns and missiles in a secondary air-to-surface strike role.
VARIANTS: *Sea King HAS/Mk 2.* ASW/SAR version for Royal Navy with two Rolls-Royce Gnome H.1400-1 turboshaft engines, each of which has a max contingency rating of 1,238 kW (1,660 shp). Twenty-one ordered. All HAS.Mk 1s converted by the Royal Navy to Mk 2 standard.
Sea King HAR.Mk 3. SAR version for Royal Air Force with Gnome H.1400-1 engines. Flight crew of two pilots, electronics/winch operator, and load-master/winchman. Accommodation for six stretchers, or two stretchers and 11 seated survivors, or 19 persons. Nav system includes Decca TANS F computer, Mk 19 nav receiver, and Type 71 Doppler. MEL radar. Sixteen ordered, with deliveries completed in 1979.
Sea King HC.Mk 4. Version of Commando Mk 2 for Royal Navy. Combines folding rotor and tail of Sea King and non-retractable landing gear of Commando. Gnome H.1400-1 engines. Decca TANS with chart display, and Type 71 Doppler. Carries 27 equipped troops, or 2,720 kg (6,000 lb) internal cargo, or 3,400 kg (7,500 lb) slung load. Can operate in Arctic or tropical conditions. Seventeen ordered, eight delivered by early 1981.
Sea King Mk 4X. Development vehicle for RAE Farnborough, generally similar to HC.Mk 4. Two ordered; delivery scheduled for 1983.
Sea King HAS.Mk 5. Developed ASW version for Royal Navy, with Gnome H.1400-1 engines, Decca TANS and Type 71 Doppler, sonobuoy dropping equipment and associated Marconi LAPADS data processing, larger radome for bigger Sea Searcher radar rotating antenna, provisions for future installation of MEL Sea Searcher radar. Cabin lengthened 1.83 m (6 ft) by internal modification to accommodate extra equipment. Seventeen ordered, four delivered by early 1981. RN HAS.Mk 2s to be updated to this standard.

Sea King Mk 41. SAR version for Federal German Navy with H.1400 engines. First of 22 ordered (89 + 50) flew on 6 March 1972. Delivery completed in 1974.

Sea King Mk 42. ASW version for Indian Navy with H.1400 engines. Twelve ordered, delivery completed in 1974.

Sea King Mk 42A. ASW version for Indian Navy with H.1400-1 engines and hauldown capability for operation on small ships. Three ordered in 1977.

Sea King Mk 43. SAR version for Norwegian Air Force with H.1400 engines. Eleven delivered.

Sea King Mk 43A. SAR version for Norwegian Air Force with H.1400-1 engines. One ordered in 1980.

Sea King Mk 45. ASW version for Pakistani Navy with H.1400 engines. Six ordered, delivery completed during 1975.

Sea King Mk 47. ASW version, with H.1400-1 engines, of which six ordered by Saudi Arabia on behalf of Egyptian Navy. Delivery completed during 1976.

Sea King Mk 48. SAR version with H.1400-1 engines for Belgian Air Force. Five ordered, one of which is convertible to have VIP interior. Delivery completed in November 1976.

Sea King Mk 50. General-purpose version for the Royal Australian Navy, with H.1400-1 engines, which was developed from the HAS.Mk 1. Ten ordered, of which the first flew on 30 June 1974, being the first Sea King to fly with the uprated Gnome engines. Used by the RAN for ASW, casualty evacuation, SAR, tactical troop lift, and vertical replenishment.

Commando Mk 1. Designation of first five Commandos, part of larger quantity ordered by Saudi Arabia on behalf of Egyptian Air Force. Powered by H.1400 engines. Accommodation for 21 troops. All delivered.

Commando Mk 2. Major production version of the Commando, with H.1400-1 engines. Seventeen built for the Egyptian Air Force, the first flown on 16 January 1975.

Commando Mk 2A. Designation of three Mk 2s ordered by the Qatar Emiri Air Force.

Commando Mk 2B. Designation of two Mk 2s with VIP interiors for the Egyptian Air Force.

Commando Mk 2C. Designation of one Mk 2 with VIP interior for the Qatar Emiri Air Force.

Westland VIP Commando, Qatar Emiri Air Force

WESTLAND/AÉROSPATIALE LYNX

First flights:
Lynx, first prototype (XW835) 21 March 1971
Lynx, fifth prototype (XX153), AH.Mk 1 development
aircraft 12 April 1972
Lynx HAS.Mk 2 prototype (XX469) 25 May 1972
Lynx French Navy prototype (XX904) 6 July 1973
Lynx AH.Mk 1 first production (XZ170) 11 February
1977
Lynx HAS.Mk 2 first production (XZ227) 10 February
1976

Royal Navy Westland Lynx lands aboard HMS *Birmingham*

TYPE: Twin-engined multi-purpose helicopter.

NOTES: The third of the helicopters that was included in the Aérospatiale/Westland co-production agreement, the WG.13, as it was known originally, was a very different proposition so far as Westland was concerned. This stemmed from the fact that the WG.13 was a Westland design, and as a result of which the British company retained design leadership. In terms of production Westland is responsible for 70 per cent and Aérospatiale 30 per cent. The first British aircraft to be designed from the outset on a metric basis, it was intended originally to be suitable for general-purpose naval and civil roles. It was soon clear, however, that this fast and manoeuvrable helicopter was suitable for general military use, and the development programme expanded the military capability as much as possible. A batch of six prototypes (XW835-XW839 and XX907) was constructed initially, the latter being allocated to Rolls-Royce for engine development and used subsequently for AH.Mk 1 development. Other airframes were built for electrical, fatigue, and static testing. The first to fly, on 21 March 1971, was XW835. This aircraft was used subsequently for engine development with Pratt & Whitney Aircraft of Canada PT6 engines, but did not enter production with this powerplant.

An additional batch of seven aircraft was built to speed the development programme, and by April 1975 the full team of prototypes had accumulated in excess of 2,000 flight hours. Very soon after that date four aircraft (two each of Army and Navy configuration) began final type testing and certification trials at the A & AEE Boscombe Down. These aircraft were XZ170/XZ171 and XZ227/XZ228 respectively: XZ171 was used subsequently for tropical trials, and XZ228 for cold trials. Service intensive flying trials units were then established: first was No.700L Naval Air Squadron, formed at RNAS Yeovilton in September 1976, which was a joint Royal Navy/Royal Netherlands Navy operational evaluation unit. It was followed in mid-1977 by formation of the Army Aviation unit at Middle Wallop, Hampshire. Following completion of the Army's intensive trials, in December 1977, deliveries of production aircraft for service with operational units began. The Army was the first to put the Lynx into active service, with its squadrons in West Germany, each division equipped with one squadron of light observation Gazelles, and one of TOW-armed Lynxes.

The versatility of the Lynx as a weapon platform had been explored effectively by Westland's demonstrator (G-LYNX). The range of weapons deployed include an AN/ALE-39 countermeasures dispenser with ECM chaff; 20 mm automatic cannon; ECM warning system; twin 7.62 mm machine-gun pods; Euromissile Hot, and Hughes TOW, anti-tank guided missiles; Matra Magic 550 air-to-surface missiles; and FZ 2.75 in, SNEB 68 mm, and SURA 80 mm air-to-ground rockets.

STRUCTURE: Four-blade semi-rigid main rotor with titanium head, and four-blade tail rotor, both of composite construction. Main rotor has a 6° negative pitch capability. Main rotor blades can be folded. Conventional semi-monocoque pod and boom fuselage structure, mainly of light alloy. Horizontal stabiliser on starboard side of tail rotor pylon. Tubular skid type landing gear, with provision for attaching ground handling wheels. Flotation gear optional.

ACCOMMODATION: Pilot and co-pilot or observer on side by side seats. Dual controls optional. Additional crew members carried according to role.

Maximum accommodation for a pilot and 10 armed troops or paratroops, or 12 lightly armed troops. Seats removed easily for carriage of up to 907 kg (2,000 lb) of internal freight, or for casualty evacuation with a crew of two, three stretchers, and a medical attendant. Up to nine survivors can be carried when deployed in SAR role. An external load of up to 1,361 kg (3,000 lb) can be carried on an under-fuselage hook.

DATA (A: AH.Mk 1; B: HAS.Mk 2):

POWER PLANT: Two 671 kW (900 shp) Rolls-Royce Gem 2 turboshaft engines, with max continuous rating of 559 kW (750 shp), mounted above the cabin aft of the main rotor shaft. Fuselage fuel tanks have a standard capacity for 733 kg (1,616 lb); two auxiliary tanks, with a combined capacity of 654 kg (1,442 lb), optional to extend ferry range.

Main rotor diameter:
A, B   12.802 m (42 ft 0 in)

Main rotor disc area:
A, B   128.69 m² (1,385.35 sq ft)

Tail rotor diameter:
A, B   2.21 m (7 ft 3 in)

Length overall, rotors turning:
A, B   15.163 m (49 ft 9 in)

Length overall:
A, main rotor blades folded   13.165 m 43 ft 2¼ in)
B, main rotor blades and tail folded
     10.618 m (34 ft 10 in)

Height overall, rotors turning:
A   3.66 m (12 ft 0 in)
B   3.59 m (11 ft 9½ in)

Skid track:
A   2.032 m (6 ft 8 in)

Wheel track:
B   2.778 m (9 ft 1¼ in)

Wheelbase:
B   2.94 m (9 ft 7¾ in)

Manufacturer's bare weight:
A   2,815 kg (6,206 lb)
B   2,761 kg (6,088 lb)

Max T-O weight:
A   4,536 kg (10,000 lb)
B   4,763 kg (10,500 lb)

Max continuous cruising speed:
A   140 knots (259 km/h; 161 mph)
B   125 knots (232 km/h; 144 mph)

Speed for max endurance:
A, B   70 knots (130 km/h; 81 mph)

Min flying speed, one engine out:
A   19 knots (35.5 km/h; 22 mph)
B   23 knots (43 km/h; 26.5 mph)

Max rate of climb at S/L:
A   756 m (2,480 ft)/min
B   661 m (2,170 ft)/min

Hovering ceiling OGE:
A   3,230 m (10,600 ft)
B   2,575 m (8,450 ft)

Typical range with reserves:
A, troop transport   292 nm (540 km; 336 miles)
B, radius of action, SAR, out and back at max sustained speed, allowances for T-O and landing, 30 min loiter in search area, 3 min hover for each survivor, 10 per cent fuel reserves at end of mission (crew of 3 and 7 survivors)
     96 nm (178 km; 111 miles)

Max range, standard fuel:
A   340 nm (630 km; 392 miles)
B   320 nm (593 km; 368 miles)

Max ferry range, standard plus auxiliary fuel:
A   724 nm (1,342 km; 834 miles)
B   565 nm (1,046 km; 650 miles)

VARIANTS: *Lynx HAS.Mk 2.* Version for Royal Navy, suitable for ASW classification and strike, ASV search and strike, SAR, reconnaissance, troop transport, fire support, communications and liaison, and vertical replenishment. Differs from AH.Mk 1 by having tail rotor pylon which can be folded manually, non-retractable tricycle landing gear with

Royal Navy Westland Lynx with Skua missiles

Battlefield Lynx firing TOW

single wheels on main units and twin wheel nose unit. Sprag units able to lock each main wheel. Flotation gear and harpoon deck-lock securing system optional. First operational unit, No.702 Squadron, formed after completion of Navy's intensive trials in December 1977. On 27 January 1981, No.815 Squadron was commissioned at RNAS Yeovilton as the Headquarters squadron for Lynx ship's flights, of which there will be an eventual total of 51, each operating one Lynx. A considerable emphasis was placed during this naval aircraft programme to develop the deck landing capability, including a comprehensive rolling platform phase, and extensive ship trials. A combination of the main rotor negative pitch capability, sprag units, flotation gear, and harpoon deck-lock system, combined with the general characteristics of this aircraft, have provided the most unrestricted shipboard capability of any helicopter.

Lynx Mk 2 (FN). Version, generally similar to HAS.Mk 2, for service with French Navy. Differs by having wheel brakes instead of sprag units, Alcatel dunking sonar, French radar and radio, and AS.12 wire-guided missiles. First of 26 delivered on 28 September 1978; delivery completed.

Lynx HAS.Mk 3. Designation of Royal Navy aircraft which have uprated transmission, and uprated power plant comprising two 835 kW (1,120 shp) Rolls-Royce Gem 41-1 turboshafts.

Lynx HAS.Mk 4. Designation of an additional 14 aircraft ordered for the French Navy in May 1980: these differ by having the uprated Rolls-Royce Gem 41-1 turboshafts as installed in the Royal Navy's HAS.Mk 3s.

Lynx Mk 23. Naval version for service with the Argentinian Navy, generally similar to HAS.Mk 2. Two delivered.

Lynx Mk 25. Designation of six aircraft, generally similar to HAS.Mk 2, for the Royal Netherlands Navy, which designates them UH-14A. All delivered, and serving with No.7 Squadron, they are used for SAR, communications, and training.

Lynx Mk 27. ASW version for the Royal Netherlands Navy, which designates them SH-14B. These have uprated Rolls-Royce Gem turboshafts, increased AUW of 4,763 kg (10,500 lb), and are equipped with Alcatel dunking sonar. All delivered.

Lynx Mk 28. General-purpose military version, similar to AH.Mk 1, for State of Qatar Police. Three ordered. These differ from the AH.Mk 1s by having uprated Rolls-Royce Gem 41-7 turboshaft engines, flotation equipment, sand-filter air intakes, and Nitesun searchlight.

Lynx Mk 80. Version for service with the Royal Danish Navy, generally similar to HAS.Mk 2. Eight ordered. The first was handed over on 15 May 1980, and a total of seven had been delivered by early 1981.

Lynx Mk 81. Eight aircraft with uprated Rolls-Royce Gem turboshafts for the Royal Netherlands Navy. These have the Dutch designation SH-14C, and carry MAD equipment. AUW of 4,763 kg (10,500 lb). All delivered.

Lynx Mk 86. Naval version for service with the Royal Norwegian Air Force Coastguard. Generally similar to HAS.Mk 2, but with uprated Gem 41-2 engines, non-folding tail cone, and AUW of 4,763 kg (10,500 lb). Six ordered, of which the first was delivered in January 1981.

Lynx Mk 87. Naval version for service with the Argentinian Navy, generally similar to Lynx Mk 23, but with uprated Gem 41-2 engines. AUW of 4,763 kg (10,500 lb). Two ordered and delivered.

Lynx Mk 88. Naval version for service with the Federal German Navy. Generally similar to Lynx Mk 86, with non-folding tail cone, but incorporating Bendix AN/AQS-18 Sonar. Twelve ordered, of which the first was delivered in June 1981.

Lynx Mk 89. Naval version for service with the Brazilian Navy, generally similar to HAS.Mk 2. Nine delivered.

ARMAMENT: (Battlefield versions) can include 20 mm cannon, 7.62 mm GEC Minigun, rockets, and Aérospatiale/MBB Hot, Hughes TOW, or Nord AS.11 missiles. (Naval versions) can include two Mk 44 or Mk 46 homing torpedoes, and six marine markers, or two Mk 11 depth charges, or BAe Sea Skua or Nord AS.12 missiles.

AVIONICS: Can include UHF/VHF with homing, standby UHF, AM/FM with homing, VHF/AM, VHF/FM, VOR/ILS, DME, Tacan, TANS, Doppler, AFCS, automatic stabilisation equipment, transponder, Ferranti Sea Spray radar, and Bendix or Alcatel sonar.

WESTLAND WG.30/WESTLAND 30

First flight: First prototype (G-BGHF) 10 April 1979

TYPE: General-purpose civil/military helicopter.

NOTES: As a private venture, Westland began design studies in early 1976 of a new helicopter that would be larger than the Lynx, but which would utilise much of the proven Lynx dynamic system. Detail design was originated during 1977, and leading in January 1978 to the decision to proceed with the construction of two prototypes. The first of these (G-BGHF) made its first flight in the Spring of 1979, and by 1 February 1981 it had accumulated 432 flight hours. The original designation of this new helicopter was WG.30, but this has since been changed to Westland 30 for those intended for the civil market, with WG.30 applying specifically to the military version.

Of generally similar overall configuration to the Lynx, the Westland 30 retains the basic dynamic system and power plant of that aircraft, but has a larger diameter main rotor, a new tail rotor, and a completely new airframe. This has a more spacious fuselage, introduces a new automatic flight control system, and incorporates as standard the uprated Rolls-Royce Gem turboshafts that have been introduced on more recent versions of the Lynx. The first customer for the Westland 30 is British Airways Helicopters, which ordered two of these aircraft in February 1981. It was anticipated that the first, due for delivery in late 1981, would be introduced into service on the airline's well-known Penzance-Isles of Scilly route, its regular passengers well versed in helicopter travel. The second aircraft was scheduled for delivery in early 1982, and Westland anticipated further orders from the same source. In addition to an obvious passenger/cargo capability, the company believes that it will find use also for VIP and executive transport, offshore gas/oil rig support, and Arctic operation.

STRUCTURE: Four-blade semi-rigid main rotor and four-blade tail rotor, both having blades of composite construction. Semi-monocoque fuselage, of pod and boom configuration, which is of conventional light alloy structure. Non-retractable tricycle landing gear with twin-wheel nose unit and single wheel on each main unit.

ACCOMMODATION: Crew of two on flight deck, and up to 17 passengers in main cabin with airline style seating. Optional layouts include high-density seating for up to 22 passengers; executive/VIP interior for six to eight, with galley, and toilet; offshore oil/gas rig support; mixed passenger/cargo; or all cargo.

DATA:

POWER PLANT: Two 835 kW (1,120 shp) Rolls-Royce Gem 41-1 turboshaft engines, each with a continuous rating of 671 kW (900 shp). Fuel capacity 998 kg (2,200 lb).

Westland WG.30 tactical transport

151

Westland WG.30 tactical transport

Main rotor diameter	13.31 m (43 ft 8 in)
Main rotor disc area	139.14 m² (1,497.7 sq ft)
Tail rotor diameter	2.44 m (8 ft 0 in)
Length overall, rotors turning	15.90 m (52 ft 2 in)
Height overall, rotors turning	4.04 m (13 ft 3 in)
Manufacturer's bare weight	3,030 kg (6,680 lb)
Max T-O weight	5,443 kg (12,000 lb)
Max level speed at S/L 130 knots (241 km/h; 150 mph)	
Hovering ceiling IGE	1,920 m (6,300 ft)
Hovering ceiling OGE	1,190 m (3,900 ft)
Range with 1,814 kg (4,000 lb) internal payload	
	123 nm (228 km; 142 miles)
Max ferry range, standard fuel with reserves	
	nearly 350 nm (648 km; 403 miles)

VARIANT: *WG.30 Lynx.* Military version, able to accommodate 14 fully-equipped troops, 17 troops with reduced equipment, or a maximum of 22 in a high-density seating layout. In a cargo configuration it can be used to carry ammunition, anti-tank missile launch teams, fuel, and supplies for battle-field support. For aeromedical use the WG.30 can accommodate six stretchers, and a maximum of ten persons seated, comprising casualties and medical attendants.

AVIONICS: IFR avionics, including ADF, DME, and VOR/ILS, under development. Three-axis AFCS with computer-based control. Communications and security systems to customer's requirements.

Westland 30 civil transport

Official Specifications of Westland Fixed-Wing Aircraft Projects

Name and/or Role	Official Specification	Powerplant	Span Metres (Feet)	Wing Area Metres^2 (sq ft)	AUW Estimated kg (lb)	Max Speed Estimated Knots (km/h; mph)	Remarks
Single-Engined Monoplane Bomber Mk 1	23/25	Bristol Orion (Jupiter VII)	18.29 (60.0)	47.38 (510)	2,631 (5,800)	—	Straight wing GA.22754 W.T. Model No. 26
Single-engined Monoplane Bomber Mk 2	23/25	Bristol Orion (Jupiter VII)	18.29 (60.0)	47.38 (510)	—	—	Swept wing W.T. Model No. 27
Experimental Twin-Engined Biplane Bomber	39/24	Armstrong Siddeley Jaguar	17.98 (59.0)	71.53 (770)	—	—	W.T. Model No. 20
Twin-Engined Sesquiplane Bomber	B9/24	Armstrong Siddeley Jaguar	19.20 (63.0)	73.95 (796)	—	—	W.T. Model No. 23
Experimental Twin-Engined Monoplane Bomber	B9/24	Armstrong Siddeley Jaguar	18.90 (62.0)	62.24 (670)	—	—	W.T. Model No. 25
Westland 7-seater/ Twin-engined Mailplane	21/28	2 × 75 kW (100 hp) Cosmos Lucifer or 112 kW (150 hp) ABC Wasp	13.94 (45.75)	51.10 (550)	1,786 (3,938)	—	Intended as a passenger or a colonial mail carrier
Limousine V Ten-Seater, High Wing Monoplane	6/29	3 × Armstrong Siddeley Lynx or 2 Jaguar	20.73 (68.0)	61.78 (665)	—	—	Development of Limousine IV W.T. Model No. 37
Single-Seat Fighter Mid/High-Wing Monoplane	F7/30	Rolls-Royce Goshawk	11.43 (37.5)	23.23 (250)	—	—	W.T. Model NR
Sesquiplane Light Bomber	P27/32	Rolls-Royce Kestrel	Upper 18.29 (60.0) Lower 8.08 (26.5)	58.25 (627)	—	—	This specification, to which the Fairey Battle was built, called for a 454 kg (1,000 lb) bombload, and a range of 868 nm (1,609 km; 1,000 miles). GA.55650
Pterodactyl VII Flying-Boat	R1/33	4 × de Havilland Gipsy VI	19.25 (63.16)	59.18 (637)	—	—	GA.53007
Single-Seat Fighter, Low/Mid-Wing Monoplane	F5/34	Bristol Perseus	11.43 (37.5)	21.37 (230)	—	—	—
General-Purpose Reconnaissance Torpedo-Bomber	G24/35 (via M15/35 to 10/36)	2 × Bristol Perseus	17.37 (57.0)	44.13 (475)	—	—	4-seat general-purpose aircraft. Recesses in both sides of lower fuselage to accommodate 4 × 500 lb bombs or 2 torpedoes. Manual dorsal turret
Single-Seat Day/Night Fighter (P9)	F37/35	Bristol Hercules	14.55 (47.75)	34.37 (370)	4,536 (10,000)	—	Design study only
Single-Seat Day/Night Fighter (P9)	F37/35	2 × 8.0 kN (1,800 lb st) Whittle W.2B Turbojets	14.55 (47.75)	34.37 (370)	4,536 (10,000)	—	Design study only
Army Co-Operation (P8)	A3/37	Bristol Perseus	15.24 (50.0)	24.15 (250)	4,536 (10,000)	—	Lysander development with retractable landing gear
Torpedo-Bomber, Level or Dive-Bomber, Reconnaissasnce (P10)	S24/37	Bristol Taurus	14.55 (47.75)	34.37 (370)	4,763 (10,500)	185 (343; 213)	Braced high-wing monoplane, tailwheel landing gear, internal weapons

Name and/or Role	Official Specification	Powerplant	Span Metres (Feet)	Wing Area Metres^2 (sq ft)	AUW Estimated kg (lb)	Max Speed Estimated Knots (km/h; mph)	Remarks
Longe-Range Fighter	F6/39	2 × 1,193 kW (1,600 hp) Rolls-Royce Griffons	18.44 (60.5)	41.81 (450)	7,348 (16,200)	344 (637; 396)	Design study. Twin tractor propellers, with tailwheel landing gear. Merlin version also
Long-Range Fighter	F6/39	2 × 1,193 kW (1,600 hp) Rolls-Royce Griffons	15.85 (52.0)	41.81 (450)	7,348 (16,200)	344 (637; 396)	Design study. Twin pusher propeller layout. Tricycle landing gear
Army Co-Operation (P11)	A7/39	940 kW (1,260 hp) Bristol Taurus	15.24 (50.0)	34.84 (375)	4,536 (10,000)	208 (386; 240)	Three-seat low-wing monoplane. Bombs carried externally
Army Co-Operation (P.11)	A7/39	940 kW (1,260 hp) Bristol Taurus	18.29 (60.0)	34.84 (375)	4,354 (9,600)	208 (386; 240)	High-wing monoplane W.T. model developed from P10 (S24/37). Retractable landing gear
Fleet Fighter	N8/39	Rolls-Royce Griffon	13.72 (45.0)	24.15 (260)	4,354 (9,600)	313 (579; 360)	Folding wings, fixed guns. Design study
Fleet Fighter	N8/39	940 kW (1,260 hp) Bristol Taurus	15.24 (50.0)	34.84 (375)	5,262 (11,600)	—	Main weapons carried in turret. Design study
Fleet Fighter	N9/39	940 kW (1,260 hp) Bristol Taurus	15.24 (50.0)	34.84 (375)	—	221 (410; 255)	Generally as N8/39 above but with fixed guns. Design study
High-Altitude Fighter (P14)	F4/40	2 × Rolls-Royce Merlin XX	19.81 (65.00)	39.48 (425)	5,670 (12,500)	300 (555; 345)	GA.84132 1st scheme
High-Altitude Fighter (P14)	F4/40	2 × Rolls-Royce Merlin XX	18.29 (60.00)	37.16 (400)	5,216 (11,500)	330 (612; 380)	Engines mounted in tandem, with shaft drive to contra-rotating propellers. Design study
High-Altitude Fighter (J8)	F4/40	2 × Whittle W.2B 700 Turbojets	18.29 (60.00)	Main Wing 35.30 (380) Delanne 16.72 (180)	7,484 (16,500)	365 (676; 420)	Tandem wing project embodying Delanne wing. SD362
Light Bomber Short-Range	B7/40	1,603 kW (2,150 hp) Bristol Centaurus	15.85 (52.0)	33.44 (360)	7,348 (16,200)	252 (467; 290)	Delanne type, bombs carried internally, crew of four
Mass Production Fighter	F19/40	1,044 kW (1,400 hp) Bristol Hercules	12.50 (41.0)	22.30 (240)	3,266 (7,200)	292 (541; 336)	All-wooden construction, alternative power plant to short supply Merlin, fixed spatted landing gear
Close-Support, with Dive-Bomber and Tactical Reconnaissance capabilities	B20/40	1,603 kW (2,150 hp) Bristol Centaurus	16.15 (53.0)	37.16 (400)	6,123 (13,500)	252 (467; 290)	Variant of B7/40 proposal without Delanne wing
High-Altitude Radar Precision Bomber	B5/41?	2 × Rolls-Royce Merlin 76/77	21.34 (70.00)	—	8,618 (19,000)	330 (612; 380)	Design study based on Welkin F4/40, with extended radar nose and provision for 2 × 2,000 lb bombs in what was originally gun bay. Mock-up built. Wing of 20% greater chord considered
Heavy Bomber	B8/41	4 × 1,119 kW (1,500 hp) Rolls-Royce Griffons	34.44 (113.0)	118.45 (1,275)	31,751 (70,000)	*261 (483; 300)	*Cruising speed. Delanne configuration, four cannon in tail turret

Name and/or Role	Official Specification	Powerplant	Span Metres (Feet)	Wing Area Metres^2 (sq ft)	AUW Estimated kg (lb)	Max Speed Estimated Knots (km/h; mph)	Remarks
High Altitude Bomber	B3/42	4× Rolls-Royce Merlins, Developing 746 kW (1,000 hp) at 12,190 m (40,000 ft)	55.78 (183.0)	260.12 (2,800)	20,412 (45,000)	*165 (306; 190)	*Cruising speed. Specification to which Vickers Windsor prototypes built. Range 1,300 nm (2,415 km; 1,500 miles). Bombload 1,814 kg (4,000 lb)
Single-Seat Jet Fighter	E5/42	13.3 kN (3,000 lb st) Halford H.1 Turbojet	14.02 (46.0)	22.30 (240)	4,354 (9,600)	426 (789; 490)	Twin boom configuration with central nacelle
Lightweight Fighter	F6/42	1,491 kW (2,000 hp) Rolls-Royce Griffon	10.82 (35.5)	19.14 (206)	3.765 (8,300)	391 (724; 450)	Specification intended to arrest growing weight of fighter aircraft
Torpedo-Bomber Reconnaissance	S6/43	2,125 kW (2,850 hp) Napier Sabre NS.53/SM	18.29 (60.0)	51.10 (550)	10,886 (24,000)	230 (426; 265)	Folding wing, and internal torpedo stowage. GA.P1005
Single-Seat Jet Fighter	N7/43	13.3 kN (3,000 lb st) Halford H.1 Turbojet	12.19 (40.0)	26.48 (285)	4,990 (11,000)	339 (628; 390)	Navalised version of the E5/42 proposal above. GA.P1013
Naval Fighter	N7/43	1,230 kW (1,650 hp) Rolls-Royce Griffon	13.41 (44.0)	25.55 (275)	5,143 (11,340)	334 (620; 385)	Wing folding, retractable tricycle landing gear, pilot's ejection seat
Torpedo Reconnaissance, with mixed powerplant	S11/43	1× 2,237 kW (3,000 hp) Pratt & Whitney Radial, 1× 13.3 kN (3,000 lb st) Halford H.1 Turbojet	16.76 (55.0)	43.66 (470)	12,066 (26,600)	321 (595; 370)	Turbojet engine to assist take-off and provide high-speed performance. External torpedo stowage. Unusual butterfly tail unit. Revision of S6/43 specification. GA.P1015
Fighter-Bomber	F12/43	2× 746 kW (1,000 hp) Rolls-Royce Merlins	13.72 (45.0)	31.59 (340)	10,433 (23,000)	443 (821; 510)	Engines in tandem within fuselage; shaft-driven contra-rotating pusher propellers aft of tail unit. This is the specification to which the de Havilland Hornet was built
Civil Transport to Brabazon IIA Recommendation	25/43	2× 746 kW (1,000 hp) Rolls-Royce or Armstrong Siddeley Engines	18.59 (61.0)	39.02 (420)	8,391 (18,500)	—	Requirement was for a short-haul transport for about 30 passengers specification to which Airspeed AS.57 Ambassador built. GA.SD530
Civil Transport to Brabazon VB Recommendation	26/43	2× 373 kW (500 shp) Gas Turbines	15.24 (50.0)	30.66 (330)	4,472 (9,860)	—	Intended as a D.H. Rapide replacement. GA.SD521
Naval Strike/ Fighter (W34)	N11/44	2,237 kW (3,000 hp) Rolls-Royce 24H46	12.19 (40.0)	29.73 (320)	7,847 (17,300)	365 (676; 420)	Original N11/44 scheme, with engine in centre fuselage and extension shaft drive to contra-rotating propellers. Pilot forward with 11° downward view over nose. Straight trailing-edge on outer wing panels
RAF Fighter/ Bomber	F13/44	2,237 kW (3,000 hp) Rolls-Royce 24H46	12.19 (40.0)	29.73 (320)	7,484 (16,500)	380 (704; 438)	Remarks as above for N11/44
Civil Transport to Brabazon VA Recommendation	18/44	—	—	—	—	—	Intended as a D.H. 86 replacement

Name and/or Role	Official Specification	Powerplant	Span Metres (Feet)	Wing Area Metres^2 (sq ft)	AUW Estimated kg (lb)	Max Speed Estimated Knots (km/h; mph)	Remarks
Interceptor for Royal Navy	F11/45	21.6 kN (4,860 lb st) Rolls-Royce Avon (AJ-65) Turbojet	10.67 (35.0)	26.01 (280)	5,670 (12,500)	—	Mid-wing monoplane with swept wings. Intended for operation from carrier with flexible deck. GA.SD516D
Interceptor for Royal Navy	F11/45	21.6 kN (4,860 lb st) Rolls-Royce Avon (AJ-65) Turbojet, plus one Liquid Fuel Rocket	10.67 (35.0)	26.01 (280)	5,670 (12,500)	—	Remarks as above for F11/45, plus bifurcated jet pipes, with rocket engine in tail. GA.SD535
Naval-RAF Strike/Fighter (W35)	N12/45	One Rolls-Royce Clyde Turboprop	13.41 (44.0)	32.98 (335)	Fighter 7,058 (15,560) Strike 8,482 (18,700)	Fighter 395 (732; 455) Strike 360 (668; 415)	Straight through tail pipe. Cockpit well forward to give improved view over nose. Short fin. Wyvern built to this specification. GA.WA3/00/001
Naval Fighter/ Interceptor (W35)	N12/45	One Bristol High Compression Turboprop	13.41 (44.0)	32.98 (355)	6,940 (15,300)	402 (745; 463)	Remarks as above. GA.SD471
Naval Fighter/ Interceptor (W35)	N12/45	One higher output Rolls-Royce Clyde Turboprop	13.41 (44.0)	32.98 (355)	8,074 (17,800)	435 (806; 501)	Deepened fuselage, with cockpit in standard Wyvern position. Otherwise, remarks as above. GA.SD476
Royal Navy Strike/Fighter	N12/45	2,237 kW (3,000 hp) Napier Nomad E125 Compound Engine	13.41 (44.0)	32.98 (355)	8,845 (19,500)	—	Fuselage and tail unit similar to W34 (N11/44). GA.PJD108
Wyvern TF4 Naval Fighter	N12/45	One Napier E141 Double Turboprop	13.41 (44.0)	34.37 (370)	9,525 (21,000)	—	Wide-chord inner wing, radar pod in leading-edge of port centre-section. GA.PJD232
Wyvern S5E Naval Strike	N12/45	2,535 kW (3,400 shp) Napier Double Eland Turboprop	13.41 (44.00)	32.98 (355)	Standard 10,024 (22,100) Max Overload 11,113 (24,500)	—	Proposal to uprate Wyvern S4. GA.PD116
Naval Strike/ Fighter (W36)	N12/45	28.9 kN (6,500 lb st) Rolls-Royce Avon (AJ-65) Turbojet	13.41 (44.00)	32.98 (355)	8,618 (19,000)	—	Fuselage and tail unit basically as W34 (N11/44), but with two alternative tricycle landing gears. GA.PJD104/106
Naval Strike (W36)	N12/45	31.1 kN (7,000 lb st) Metropolitan Vickers F.9, or Rolls-Royce Avon Turbojet	13.41 (44.0)	33.44 (360)	Max Strike 9,072 (20,000)	—	Low-wing turbojet development of Wyvern with wide-chord inner wing, four fuselage mounted 30 mm Aden guns, tricycle landing gear. Proposal only. GA.PJD130/134
Anti-submarine Patrol	GR17/45	—	—	—	—	—	Design study only. This specification led to production of Fairey Gannet, manufacture of which continued after acquisition of Fairey
Civil Transport	15/46	—	—	—	—	—	Design study only. Brabazon IIB specification

Name and/or Role	Official Specification	Powerplant	Span Metres (Feet)	Wing Area Metres^2 (sq ft)	AUW Estimated kg (lb)	Max Speed Estimated Knots (km/h; mph)	Remarks
Naval All-Weather Day/Night Fighter	N40/46	2 × 21.6 kN (4,860 lb st) Armstrong Siddeley F8 Beryl Turbojets	15.54 (51.0)	56.67 (610)	10,659 (23,500)	—	Engines mounted one above the other in aft fuselage. The D.H.110 Sea Vixen was the successful contender to this specification. GA.PJD129
Naval All-Weather Day/Night Fighter	N40/46	2 × 21.6 kN (4,860 lb st) Armstrong Siddeley F8 Beryl Turbojets	16.76 (55.0)	69.21 (745)	11,022 (24,300)	—	Alternative proposal to above with engines mounted side by side in aft fuselage, folding wings, swept fin and rudder, no tailplane. GA.PJD142
Naval All-Weather Day/Night Fighter	N40/46	Powerplant as above	16.26 (55.0)	69.21 (745)	11,022 (24,300)	—	Generally similar to PJD142 above, but incorporating a T tail. GA.PJD143
Naval All-Weather Day/Night Fighter	N40/46	Powerplant as above	16.76 (55.0)	69.21 (745)	11,022 (24,300)	—	Generally similar to PJD129, but larger tail warning radar in trailing-edge of stbd wing. GA.PJD144
Basic Trainer	T16/48	Alternative proposals with one Armstrong Siddeley Cheetah, de Havilland Gipsy Queen 51, or Alvis Leonides	14.02 (46.0)	27.87 (300)	—	—	—
15-Passenger Civil Transport	26/49	4 × 108 kW (145 hp) de Havilland Gipsy Major 10	21.34 (70.0)	41.81 (450)	with 12 passengers 4,309 (9,500)	—	Small short-haul transport with tricycle landing gear. All cabin seats rear facing. GA.PJD202
15-Passenger Civil Transport	26/49	4 × 186 kW (250 hp) de Havilland Gipsy Queen 30	24.38 (80.0)	53.88 (580)	with 15 passengers 5,670 (12,500)	—	Alternative proposal to above with slightly larger dimensions. GA.PJD203
Naval General-Purpose Light ASW Aircraft	?	984 kW (1,320 shp) Armstrong Siddeley Mamba ASM3, or 1,044 kW (1,400 shp) Rolls-Royce RDa3 Dart Turboprop	16.76 (55.0)	46.45 (500)	6,042 (13,320)	—	Inverted gull-wing configuration, folding wings, T tail, tricycle landing gear. GA.PJD235 with fixed landing gear. GA.PJD236 with retractable landing gear
Rocket-Propelled Interceptor A	F124T	Two de Havilland Spectre Rocket Engines (mounted side by side	8.84 (29.0)	30.66 (330)	—	—	Swept delta wing in a high-wing configuration. Initial tests would have been flown with two Armstrong Siddeley Viper turbojets. GA.PJD306/311
Rocket-Propelled Interceptor B	F124T	As above, but engines mounted one above the other	8.72 (28.6)	Main 19.04 (205) tail 11.61 (125)	—	—	Alternative proposal to above with large Delanne type delta tailplane set low on fuselage, with endplate fins and rudders
Two-Seat Carrier-Based Naval Strike Aircraft	M148T	2 × 31.1 kN (7,000 lb st) de Havilland Gyron Junior, or two Rolls-Royce BE 33 turbojets	13.00 (42.67)	74.32 (800)	—	—	Swept wings, twin fins and rudders, tricycle landing gear. Max weapon load 3,629 kg (8,000 lb). GA.PD180/183

Name and/or Role	Official Specification	Powerplant	Span Metres (Feet)	Wing Area Metres[2] (sq ft)	AUW Estimated kg (lb)	Max Speed Estimated Knots (km/h; mph)	Remarks
Basic Jet Trainer	?	7.3 kN (1,640 lb st) Armstrong Siddeley ASV.5 Viper turbojet	9.45 (31.0)	15.79 (170)	—	—	Swept wings, tricycle landing gear. Specification to which BAC Jet Provost T5 was built. GA.PD129
Operational Trainer (W.37-1) Two-Seat	?	Armstrong Siddeley Sapphire turbojet	12.73 (41.75)	43.20 (465)	External Weapons 8,750 (19,290) Internal Weapons 8,940 (19,710)	—	Swept folding wings, swept tail surfaces, tricycle landing gear, airbrakes in fuselage sides. Two variants of each, with external or internal weapon carriage. GA.PJD230 GA.PJD225 GA.PJD223
Operational Trainer (W.37-2) Single-Seat	?	Armstrong Siddeley Sapphire Turbojet	12.73 (41.75)	43.20 (465)	External Weapons 10,000 (22,047) Internal Weapons 10,046 (22,147)	—	
Naval Target Aircraft	?	Rolls-Royce W2B Turbojet	9.75 (32.0)	17.65 (190)	1,860 (4,100)	—	Unidentified GA of 1941/42 vintage
Gannet AEW Development	?	Bristol Siddeley Double Mamba 112	16.63 (54.57)	43.66 (470)	11,730 (25,860)	Cruising 126 (233; 145)	Pancake radome with AN/APS-20 radar above rear fuselage, tail unit incorporating large endplate fins and rudders. Mid-1965 vintage

Westland Rotary-Wing Aircraft Projects

Identification	Role	Powerplant	Main Rotor Diameter Metres (Feet)	AUW Estimated kg (lb)	Remarks
WG.1	ASW/Heavy Logistics	4 × Bristol Siddeley Gnome Turboshafts	17.07 (56.0)	16,216 (35,750)	Accommodation for 33 troops, or 18 stretchers, or 3 × 1,814 kg (4,000 lb) containers
WG.3	Light Tactical Transport	2 × Bristol Siddeley Gnome turboshafts	13.72 (45.0)	4,990 (11,000)	Accommodation for 15 troops, or 9 stretchers plus 2 attendants
WG.4	ASW/Medium Logistics	Two Turboshaft Engines	18.55 (60.86)	7,893 (17,400)	Accommoadation for 24 troops or 12 stretchers, or one 1,814 kg (4,000 lb) container
WG.5	Lightweight Utility	One Turboshaft Engine	9.75 (32.0)	1,089 (2,400)	Three-seat turbine engine development of the Saro Skeeter
Sikorsky S-56 Development Sikorsky S-56 Development	— —	Two Rolls-Royce RB.109 Turboshafts Two Napier Eland Turboshafts	21.95 (72.0)	—	Engines in nacelles at end of stub wings, tailplane with elevators, five-blade main rotor, four-blade tail rotor, tailwheel landing gear
Sikorsky S-58 ASW Development Sikorsky S-58 ASW Development	ASW ASW	One Napier Gazelle Turboshaft One Rolls-Royce Dart Turbine	17.07 (56.0)	—	Folding main rotor blades, folding tail pylon, four-blade main and tail rotors, tailwheel landing gear. Armed with two torpedoes
BEA Specification BEA Specification	Transport Transport	Four Rolls-Royce Dart Turbines Three (?) Napier Eland Turboshafts	26.05 (85.45)	—	—
W.80	Transport	Two Turbines	22.86 (75.0)	—	—
Twin-Engined Helicopter	30-Seat Transport	One Armstrong Siddeley Double Mamba	22.86 (75.0)	—	—
WB.6 Westminster	Flying Crane	Two Rolls-Royce Tyne Turbines	21.95 (72.0)	—	—

INDEX